THE ETHNOGRAPHIC EYE

REFERENCE BOOKS IN INTERNATIONAL EDUCATION
VOLUME 47
GARLAND REFERENCE LIBRARY OF SOCIAL SCIENCE
VOLUME 922

THE ETHNOGRAPHIC EYE

INTERPRETIVE STUDIES OF EDUCATION IN CHINA

EDITED BY
JUDITH LIU, HEIDI A. ROSS, AND DONALD P. KELLY

FALMER PRESS
A MEMBER OF THE TAYLOR & FRANCIS GROUP
NEW YORK AND LONDON
2000

Published in 2000 by
Falmer Press
A member of the Taylor & Francis Group
19 Union Square West
New York, NY 10003

10 9 8 7 6 5 4 3 2 1

Library of Congress Cataloging-in-Publication Data

The ethnographic eye : interpretive studies of education in China /
    edited by Judith Liu, Heidi A. Ross and Donald P. Kelly.
        p. cm. — (Garland reference library of social science ;
    v. 922. Reference books in international education ; v. 47)
        Includes bibliographical references and index.
        ISBN 0-8153-1471-X (alk. paper)
        1. Educational anthropology—China Case studies. 2. Education—
    Social aspects—China Case studies. I. Liu, Judith, 1950- .
    II. Ross, Heidi A., 1954- . III. Kelly, Donald P. IV. Series:
    Garland reference library of social science ; v. 922. V. Series:
    Garland reference library of social science. Reference books in
    international education ; vol. 47.
    LB45.E837 1999
    306.43—dc21   99-39740
                                                                     CIP

Printed on acid-free, 250-year-life paper.
Manufactured in the United States of America

Contents

Series Editor's Foreword

This series of scholarly works in comparative and international education has grown well beyond the initial conception of a collection of reference books. Although retaining its original purpose of providing a resource to scholars, students, and a variety of other professionals who need to understand the role played by education in various societies or world regions, it also strives to provide accurate, relevant, and up-to-date information on a wide variety of selected educational issues, problems, and experiments within an international context.

Contributors to this series are well-known scholars who have devoted their professional lives to the study of their specializations. Without exception these men and women possess an intimate understanding of the subject of their research and writing. Without exception they not only have studied their subject in dusty archives but have lived and traveled widely in their quest for knowledge. In short, they are "experts" in the best sense of that often overused word.

In our increasingly interdependent world, it is now widely understood that it is a matter of military, economic, and environmental survival that we understand better not only what makes other societies tick, but also how others, be they Japanese, Hungarian, South African, or Chilean, attempt to solve the same kinds of educational problems that we face in North America. As the late George Z. F. Bereday wrote in *Comparative Methods in Education* more than three decades ago: "[E]ducation is a mirror held against the face of a population. Nations may put on blundering shows of strength to conceal public weakness, erect grand façades to conceal shabby backyards, and profess peace while secretly arming for conquest, but how they take care of their children tells unerringly who they are" (New York: Holt, Rinehart and Winston, 1964, p. 5).

Perhaps equally important, however, is the valuable perspective that studying another education system (or its problems) provides us in understanding our own system (or its problems). When we step beyond our own limited experience and our commonly held assumptions about schools and learning in order to look back at our system in contrast to another, we see it in a very different light. To learn, for example, how China or Belgium handles the education of a multilingual society, how the French provide for the funding of public education, or how the Japanese control access to their universities enables us to better understand that there are reasonable alternatives to our own familiar way of doing things. Not that we can borrow directly from other societies. Indeed, educational arrangements are inevitably a reflection of deeply embedded political, economic, and cultural factors that are unique to a particular society. But a conscious recognition that there are other ways of doing things can serve to open our minds and provoke our imaginations in ways that can result in new experiments or approaches that we may not have otherwise considered.

Since this series is intended to be a useful research tool, the editor and contributors welcome suggestions for future volumes, as well as ways in which this series can be improved.

Edward R. Beauchamp
University of Hawaii

THE ETHNOGRAPHIC EYE

CHAPTER 1

Introduction
A Discursion on Ethnography

DONALD P. KELLY

This volume is somewhat Janus-faced. On the obverse, it deals with the merits of doing ethnographic research; on the reverse, it deals with education in China. Yet not all of the studies included in this volume used ethnographic research methods, nor do all the research cases included here involve studies of modern Chinese education. Needless to say, the ambivalent structuring of this work produces a conundrum: What is the value of a book that purports to use various ethnographic studies to shed light on Chinese schooling, when not all the chapters in it fit within this parameter?

The answer to this question rests on several points. First, this work makes clear that education entails more than the inculcation of facts per se. The very act of attending school places an individual within an institution that is designed to acculturate and socialize students to accept as valid the tenets of a specific culture and to fit unquestioningly into prescribed social roles. In the call for the development of national standards that is frequently voiced in the United States, this function of schooling is largely ignored; yet in China moral education is invariably considered to be an integral part of schooling. Educational research on China must always take this conception of schooling into account, particularly when Chinese education is viewed in light of the monumental cultural and social changes that have occurred since the implementation of market socialism.

Second, ethnographic methods are not always appropriate for conducting educational research. At the most basic level, employing

I wish to thank Judith Liu, Vandra Masemann, and Linda A. M. Perry for their assistance with this chapter.

ethnographic methods requires a knowledge of the language used by informants. If a researcher does not know the language (or is funded by an agency that wants easily compared statistical analyses), then the data to be analyzed must be "hard," and consequently, the use of quantitative methods is more applicable to this situation. Even quantitative researchers, however, must have some awareness of the cultural and social settings they are going to encounter. After all, data produced in the absence of cultural and social contexts can provide little more than a general picture of a research setting. Ethnography's value lies in providing detailed interpretations, while quantitative work's value lies in producing numerical explanations.

Lastly, schooling is something we have all experienced and understand, and examining a foreign situation makes us more aware of the "hidden" curricular components that shaped our educations. Ability grouping and tracking procedures are not used solely to differentiate levels of academic skills; they have cultural and social outcomes as well. In many ways, these elements become more noticeable through comparative education because understanding another culture and society necessitates that we question concepts that normally go unquestioned. Asking "Why?" is at the heart of ethnographic research. Thus, in true ethnographic fashion, by looking at educational practices in China, we are given an opportunity to reflect back upon our own.

SERENDIPITY

While Judith Liu interviewed women who had attended St. Hilda's School for Girls in Wuhan, Heidi Ross studied the McTyeire School for Girls in Shanghai. Despite this similarity in research interests, their paths did not cross until they met as Luce Fellows during a seminar at the 1989 Henry Luce Foundation's "History of Christianity in China" program held in Lawrence, Kansas. As it happened, not only had they both done ethnographic work on missionary girls' schools in China but also both were interested in acculturation and socialization processes—Judith on moral education and Heidi on gender socialization—and both of them were fascinated by the ways in which external social and cultural forces shape people's lives—Judith in the generalized form of "structures" and Heidi in the specific form of patriarchy. The serendipity of their meeting and then discovering the similarity of their ideological perspectives led Judith and Heidi to conclude that a volume dealing with various studies of Chinese schooling would be an excellent way to examine the applicability of doing ethnographic work on education in China. In this introduction, a theoretical discussion of ethnography as a methodological tool is offered, as well as a brief overview of each substantive chapter.

ETHNOGRAPHY

While ethnography is a *process* that entails the use of qualitative research methods—doing fieldwork and compiling fieldnotes—it is also a *product:* the written text that details one's encounters with an "other."[1] In essence, an ethnography is a descriptive textual account of a researcher's experiences in what are frequently unfamiliar cultural and social settings.

To paraphrase the work of Robert Sherman and Roman Webb (1988), ethnography (as opposed to other forms of qualitative research) should include five elements: four dealing with the ethnographic process, the fifth with the ethnographic product. First, what is being studied is context-bound. Therefore, ethnographers must immerse themselves in a culture to better perceive and understand the observed people and events. Second, the act of observation must not change the context. That is, the fieldwork must occur naturally and not be contrived. Third, the informants must believe they can speak freely and for themselves. Ethnographers, in other words, must not influence informants in ways such that the informants' perception of reality might be altered. As such, a reflexive relationship between investigators and informants should evolve in which informants teach investigators about their cultural beliefs and social practices. Fourth, ethnographers must look at their interactions from a "systems perspective," because any event, phenomenon, or person being studied is part of a complex web of meaning that is dependent solely upon its context. Finally, ethnographers must become cultural workers by finding coherence in what they have studied, find some insights, and re-present their insights to an audience in a written text.[2]

These five points idealize the ethnographic method, and some qualifications need to be added to them, especially if ethnographic work is being done in a culture other than one's own. That is, a common ground exists between researchers and informants when ethnographic work is done in "familiar territory." For example, while "American culture" is not as unified a category as the name would imply, one can still see a thread that holds Western society—not just American society—together. This thread is what Marshall Sahlins referred to as "La Pensée Bourgeoise,"[3] or the near-doxic acceptance of the political economy of capitalist production as *the* organizing principle of Western society.[4]

What happens then, when a Western-educated and -trained ethnographer is engaged in studying a cultural and social system that represents a way of life distinctly different from that of the ethnographer? In this case, "[e]thnography is actively situated *between* powerful systems of meaning,"[5] where the ethnographer must exhibit "a tolerance for ambiguity, multiplicity, contradiction, and instability."[6] Amid all these contingencies, however, is a belief that there exists a commonality between and among human social groups. This reflects the power and attraction of doing ethnographic work. The mysteriousness of the "other" becomes comprehensible and even familiar to us during ethnographic fieldwork. As James Clifford writes: "What one *sees* in a coherent ethnographic account, the imaged construct of the other, is connected in a continuous double structure with what one *understands*."[7]

For a coherent ethnographic account to emerge, an ethnographer must, in turn, produce an ethnographic text—a distinct writing genre where the "scientific principle of participant observation [becomes] incorporated into a literary description of another culture and social order."[8] This fusion of the literary to the scientific within an ethnography marks its departure from travel or personal journal accounts of encounters with some distinct "other" that characterized anthropological work until the twentieth century.

Like travel accounts, the writing within an ethnography still entails the use of a personal narrative, but with a near-schizophrenic twist, because ethnographers must assume two frequently contradictory roles. Thus, when conducting ethnographic fieldwork, the role assigned to the author's personal experiences (that is, being an active participant) frequently stands in opposition to the role assigned to science (namely, being an unbiased observer).[9] The ethnographer must decide which role (active participant or detached observer) will assume the author(ity) for structuring the final ethnographic text. This role conflict has framed the theoretical debate that surrounds the meaning of doing ethnographic work today, and depending upon one's ideological bent, it determines whether the final product will tend to be a classical, postmodern, feminist, or critical ethnography.

CLASSICAL ETHNOGRAPHY

One: Experiential Authority and the Explanation of Culture[10]

As with any intellectual pursuit, views on the meaning (or purpose) of ethnographic work have changed over time. When Melford Spiro analyzed the changes in classical ethnography, he detected one element that has been constant: the notion of cultural relativism.[11] From an anthropological perspective, looking at different cultures has entailed three types of cultural relativism: descriptive, normative, and epistemological.

The first, descriptive relativism, was based upon "the theory of cultural determinism."[12] That is, since cultures are constitutive of their social orders and of the psychological traits of their peoples, the differences between human groups are the consequences of their cultural variations. By cataloging these differences, early anthropologists believed that a "Science of Man" could be developed. Inherent within this view, however, is a belief that cultural development is teleological and that over time and through the inevitability of progress, all cultures would (and could) attain the cultured "sophistication" of the West. In this perspective, the participant side of being a participant-observer was more important because cultural knowledge came from personal interaction with the "other."

Beginning in the 1930s, this perspective on anthropological investigation was seriously challenged. Anthropologists were still studying "primitive" peoples, but the ideological context that provided the direction for their studies was being radically transformed. First, disillusionment with the view that "material progress" is necessarily "progressive" was increasing. This disillusionment was sparked by a critical reassessment of the causes and consequences of World War I. Next, Woodrow Wilson's idealistic call for a worldwide acceptance of the goal of national self-determination was going unheeded. And, finally, the presence of colonial powers in "underdeveloped" areas of the world was continuing, particularly in those areas that were inherently fascinating to ethnographers. The result was that anthropological fieldworkers began to question the contradiction between Western liberal ideals and how they actually were being applied in other parts of the world. The questioning of these cultural and social conditions, when conjoined with a growing faith in the value of the scientific method, combined to transform the ideological basis for anthropological fieldwork. To be considered of intellectual value, fieldwork now was seen as the purview of the scientifically trained, emotionally detached observer. From this perspective, the participant-observer method for doing ethnographic fieldwork changed from focusing on the participant to focusing on the observer, where the scientifically based objectivity in recording what the researcher had seen would result in an "unbiased" account.

Not surprisingly, this unbiased reporting of the lives of "primitive" peoples served as a critique of the West. According to George Marcus and Michael Fischer, the new, normative relativistic ethnography developed three broad critiques of the West: "They—primitive man—have retained a respect for nature, and we have lost it (the ecological eden); they have sustained close, intimate, satisfying communal lives, and we have lost this way of life (the experience of community); and they have retained a sense of the sacred in everyday life, and we have lost this (spiritual vision)."[13]

Accompanying these critiques of the West was a strong belief in the power of science to rationally and objectively arrive at the "truth." As Michel de Certeau asserts, scientific discourse is "univocal"[14] because it asserts that for any given situation there is one and only one acceptable meaning—the one regarded as true. As such, scientific language is an "artificial language" that seeks to circumscribe the contingent, intersubjective, and negotiated aspects of language usage that mark everyday human communicative interaction. Further, adherence (or mere tacit acceptance) of the scientific method has "excluded certain expressive modes from its legitimate repertoire: rhetoric (in the name of 'plain,' transparent signification), fiction (in the name of fact), and subjectivity (in the name of objectivity). The qualities eliminated from science were localized in the category of 'literature.' " [15]

The combination of the scientific method with a rigorous description of fieldwork observations resulted in the belief that an ethnographer's written cultural representations were nothing more than pure, objective facts. From this perspective, the ethnographer becomes an *authority* whose textual representations are, in reality, the truth. Adherence to this transcendental position for the researcher reached the degree that E. E. Evans-Pritchard could write about the totality of Nuer culture without ever referring to any individual Nuer informant by name.[16] Adherence to the scientific method made it possible for Evans-Pritchard to believe that his observations were objectively true. Since he knew where the Nuer "were coming from," adherence to this perspective made it possible for him to paint what he "knew" as a realistic portrait of Nuer life without having to worry about any contingent, cultural irregularities blurring the details of his realist masterpiece.

By seeking to tell only the "truth" and by maintaining a position of value neutrality, scientific discourse becomes univocal; consequently, the author tends to disappear from a scientifically based, normative relativist ethnographic text. Thus, the power that emanates from this type of ethnographic account is attributable to its scientific pretensions. First, the ethnographer must establish that fieldwork was done in order to authenticate an "experiential authority" that makes the ethnographer eminently qualified to speak about the culture or for the social group being studied.[17] Second, the ethnographer must "transcend" the text in order to validate the univocal nature of science. In this manner, normative relativist ethnographic texts have the tendency to become locked into a time-less synchronic present. Because the goal of scientific inquiry is to explain, history needs to be bracketed in order to make sense of the "deeper" structures at play in a given cultural or social system.

It is the rare ethnographer, as with Margery Wolf in her book *A Thrice-Told Tale,* who challenges the scientific notion of absolute truth that underlies normative relativist ethnographic work. In her book, Wolf analyzes an incident that occurred in Taiwan in 1960. In the first account of the incident, Wolf wrote a story that was fiction; in the second account, she wrote as a feminist anthropologist who transcribed the event from "a jumble of field observations and interviews" while giving special attention to the woman who was her assistant and translator; and in the third account, Wolf wrote as a more "traditional" anthropologist as she attempted to place the incident within the larger "context of shamanism in Taiwan."[18]

What is intriguing about Wolf's book is that not only did her historical record of the event—the short story and her journals and fieldnotes—tell a "quite different version of what had happened,"[19] but also she, too, was not the "same person" who had written those various accounts of the incident. What Wolf portrays in *A Thrice-Told Tale* is the notion that ethnographic texts do not necessarily represent a one-to-one correspondence with the events they detail. Rather, normative relativist ethnographers, despite their scientific pretensions, are not really engaged in *explaining* what has happened during their fieldwork as much as they are in *interpreting* what happened. Further, it should be clear that other voices are engaged in fashioning the final product; it should also be clear that the ethnographer needs to be acutely aware of the dialogic (or polyphonic) nature of ethnographer-informant communicative interaction and how this interaction, in turn, affects both (or all) of them. From this awareness, a more sophisticated view of ethnographic work emerged.

Two: Interpretive Authority and the Understanding of Culture

With the realization that, at base, ethnography deals more with interpretation than with explanation, epistemological relativism is now the predominant ethnographic form.[20] As with descriptive and normative relativism, the goal is the production of an ethnographic text, but the text's meaning has changed. Whereas descriptive and normative relativism assumed that general precepts could be applied holistically to discern transcultural regularities, epistemological relativism uses "the ethnographer's empathy, *Verstehen,* insight, imagination, [and] understanding" as the means to study a particular culture.[21] By no longer looking for cultural universals, interpretive ethnography also questions the role of science.

In examining the role of science, interpretive ethnographers began to realize that the social conditions underlying the way that fieldwork is conducted are no longer the same as they were when experiential authority guided ethnographic work. We are now in a postcolonial world where the implicit ability of a researcher to "accurately" represent the "other" no longer goes unquestioned because the power differentials separating researcher from informant have become explicit and must be taken into account in any interaction. Consequently, the interaction between researcher and informant is no longer seen as incidental to the fieldwork but as "multisubjective, power-laden, and incongruent"[22] and, hence, crucial to the success of the entire ethnographic process. What becomes "realized" in the text of an epistemological relativistic ethnography is the result of negotiations over cultural meanings that have taken place between researcher and informants.

Accompanying this implicit (and at times, explicit) critique of the univocal nature of science is the virtual abandonment of belief in the tenets of positivism. The rediscovery of the work of Wilhelm Dilthey and the distinction he made between *Geisteswissenschaften* (the human sciences) versus *Naturwissenschaften* (the natural sciences) has had a significant impact on ethnographic work through the promulgation of theoretical alternatives to positivism. Phenomenology, with the goal of achieving an intersubjective understanding between researchers and informants over the implicit meanings "existing" within a culture, and hermeneutics, with the view that the meaning of most cultural products or constructs—verbal, written, or "fashioned" in some form—can be deciphered as a text, have refocused ethnographic work. The slipperiness of context can now be understood through a process of interpretation. In this process, the position of the ethnographer becomes crucial. By no longer privileging the observer over the participant, interpretive ethnography stresses "that social life must fundamentally be conceived as the negotiation of meanings."[23] As such, cultural and personal values—both the researcher's and the informant's—play a significant role in shaping the ethnographic encounter. This negotiation of meanings forces the ethnographer to do something experiential ethnography never did: to seriously question his or her position vis-à-vis the informant concerning the production of the final text. Admittedly, the ethnographer is the one who writes the text and has the ultimate say about what is or is not included in the final product, but what is said is no longer seen to transparently represent reality. Thus, from the perspective of interpretive ethnography, cultures (depicted through a process that Clifford Geertz refers to as "thick description"[24]) are inventions, not representations, that result from intersubjective conflict and cooperation between researchers and informants.[25]

This conception of the ethnographic invention of cultures gives new meaning to what an ethnographic text is. If the intent of experiential authority focused on the author's ability to accurately transcribe observations into valid descriptions, then interpretive authority centers on the ethnographer's intentional creation of a negotiated, contingent reality. That is, under the rubric of interpretive authority, ethnographies are not seen as realistic representations of cultural facts, but, rather, they are seen as creative fictions. As de Certeau frames it, "fiction . . . is a discourse that 'informs' the 'real' without pretending either to represent it or to credit itself with the capacity for such a representation."[26] Ethnography, from this perspective, is "something made or fashioned" that is not inherently false—but neither should it necessarily be considered inherently true.[27]

By questioning science and its quest for truth, interpretive ethnography has made truth, as well as culture, something that is contingent, negotiated, and subjective. With no credence for (or no willing acceptance of) the conception of cultural universals as its theoretical foundation, interpretive ethnography has no moorings with which to anchor itself. With the advent of postmodernism, this free-floating state of ethnographic inquiry results in an even more fluid situation.

POSTMODERN ETHNOGRAPHY

The postmodern assault on positivistic science has had far-reaching consequences in the humanities and the social "sciences." To attack science is, in many ways, to attack truth, and with it the very foundations of Western knowledge. With a hierarchy of knowledge ranging from the cause and effect relationships of the natural sciences to the correlations of the social sciences, and further to the rhetorical devices of the humanities, the goal of all these inquiries has been to produce a "factual" representation of reality. If life is based upon contingent situations and negotiated meanings, then how can anything be represented as real? If nothing can be taken for granted, then is it possible that no metanarratives exist to legitimize notions of beneficial societal progress or the possibility of human emancipation? In a sense, postmodernism arose as a way of trying to deal with the existential angst that this crisis in representation produced.

Postmodernism emerged to question the foundations of Western thought, the scientific method, their concomitant quest for universal truths, and the certainty surrounding taken-for-granted meanings—in other words, the whole of Enlightenment epistemology.[28] This philosophical debate is being played out within ethnographic work through an increased awareness of the implicit and explicit power relations that exist between researchers and informants, and through a growing acceptance of the discursive nature of ethnographic fieldwork.

The work of Michel Foucault has been exceedingly influential in reconceptualizing the cultural links between power and truth. According to Foucault, a "regime of truth" exists in the West that is culturally tied to the constitution of Western social practices. Thus,

> "Truth" is to be understood as a system of ordered procedures for the production, regulation, distribution, circulation and operation of statements.
>
> "Truth" is linked in a circular relation with systems of power which produce and sustain it, and to effects of power which it induces and which extend it. A "regime" of truth. [*sic*]
>
> This regime is not merely ideological or superstructural; it is a condition of the formation and development of capitalism.[29]

Under this schema, *science* is tied inexorably to *truth;* whereas *ideology* is tied inexorably to *power.*[30] In a sense, ethnographers (and other intellectuals), by adhering to an ideology that legitimates the power of science, have supported the existing "regime of truth." By not examining how power is tied to the hegemonic conceptions that legitimate the existing social, economic, political, and cultural systems, Western intellectuals have abrogated their responsibility to question the taken-for-granted aspects of Western thought. In a way, Foucault is advocating the deconstruction of the unquestioned, universalistic, doxic "truths" of modern thought. In this manner, conceptions of truth enter into the world of orthodox/heterodox debates,[31] where the arbitrary nature of cultural and social constructions becomes manifest. Researchers who accept this postmodern ideological stance must, in turn, take a more self-conscious, "reflexive" position toward the process and product of ethnographic work.

While postmodern ethnographers would want us to believe that they have stumbled onto something important, the notion of reflexivity is nothing new, nor is it necessarily postmodern. In the field of sociology, at least four conceptions of reflexivity have emerged. First is Max Weber's *Verstehen* method in which the "consciousness of induced consciousness"[32] is employed. In a sense, Weber's view of reflexivity boils down to an ethnographer being able to understand what is happening in a foreign context. Unlike the explicitness of scientific attempts to explain things, Weber's notion of reflexivity is far more implicit—as so much of life usually is. Next is Bennett Berger's more "scientific" approach to reflexivity, in which the ethnographer "attempts to cope with one's own consciousness of the consequences of other-direction and role-taking in oneself," with the idealized goal of becoming "the utterly detached observer."[33] Third is Alvin Gouldner's stance from which researchers must "acquire the ingrained *habit* of viewing our own beliefs as we now view those held by others."[34] In all three views, reflexivity "requires an 'I,' and no apologies for the first person are needed."[35] These definitions hold the ethnographer responsible for understanding, interpreting, and describing the "other."

The fourth view of reflexivity comes from Pierre Bourdieu, who takes the idea of reflexivity to its furthest limits. Bourdieu's reflexivity is epistemological, as he is not particularly interested in what "others" can tell him about their culture or society, but rather what they can tell Bourdieu about his own culture or society. For Bourdieu, if a researcher can grasp the arbitrary nature of another's culture or society, then this understanding can be used as a means to uncover the normally unreflected, arbitrary nature of the researcher's culture or society.[36]

All of these sociological views on reflexivity are clearly not postmodern in their theoretical orientations.[37] As such, they contrast markedly with the postmodern turn that inspires many recent anthropological ethnographies. This postmodern turn takes a hermeneutic approach to research, which holds that all cultural and social interactions can be "read" and interpreted as if they were written texts. Further, "others" are implicated in the construction of the text. Ethnography becomes, then, the textual reconceptualization of a living "text" that seeks to be compelling in its retelling. Ironically, postmodern ethnographies tend to be multivocal on paper; yet the stories they purport to tell appear distanced from the actual fieldwork experience. That is, "the notion of reflexivity recognizes that texts do not simply and transparently report an independent order of reality. Rather, the texts themselves are implicated in the work of reality-construction."[38]

Thus, reflexivity in anthropological approaches tends to be concerned with how it affects the ethnographic textual product; whereas reflexivity in sociological approaches tends to be concerned with how it affects the ethnographic methodological process. In either case, ethnographers who wish to be reflexive should attempt to address both the *process* and the *product*—the dual meanings implied in the etymology of the word *ethnography*.

Nowhere is the postmodern conception of the interplay between power and reflexivity in ethnographic work more analyzed than in their relation to discourse. As with interpretive ethnography, postmodern ethnography, whether it stresses dialogism or polyphony,[39] is concerned with how language shapes self/other encounters. But whereas interpretive ethnography is predicated on the idea of "dialogical egalitarianism," postmodern ethnography is aware of both latent and manifest "power relations" that undergird any ethnographic encounter. As Vincent Crapanzano writes: "There is a double indexing that occurs within any exchange: an intra- and extra-dialogical indexing of the participants, for example, as equal within the dialogue but as unequal outside the dialogue, in real life, as we say."[40] While Crapanzano's observation can apply to *all* social encounters, it is particularly important to be aware of the power differentials operating within the discourse when conducting ethnographic work across cultures. Thus, ethnographers must become acutely aware of how these power differentials can affect the course of their discursive practices and social interactions with the "other."

At another level, it has also become clear to postmodernists that language itself is not a transparent medium for communication. Drawing on the work of Mikhail Bakhtin (and others), postmodernists have come to embrace the belief that "The word in language is half someone else's."[41] For Bakhtin,

At any given time, in any given place, there will be a set of conditions—social, historical, meteorological, physiological—that will insure that a word uttered in that place and at that time will have a meaning different than it would have under any other conditions; all utterances are heteroglot in that they are functions of a matrix of forces practically impossible to recoup, and therefore impossible to resolve.[42]

If this summation of Bakhtin's view on the heteroglot nature of dialogic interaction is accepted, then how in such a contextual and contingent world is it possible for ethnography to be done in a meaningful way? According to Paul Ricoeur, the discourse between ethnographer and "other" must become "autonomous" from both the intention of either speaker and the actual utterance itself.[43] Thus, for a fieldwork encounter to become a text, it must be removed from the interlocutionary context (namely, it must be "translated") and then transcribed. Ultimately, ethnographies are texts not dialogues, and for postmodernists, this position is angst-producing. By taking an ideological position that seeks to uncover the hidden recesses of power, it is ironic that in order to produce a text, the ethnographer has the final say over creating the final written product. Thus, the postmodern movement began as a questioning of how the West represents itself and the world;[44] yet even if postmodern-inspired, reflexive ethnographies "cast encounters between two individuals" in such a way as to "successfully dramatize the intersubjective give-and-take of fieldwork and introduce a counterpoint of authorial voices, [ethnographic texts] remain *representations* of dialogue."[45]

How does one escape this conundrum? If ethnographies are capable of producing only representations of encounters with others, and if the epistemological basis of representation itself is no longer taken for granted, then what value is there in reading or writing a postmodern ethnography? According to de Certeau:

> If the professional applies himself to the task of listening to what he can see or read, he discovers before him interlocutors, who, even if they are not specialists, are themselves subject-producers of histories and partners in a shared discourse. From the subject-object relationship, we pass to a plurality of authors and contracting parties. A hierarchy of knowledges is replaced by a mutual differentiation of subjects. From that moment, the particular place of the relationship that the technician maintains with others introduces a dialectic of all these places, that is, an experience of time.[46]

This quotation eloquently expresses the ideological basis of postmodern ethnography. The ultimate goal is the creation of a dialogic (or polyphonic) text that richly weaves the various threads of the subject's story and the ethnographer's analysis into a tapestry that minimizes the "symbolic violence" done to the "other."[47] To be sure, no reconstruction of fieldwork is totally free from the effects of symbolic violence, because the very nature of the ethnographic endeavor, no matter how reflexive it might be, is layered with power differentials. However, if the endeavor is one of negotiation and collaboration with the "other" so that the "discourse about the other [becomes] a means of constructing a discourse authorized by the other,"[48] then the severity of the symbolic violence done to the "other" will be minimized. If this construction of an "authorized" discourse is done well, what results is a compelling representation that engages and informs the reader.

There is one possible problem that can adversely affect the value of a postmodern ethnography, however, and that occurs when the text becomes too confessional or too reflexive. As Renato Rosaldo states: "If classic[al] ethnography's vice was the slippage from the ideal of detachment to actual indifference, that of present-day reflexivity is the tendency for the self-absorbed Self to lose sight altogether of the culturally different Other."[49] If postmodern ethnography can overcome this potential descent into bathos, then the contingent view of life held by postmodern ethnographers can be used to introduce the contextual, rhetorical, and political dimensions that undergird another culture and social system, which may, in turn, be used to reflect upon our own. Can we ask anything more from the pursuit of knowledge?

FEMINIST ETHNOGRAPHY

In 1986, an anthology, *Writing Culture: The Poetics and Politics of Ethnography,* appeared. This book, edited by James Clifford and George Marcus, had an immediate impact upon the meaning of doing ethnography. Postmodern in nature, the book made the startling observation that doing ethnographic work entailed writing; not writing as merely inscribing notes and publishing results, but writing as a literary process imbued with political overtones. As Clifford phrased it: "[The authors in this anthology] see culture as composed of seriously contested codes and representations; they assume that the poetic and the political are inseparable, that science is in, not above, historical and linguistic processes."[50] Further, Clifford asserted that "Most of the essays, while focusing on textual practices, reach beyond texts to contexts of power, resistance, institutional constraint, and innovation."[51] These ideas were akin to placing fire near a powder keg, and exemplified a growing awareness of the postmodern impact upon ethnographic work. It was becoming increasingly clear that since ethnography involved writing, then the postmodern turn toward literary processes involving the use of metaphor and figure and the narrative nature of life was probably more appropriate for ethnography than classical ethnography's attempts to render ethnography a scientific, value-free, Western experience. That is, the canon of Western discourse—specifically, the adherence to objective, factual, prosaic signification—was inappropriate for guiding ethnographic work. Henceforth, the goal would be to "think of a cultural poetics that is an interplay of voices, of positioned utterances."[52] Yet despite this observation, certain voices are absent from the text, which caused Clifford to ask: "Why, then, are there no essays in this book written from primarily feminist standpoints?"[53]

His answer, needless to say, set off a feminist maelstrom. According to Clifford, the book was the outcome of an "advanced seminar" for participants "who had already contributed significantly to the analysis of ethnographic textual form,"[54] and in a tautological justification derived after the fact, it was concluded that "feminist and non-Western writings have made their greatest impact"[55] on ethnographic content. Thus, it appears that feminist (and non-Western) writers were excluded from being invited because the seminar was "advanced"; then their exclusion was justified because they were making contributions to ethnography only in what they write as opposed to how they write.

According to Ruth Behar, "*Writing Culture*'s effect on feminist anthropologists was to inspire an empowering rage."[56] It appears that Clifford and the others, although aware of the problem of excluding feminists, were unable to escape the very patriarchal structures that feminism seeks to question—that, at that time, "gender and genre" were still inextricably linked. The result was that in 1990 Lila Abu-Lughod asked: "Can there be a feminist ethnography?"[57] The answer was yes, but if and only if a context arises where "ethnography has become separated from anthropology."[58] According to this view, there is something insidious in the structure of anthropology that renders feminist ethnography, at best, marginalized.

The upshot of this debate concerning feminist ethnography is an increased awareness concerning issues of gender, color, voice, and power, and how these issues impact the "field" and the final ethnographic product. Feminism, with its notion of "sisterhood," has placed these issues into even sharper focus than postmodern ethnography was able to do. That is, if feminists practice sisterhood, then how do the ethnographer's special positions of privilege and power affect her relationships with her informants? How can the voices of women of color be accurately heard (and truthfully represented) if the ethnographer herself is white? Since feminist ethnography is still in its infancy, these issues (and many others) have yet to be resolved; yet the fact that feminist ethnography has broached them means that the process and product of ethnographic endeavors will only be enhanced through an increased awareness of the politically gendered nature of cultural and ethnographic representations.

CRITICAL ETHNOGRAPHY

Critical ethnography seeks to make the implicit nature of power relations more explicit. Whether the theoretical stance is Marxian and based on class struggle or Foucaultian and based on "a plurality of autonomous struggles waged throughout the microlevels of society,"[59] a critical stance is taken toward the hegemonic nature of established social and cultural hierarchies. Since no society exists where the few do not benefit at some social cost to the many, deconstructing the epistemological bases for systems of domination and subordination has the potential to increase individuals' awareness of how the world "is," and how critical ethnographers think it "could be."[60] As Vandra Masemann notes, critical ethnography tries to "blur the objective/subjective distinction and thus make necessary the redefinition of social research itself"[61] by constructing "a theory of ethics and politics."[62]

The combining of ethics with politics can be seen in the way, as Michael Apple has observed, that critical ethnographers are concerned with the dual meaning embodied in the word *subject*. That is, individuals can be *subjected* to any number of authorities, and they can also be *subjects,* active participants in shaping their own lives.[63] As Apple states: "It is [critical ethnographers'] opposition to the former and their conscious embrace of the latter that sets [them] apart from so much of the existing research community."[64]

Critical ethnography can be used as a tool for critiquing the status quo by uncovering the many layers of cultural and social oppression that individuals confront. As "transformative intellectuals,"[65] critical ethnographers tend to question those cultural beliefs and social practices that normally go unquestioned.

If critical ethnography seeks to render the implicit as explicit, then this raises an important question: How does one go about doing critical ethnographic research? According to Joe Kincheloe and Peter McLaren, a critical approach entails the following:

> We are defining a criticalist as a researcher or theorist who attempts to use her or his work as a form of social or cultural criticism and who accepts certain basic assumptions: that all thought is fundamentally mediated by power relations which are socially and historically constituted; that facts can never be isolated from the domain of values or removed from some form of ideological inscription; that the relationship between concept and object and signifier and signified is never stable or fixed and is often mediated by the social relations of capitalist produc-

tion and consumption; that language is central to the formation of subjectivity (conscious and unconscious awareness); that certain groups in
any society are privileged over others and, although the reasons for this
privileging may vary widely, the oppression which characterizes contemporary societies is most forcefully reproduced when subordinates
accept their social status as natural, necessary or inevitable; that oppression has many faces and that focusing on only one at the expense of
others (e.g. class oppression versus racism) often elides the intercon-
nections among them; and finally, that mainstream research practices
are generally, although most often unwittingly, implicated in the reproduction of systems of class, race and gender oppression.[66]

When a critical researcher applies this definition to conducting
ethnographic work, he or she does so by means of a three-pronged ideological strategy. That is, critical ethnographers (1) seek a more equitable
social order, (2) see political action as the means to accomplish that end,
and (3) believe that this method can be used to study culture and society
in order to bring about substantive cultural and social change. Thus, a
critical ethnographer accepts a huge responsibility by seeking to promote
democratization through his or her "engaged activism." Interest in this
position comes from a "value-laden" perception concerning the meanings of freedom and emancipation. As with interpretive ethnography, the
goal is to create an intersubjective world between the researcher and the
informants being studied, but "critical ethnographers . . . accept an
added research task of raising their voice to speak *to* an audience *on behalf* of their subjects as a means of empowering them by giving more authority to the subjects' voice."[67]

What hubris! In countries where individualism predominates, we tend
to forget that the basis for critical analyses rests on a theoretical foundation
that promotes *collective* political action. By taking a distinctly individualistic political stance toward the necessity of advocating social change, this
use of the critical ethnographic method has the potential to destabilize both
the researcher and the "other." The reason for this potential instability in
critical ethnographic work is that it is perched precariously between ad-
vancing a collective program for substantive social change and merely encouraging a vapid, individualistic ideological position.

One final point needs to be expressed concerning ethnographic
work. While this discussion has delineated the differences among the
various ethnographic forms typically used, these delineations are rarely
this clear-cut. That is, all postmodern ethnographies are interpretive in

nature, with the major difference between them being a question of voice. Experiential ethnographies and critical ethnographies both give authority to the ethnographer; however, the first speaks *about* and the second *for* the "other." Experiential ethnographies can have dialogic moments within them, while polyphonic ethnographies are more a desired goal than an actualized practice. Further, any ethnography that examines those at the bottom of the socioeconomic pyramid implicitly takes on the role of social advocacy inherent in critical ethnographies. This advocacy role exists whether the ethnographer intends it or not. Consequently, elements of the various "newer" ethnographic types will be seen throughout the following chapters depending on the situations in which the authors found themselves in the context of studying education in China.

ETHNOGRAPHIES ON SCHOOLING IN CHINA: A METHODOLOGICAL OVERVIEW

The present Chinese educational system has its roots in the West.[68] The obvious failure of the Confucian-based Mandarinate to produce an educated elite that could create and mount a successful campaign to combat Western economic, political, and social imperialism led to its abandonment. In response, the Chinese attempted to adopt and adapt Western-style education to Chinese purposes. This Westernization of Chinese education is but one example of the process by which Western ideas have challenged existing, non-Western ones. It is also an example of the trend toward the development of a Western-inspired, global educational subculture. As James Clifford has observed, vast cultural differences are increasingly becoming mitigated through a process of "inventive syncretism"[69] as the world becomes more and more interconnected. Consequently, cultures freely adopt from one another "precious piece[s] of culture,"[70] which they adapt to fit their own cultural needs. The use of inventive syncretism is patently evident in the evolution of the Chinese educational system, and elements of this borrowing are noticeable in the various studies examined in this volume.

   Doing fieldwork in China is not an easy task. Scholars are not given carte blanche to go anywhere and study anything. Permission must be granted for any proposed work, and even when it is granted, it does not necessarily mean that researchers are going to be able to study what they had intended. This is particularly evident when fieldwork cannot take place over an extended period of time, but must be done within the confines of a fixed, government-approved schedule. Government "influence" is seen in five of the studies presented in this volume: directly in those by Kai-ming Cheng, Gerard Postiglione, Irving Epstein, and Lynn Paine and Brian DeLany, and more indirectly in the work of Heidi Ross. In one form or another, the government controlled access to sites, length of study, and interview sources. Although this affected the results, some valuable information was found nonetheless.

Cheng's study was, in theory, the least amenable to ethnographic work. Commissioned by the International Institute for Educational Planning to look at basic education in China, it was part of a larger comparative study that included Mexico, Guinea, and India. At first glance, this would appear to be a relatively easy quantitative study comparing basic education achievements and informants' perceptions about basic education. It soon became apparent, however, that Chinese perceptions of basic education tended to ignore "traditional" academic concerns held by Western experts on school curriculum. The content matter of course work was less important to parents than the moral education components of schooling—for example, would their children be able to fit within Chinese society? The Western educational practices that framed the study favor individual educational outcomes that are measurable, but these same procedures cannot be used to assess the effects of moral education. As Cheng found, if the research overlooked local Chinese concerns, then it would have produced meaningless responses. This revelation points out that despite Chinese schooling's Western basis, the culture maintains strong links to a Confucian past. Consequently, unless survey research methods have a qualitative component that is able to place the study within the perceptions and practices of the people being studied, they will produce results that are not reflective of actual social and cultural conditions.

Postiglione's glimpse at minority education, like Cheng's on basic education, shows the difficulties involved in doing research within the confines of a rigidly prescribed schedule. True ethnographic methods cannot be used when time is short because ethnographic work entails adequate time to observe and gain rapport with informants. This situation becomes even more challenging when unfamiliar languages and customs are added to the research milieu. If a researcher cannot speak the informants' language, then translators are needed. In any social situation where translators are employed, only they know what has actually transpired, and because translation from one language to another does not occur through a one-to-one correspondence, meaning and intention become highly elastic. This problem is compounded in China, where translators tend to give researchers either responses they think the researchers want to hear or responses that adhere to the Communist Party line. Within this methodological quagmire, research will necessarily tend to be quantitative in focus and general in conclusions.

With a strong quantitative core structuring their research, both Cheng and Postiglione tend to employ experiential authority in their narratives because they were able to interview so few people. Given that both had to rely on translators to overcome the problem of local dialect or minority language, they were further divorced from their informants. As a result, the reader must rely upon the accuracy of their observations, because there tend to be so few other voices to hear.

Epstein's look at delinquency and reformatory education is based upon research that was conducted in 1983. Research and interview protocols were even more structured than those encountered by Cheng or Postiglione. While all had research subjects who were preselected, Epstein was limited to one-time-only site visits. This clearly limited the amount of information he was able to obtain and necessitated a rigorous research design. Thus, his research was guided by existing (Western) scholarship on the causes of delinquency and the role of reformatory education. Today, Epstein feels that his conclusions were, at best, naïve. With its strong emphasis on reflection, Epstein's work tends toward postmodern ethnography even though it is not multivocal. Given the serious methodological constraints faced by Epstein, the initial research itself was conducted experientially, even though he now advocates—but not without reservations—that a critical ethnographic approach might be better suited for studying reformatory education. How does one account for this change in his perceptions? Like Wolf's aforementioned *A Thrice-Told Tale,* Epstein and the world have changed. While the facts of his research have remained constant, their meanings have been transformed. Yet according to Epstein, present research on delinquency in China still seems to be conducted using the same rubrics of the past. The consequences of this chapter are thought-provoking, given the synchronic framing of his original research and the diachronic framing of his reinterpretation. Is any knowledge truly fixed?

Paine and DeLany's look at rural education places the role of the researcher front and center. Given their education and experience, they had little in common with the Chinese peasants they studied in Burntwood Township, but, as they note, basic education in China is predominantly rural. Yet almost all educational policies are designed to nurture the "best and brightest" of Chinese urban youth. This situation places researchers who study rural education at the margin and problematizes their role as researchers, as they are separated experientially from the people they study and positionally from Chinese educational concerns. As a consequence, Paine and DeLany are highly reflexive on their roles as educators and as researchers as they deal with the angst that studying rural education can produce. This places their work within the nexus between postmodern and interpretive ethnography, and offers a view of Chinese education that is rarely seen.

One common thread joins all of these chapters together. Implicitly or explicitly, they all question the validity of Western-style education in its Chinese variant. As Cheng points out, Chinese parents want their children to fit into society and education is crucial in accomplishing that goal. Further, minority and rural children and delinquents are all being taught information that is not totally applicable to their lives, as few will ever be able to apply that knowledge. It seems to elude Chinese educational authorities that, despite the vast social and economic upheavals it is undergoing, China is still a rural, agrarian, peasant society where farming is the predominant occupation. By creating an educational system that guarantees that the majority of students will ultimately fail, is China doing the right thing?

Ross's chapter is a compilation of four separate experiences ("moments") she has encountered while researching education in China. Originally schooled as a critical ethnographer, Ross came to find that an initial idealism about her ability to construct "social alternatives" for her students in China and for her eventual audience in the United States was somewhat naïve. One gets the impression that change was not necessarily in the direction that critical ethnographers would desire, as Ross was affected by the experience as much, if not more, than her students. Depending upon the direction of interpretive arrows, each served as the other's "other." In her second experience, Ross, as well as Liu in her chapter, encountered the vagaries of doing dialogically based, historical ethnographic work. Recollections of past events are so fluid that constructing a coherent explanation of those events is a difficult task at best. In Ross's case this tenuous situation was complicated by the fact that her audience and informants were one and the same group—not an enviable position for any ethnographer to be in. In her third experience, Ross confronts the changes affecting Chinese education wrought by the implementation of market socialism or, as Ross terms it, the creation of the "material school." Nowhere is the conflict between a socialist, collectivist worldview being confronted more openly by a capitalist, individualist worldview than in Chinese schools. Ross's last

experience deals with her role as the "talking head" on Chinese education in a PBS series on comparative education. In the flux that characterizes the presentation of facts within the time constraints of television
programming, information can still be exchanged that permits an understanding of similarities and differences that exist between American and
Chinese education.

Ross's various research projects employed several ethnographic
styles: interpretive, postmodern, critical. Yet the chapter, in its final narrative form, is mostly postmodern in character. Ross has had time to reflect
upon her various experiences and has created a work that is confessional
in character. While we get snippets of information about how contradictory the structural changes occurring in Chinese education are, we get an
education on the practical and intellectual problems (and their solutions)
that plague ethnographers. As Ross shows, fieldwork is rife with compli-
cations that are only compounded with the transformation of fieldnotes to
narrative text. This results in the most reflexive account of the trials and
tribulations of doing ethnographic work included in this volume.

Liu's chapter is the most personal work presented in this book. She
looks at the impact of missionary education on the lives of a cohort of
women who attended St. Hilda's School for Girls in Wuhan during the
1920s and 1930s. An ethnographic work relying on oral histories, the text
is strongly dialogic in content and interpretive in form. Since Liu relied
upon oral histories of older women, she did not have the "power" that most
Western researchers have over the social interaction because her position
with the women she interviewed was rigidly fixed. These women were all
deferentially referred to as "Auntie," and her research was tolerated out of
respect for her mother. As with all oral histories, these women's stories are
dependent upon the fragile nature of memory. Given this fragility, how can
any researcher know if what he or she is being told has any validity if factual historical errors and inconsistencies between personal recollections
are frequently encountered? What comes across in the text is the need to
position any reminiscence within a larger context—in this case, within the
context of Chinese social history, American missionary history, and the
cultural interplay between the two. Nonetheless, these women's voices are
heard in the text as they relate the effects that a Western-style education
had upon their lives. Here, too, the moral component of their schooling is
the most salient feature they can recall about their educations.

One other aspect is salient in Liu's chapter. Since reports to missionary boards were required of mission schools, the teachers and administrators of St. Hilda's left behind archival materials that enabled Liu to

access information unknown by her respondents.[71] The result is an awareness that missionary education occurred within a larger context, which was, in fact, a set of contexts shaping Eastern and Western views of the events that helped construct Liu's interpretations. Thus, the combining of oral history with archival information separates Liu's chapter from the others in this volume and gives it a historical grounding that departs from the synchronic bias of most ethnographic work.

In the Conclusion, Vandra Masemann returns again to the Janus-faced nature of this volume and looks at the duality of doing ethnographic work in general and of studying education in China in particular. This leads Masemann to ask, "What have we learned about doing ethnographic studies of education in China?" She breaks down each of the substantive chapters into three sections: (1) Doing Ethnography, (2) Studying Chinese Education, and (3) Doing Ethnography in China. By placing all the substantive chapters within this rubric and by looking at them through the lens of a critical analysis, Masemann is able to lend a coherence to what otherwise might be a disjointed text. In this way she notes that the substantive chapters go from large-scale surveys with ethnographic underpinnings that help contextualize the research (Cheng and Postiglione) to more mid-range studies that have implications for comparative work (Paine and DeLany; Epstein) to very personal, phenomenological studies that grapple with the social construction of meaning and truth (Ross and Liu). The text shows various ways that ethnographic methods can be used to catch a glimpse of that ever-elusive specter that is called, simply, "education in China."

NOTES

1. While the word *other* is used frequently in the text, it must be understood that this is primarily a postmodern term that has come to be used in place of *informants* or *natives*. The difference, however, is more than merely one of semantics. Thus, from the postmodern perspective, informants/natives are studied as objects; whereas "others" are seen as subjects—somehow different from, but nonetheless inexorably linked to, the researcher/ethnographer.

2. Adapted from Robert R. Sherman and Roman B. Webb, *Qualitative Research in Education: Focus and Methods* (London: Falmer Press, 1988), 5–8.

3. Marshall Sahlins, *Culture and Practical Reason* (Chicago: University of Chicago Press, 1976).

4. For a discussion of doxa, see Pierre Bourdieu, *Outline of a Theory of Practice,* trans. Richard Nice. Cambridge Studies in Social Anthropology, ed. Jack Goody, no. 16 (Cambridge: Cambridge University Press, 1977 [1972]), 159–171.

5. James Clifford, "Introduction: Partial Truths," in *Writing Culture: The Poetics and Politics of Ethnography,* eds. James Clifford and George E. Marcus (Berkeley: University of California Press, 1986), 2.

6. Margery Wolf, *A Thrice-Told Tale: Feminism, Postmodernism, and Ethnographic Responsibility* (Stanford: Stanford University Press, 1992), 129.

7. James Clifford, "On Ethnographic Allegory," in *Writing Culture: The Poetics and Politics of Ethnography,* eds. James Clifford and George E. Marcus (Berkeley: University of California Press, 1986), 101.

8. See Robert Thornton, "Narrative Ethnography in Africa, 1859-1920," *Man* 18 (1983): 502–520. The theoretical basis for conducting a scientific approach to ethnographic work was laid out by Bronislaw Malinowski in his *Argonauts of the Western Pacific: An Account of Native Enterprise and Adventure in the Archipelagoes of Melanesian New Guinea* (New York: E. P. Dutton, 1961 [1922]).

9. Mary Louise Pratt, "Fieldwork in Common Places," in *Writing Culture: The Poetics and Politics of Ethnography,* eds. James Clifford and George E. Marcus (Berkeley: University of California Press, 1986), 32.

10. The types of "authority" that are being used to reflect the variations in the ways ethnographies are conceived and conducted are borrowed from James Clifford, *The Predicament of Culture: Twentieth-Century Ethnography, Literature, and Art* (Cambridge, Mass.: Harvard University Press, 1988), 21–54.

11. See Melford E. Spiro, "Cultural Relativism and the Future of Anthropology," in *Rereading Cultural Anthropology,* ed. George E. Marcus (Durham, N.C.: Duke University Press, 1992), 124–151.

12. Ibid., 124.

13. George E. Marcus and Michael M. J. Fischer, *Anthropology as Cultural Critique: An Experimental Moment in the Human Sciences* (Chicago: University of Chicago Press, 1986), 129.

14. See Michel de Certeau, *Heterologies: Discourse on the Other,* trans. Brian Massumi with a Foreword by Wlad Godzich. Theory and History of Literature Series, eds. Wlad Godzich and Jochen Schulte-Sasse, no. 17 (Minneapolis: University of Minnesota Press, 1986), 202–3.

15. Clifford, "Introduction," 5.

16. E. E. Evans-Pritchard, *The Nuer* (Oxford: Oxford University Press, 1969 [1940]).

17. Paul Rabinow, "Representations Are Social Facts: Modernity and Post-Modernity in Anthropology," in *Writing Culture: The Poetics and Politics of Ethnography,* eds. James Clifford and George E. Marcus (Berkeley: University of California Press, 1986), 244.

18. Wolf, *Thrice-Told Tale,* 9.

19. Ibid., 2.

20. See Spiro, "Cultural Relativism," 126–8.

21. Ibid., 128.

22. Clifford, "Introduction," 15.

23. Marcus and Fischer, *Anthropology as Cultural Critique,* 26.

24. Clifford Geertz, "Thick Description: Toward an Interpretive Theory of Culture," in *The Interpretation of Cultures* (New York: Basic Books, 1973), 3–30.

25. See Roy Wagner, *The Invention of Culture* (Chicago: University of Chicago Press, 1975).

26. de Certeau, *Heterologies,* 202.

27. Clifford, "Introduction," 6.

28. For one side of the philosophical debate that has occurred from the postmodern attack on Enlightenment epistemology, see Richard Rorty, *Philosophy and the Mirror of Nature* (Princeton: Princeton University Press, 1979).

29. Michel Foucault, *Power/Knowledge: Selected Interviews and Other Writings 1972–1977* (New York: Pantheon Books, 1980), 133.

30. Ibid., 132.

31. See Bourdieu, *Outline,* 159–171.

32. In Bennett M. Berger, *The Survival of a Counterculture: Ideological Work and Everyday Life Among Rural Communards* (Berkeley: University of California Press, 1981), 209.

33. Ibid., 222.

34. Alvin W. Gouldner, *The Coming Crisis of Western Sociology* (New York: Basic Books, 1970), 490.

35. Berger, *Survival,* 221.

36. For a more in-depth discussion along this line of thought on reflexivity, see Loic J. D. Wacquant, "Toward a Social Praxeology: The Structure and Logic of Bourdieu's Sociology" in *An Invitation to Reflexive Sociology* by Pierre Bourdieu and Loic J. D. Wacquant (Chicago: University of Chicago Press, 1992), 36–46.

37. While Weberian theory has influenced the phenomenological and ethnomethodological precursors of postmodernism through Weber's notion of *Verstehen,* Weber himself could never be considered a postmodernist.

38. Paul Atkinson, *The Ethnographic Imagination: Textual Constructions of Reality* (London: Routledge, 1990), 7.

39. The difference between a dialogic ethnography and a polyphonic one is more than merely a case of the number of subjects "speaking." While the "other's" voice may be heard in a dialogic ethnography, authority rests squarely with the ethnographer. A polyphonic ethnography idealizes the writing of the text to be one where ethnographer and informants are given equal weight in inscribing the final product.

40. Vincent Crapanzano, "The Postmodern Crisis: Discourse, Parody, Memory," in *Rereading Cultural Anthropology,* ed. George E. Marcus (Durham, N.C.: Duke University Press, 1992), 92.

41. M. M. Bakhtin, *The Dialogic Imagination,* ed. Michael Holquist, trans. Caryl Emerson and Michael Holquist (Austin: University of Texas Press, 1981), 293.

42. Michael Holquist in *The Dialogic Imagination,* 428.

43. Paul Ricoeur, "The Model of Text: Meaningful Action Considered as a Text," *Social Research* 38 (1971): 529–562.

44. See Jean-Francois Lyotard, *The Postmodern Condition: A Report on Knowledge,* trans. Geoff Bennington and Brian Massumi with a Foreword by Fredric Jameson. Theory and History of Literature, eds. Wlad Godzich and Jochen Schulte-Sasse, no. 10 (Minneapolis: University of Minnesota Press, 1984 [1979]).

45. Clifford, *Predicament,* 43.

46. de Certeau, *Heterologies,* 217.

47. For a discussion of symbolic violence, see Bourdieu and Wacquant, *Invitation,* 167–8.

48. de Certeau, *Heterologies,* 68.

49. Renato Rosaldo, *Culture and Truth: The Remaking of Social Analysis,* (Boston: Beacon Press, 1989), 7.

50. Clifford, "Introduction," 2.

51. Ibid.

52. Ibid., 12.

53. Ibid., 19.

54. Ibid., 20.

55. Ibid., 21.

56. Ruth Behar, "Introduction: Out of Exile," in *Women Writing Culture,* eds. Ruth Behar and Deborah A. Gordon (Berkeley: University of California Press, 1995), 6.

57. See Lila Abu-Lughod, "Can There Be a Feminist Ethnography?" *Women and Performance: A Journal of Feminist Theory* 5 (1990): 7–27.

58. Deborah A. Gordon, "Conclusion: Culture Writing Women: Inscribing Feminist Anthropology," in *Women Writing Culture,* eds. Ruth Behar and Deborah A. Gordon (Berkeley: University of California Press, 1995), 437.

59. Steven Best and Douglas Kellner, *Postmodern Theory: Critical Interrogations* (New York: Guilford Press, 1991), 56.

60. See Jim Thomas, *Doing Critical Ethnography.* Qualitative Research Methods, no. 26 (Newbury Park, Calif.: Sage Publications 1993), 3–7.

61. Vandra Lea Masemann, "Critical Ethnography in the Study of Comparative Education," in *New Approaches to Comparative Education,* eds. Philip G. Altbach and Gail P. Kelly (Chicago: The University of Chicago Press, 1986 [1982]), 11. In essence, Masemann compares three approaches for conducting ethnographic research: (1) positivistic, (2) interpretive, and (3) critical. (Because her analysis is different from mine, her chapter is well worth reading for comparative purposes.)

62. Ibid.

63. See Michel Foucault, "The Subject and Power," in Hubert L. Dreyfus and Paul Rabinow, *Michel Foucault: Beyond Structuralism and Hermeneutics* (Chicago: University of Chicago Press, 1982), 208–226.

64. Michael W. Apple, "Series Editor's Introduction," in *Power and Method: Political Activism and Educational Research,* ed. Andrew Gitlin (New York: Routledge, 1994), xi.

65. See Henry A. Giroux, *Teachers as Intellectuals: Toward a Critical Pedagogy of Learning,* (Granby, Mass.: Bergin and Garvey, 1988), xxxii–xxxvi.

66. Joe Kincheloe and Peter McLaren, quoted in Phil Francis Carspecken, *Critical Ethnography in Educational Research: A Theoretical and Practical Guide* (New York: Routledge, 1996), 4. (Note that although Carspecken uses "Joe Kinchloe" throughout his book, I believe he is referring to Joe Kincheloe.)

67. Thomas, *Doing Critical Ethnography,* 4.

68. For a thorough discussion of modern Chinese education, see Suzanne Pepper, *Radicalism and Education Reform in 20th-Century*

China: The Search for an Ideal Development Model (New York: Cambridge University Press, 1996).

69. Clifford, *Predicament,* 23.

70. Bennett M. Berger, *An Essay on Culture: Symbolic Structure and Social Structure* (Berkeley: University of California Press, 1995), 9.

71. The archival aspect of Liu's research is also applicable to Ross's chapter in regard to its McTyeire "moment."

CHAPTER 2

Understanding Basic Education Policies in China
An Ethnographic Approach

KAI-MING CHENG

INTRODUCTION

China has the world's largest educational system: a total of over 220 million students in 1995. Eighty percent of the students are in primary and junior secondary schools; these nine grades constitute China's formal basic education *(jichu jiaoyu)*.[1] Meanwhile, because of the financial reforms implemented by the government in the mid-1980s, basic education has become increasingly a local endeavor. Primary schools, for example, are sponsored and operated by villages in the rural areas or by neighborhoods in the cities. Basic education is more a grassroots endeavor in China than any of the other levels of education, and hence, understanding policies dealing with basic education in China is essential to understanding education in China.

Policy-related studies in education are often interpreted as little more than numbers-crunching exercises dealing with the manipulation of financial and enrollment figures, or as issues involving expanding education's scope in society, changing its structure, or studying its financing mechanisms. However, we are aware that measuring the scope, structures, and financing formulas of educational systems does not explain the totality of education. Education is a process, and unless we understand that process in schools, we do not really understand how the educational system actually functions. Further, understanding this process inevitably involves gaining an understanding of the contexts in which this process takes place. Studies of education policies therefore should not be solely a matter of numbers crunching. In other words, ethnographic methods must play a role in policy-related research. This chapter describes how qualitative methods were used in combination with quantitative methods in order to obtain a more realistic overview of basic educational policies in China.

If quantitative methods dealing with education are frequently reduced to mere numbers, then qualitative research on education is often reduced to looking solely at classrooms and schools—the so-called microscopic aspects of educational research. The present study shows that qualitative research can be equally applicable to macroscopic policy-related research. Policy research, in the final analysis, tends to be either prescriptive or descriptive in nature. Prescriptive studies aim at finding solutions to problems in creating policy goals. They require that the research findings be "realistic" and practical. Descriptive studies aim at understanding the policy process by trying to accurately reflect what is happening and why. In both cases, the general purpose of the research is to obtain information that reflects reality. Although what constitutes reality is always open to philosophical debate,[2] most policy-related studies, by their very nature, assume the existence of a reality that is independent of the researcher. Ethnographic approaches are used in policy research studies as a means to better understand this reality by either analyzing *policies* that need to be formulated or by analyzing the *policy processes* that need to be understood.

THE STUDY

This study is part of a project that looked at basic education in four countries: China, India, Guinea, and Mexico.[3] I was in charge of the China segment, which was carried out in Zhejiang province. The project was prompted by the same considerations that led to the Jomtien conference Education for All, and was started in 1989 as the conference was being prepared.[4] If the spread of basic education is to become a focus in national policies, then it is necessary to understand how basic education is being delivered in developing countries. Hence, the research concerned educational policy and planning. The project chose China and India as the starting points because they represent the world's largest educational systems. Guinea and Mexico were then chosen to expand the case studies to include other developing countries on different continents.

The purpose of the study was to answer two questions: (1) What do students gain from basic education? and (2) How is basic education provided? The study chose not to start from a framework centered on formal curricula but to focus upon *basic educational needs* as perceived by the local community. The previous questions were, therefore, really asking: Are basic educational needs being met? and How are these basic educational needs met or not met? Hence, although much of the study dealt with the formal school system, the general approach that was used adopted a perspective that was not bound solely by the perceptions of teachers or educational planners.

Although there was no requirement for an ethnographic dimension in the study, the researchers were conscious that differences existed among the countries so that a strictly uniform framework would not be applicable for analyzing all the countries. Nonetheless, the individual studies followed a common structure. First, schools were chosen in each of five localities located within a given province or state, based upon differing economic levels. Second, all students in Grade Four and the last grade of primary schooling (i.e., Grade Five or Six in the case of China) were used as the subjects of the research. The research comprised two major components: (1) a test instrument was devised to measure basic educational achievements, and (2) a series of questionnaires and interview questions were employed to understand how people perceived the process of basic education. These were the only elements common in the four country studies; otherwise, the design was totally dependent upon the local team of researchers.

Although the overall research dealt with policy concerns, there was a consensus among the researchers that these were fundamentally case studies that could be used to improve our understanding about basic education. Hence, there was ample room in the design to allow for the analysis of the contextual factors and processes that affect basic education, and this is where ethnographic methods were used.

WHAT IS RESEARCH?

Negotiating entry into a research site is often a crucial step in doing qualitative work. In the Zhejiang project, the issue was not so much a matter of gaining physical entry as it was a matter of securing genuine cooperation from Chinese educators. The project was assigned a designated provincial counterpart, the Zhejiang Institute for Educational Research—a provincial research institute that appeared to be ideal for assisting in our proposed research. Not only was it the "proper" institution for helping us with the proposed research, but it also possessed the necessary authority to permit us to conduct our research at the various local research sites.

Problems arose, however, over the meaning of the term *research*. What was seen as research at the Institute largely fell into four distinct categories:

1. *The Questionnaire Survey*: Survey methods had been tried a few times in the province, and they were seen as a modern way of doing research in their use of computerized statistical analyses. This was seen as the most sophisticated approach for doing educational research.
2. *The Experiment*: Educational experiments had been used as a means for promoting reforms in schools or localities for a number of years. A researcher would be sent into the field to *direct* a project. The role of the researcher was to make sure that the project would accomplish the outcome anticipated by the designer of the reform.
3. *The Collation*: Often, a project's goal was the compiling of a monograph written by writers famous in the field. The Institute would collate the articles and publish the text. This project was also known as "research" *(yanjiu)*.
4. *The Reflection*: The institute was also asked to ponder policy issues in the name of *yanjiu*. It was expected that a paper containing opinions about an issue and recommendations for its implementation would be written.

Apart from survey methods, all the other categories are not normally regarded as research per se. Even in the surveys the institute had conducted, little attention was paid to observing the methodological procedures I was trained to follow. This difference in the meaning of research posed a potential problem for the project. Two approaches were considered as means to overcome this possibly insurmountable problem. The first would have involved bringing researchers from outside China to do the fieldwork.[5] The second involved working out a way to cooperate with the local researchers.

For several reasons, I adopted the latter approach. First, researchers were readily available, although they adhered to a research convention that was different from ours. This difference in the interpretation of what research "should be" can be seen as a matter of perspective, rather than as a difference in ability. Second, the study sought to look at the culture surrounding basic education in China. As such, Chinese research procedures were but one dimension of the larger culture; thus, I concluded that it would be beneficial to the aims of the study if local researchers were included. It would have been contradictory to the aims of the study if the Chinese researchers had been excluded simply because they worked within a different methodological framework.

This inclusion created a practical problem, however, in that the local researchers were not prepared to follow the "standard" research convention that we were using, and consequently, the conclusions we would draw from the research might not be accepted by the international educational community. Despite this potential problem, I was convinced that even though both research teams were accustomed to different conventions, we could still share some "common denominator" in approaching the research. I was also convinced that such a common denominator could be found in actual practice.

It was with these convictions that I decided to involve the local researchers in the design of the research instruments. The project was to develop eleven questionnaires and interviewing schemes for the main survey. We did a crude draft of the questionnaires and interviewing schemes, and went into a township that was similar to one of the designated research sites. We invited all of those who would be involved in the project from the Institute as well as the local researchers who would be doing the actual fieldwork. We worked for two full days in the township interviewing a small sample of parents, teachers, principals, and local leaders. The team would meet each evening to discuss and modify the instruments and the ways to use them based on the answers we were getting from the daily interviews. This became a training session for everybody on the team, and by the end of the two days, we arrived at a consensus on what methods we would employ.

During these two days of intensive problem solving, it became apparent that the difference between our research conventions was not so much a question of *methods* as much as a question of *purposes*. Most of the research projects done by the Institute were *prescriptive* in nature, aiming at definitive conclusions that would lead to immediate recommendations about educational policy. Its members were not accustomed to *descriptive* studies aimed at general understanding and developing insights regarding educational processes. There was, however, little disagreement about methodological concerns. The local researchers had no problem in accepting unstructured interviews starting with only a "grand tour" question. They also demonstrated a capacity for assessing the opportunities for further probing in open-ended interviews. They entered discussions about the proper way to ask a questionnaire question as well, and showed high levels of professional expertise.

Consensus-building was further achieved at the first research location in Longquan county. We deliberately singled out one of the sites to study before we visited the other proposed sites. At the first site, we carried out the entire procedure as designed; however, we invited two members from each of the other four sites to join us. In other words, there was a slightly larger team at the first site as the team members came from all five sites. The study of this first site became the training ground for the core researchers from the other sites. The core members were then expected to do a similar pilot project in their respective counties in order to train the other researchers at that site. By so doing, the essential principles and methods of the study, including the qualitative dimensions, were disseminated to all of those participating in the research.

WHAT IS BASIC EDUCATION?

It is common in the literature on schooling to identify basic education as achieving some level in literacy and numeracy. It is assumed that literacy and numeracy are the basic educational needs. But are they?

I was first alerted to this question when my Chinese counterparts from the Institute wondered if literacy and numeracy should be used to measure educational achievement. "You may not understand that in China's education, we do not see intellectual attainments as the only aim of education, and indeed they are sometimes not the most essential," they said. They raised the possibility of including within the parameters of the research questions concerning moral norms, life skills, and other factors that they considered essential for participating fully in the social life of China. This concern prompted me to launch an additional study involving two focus groups—one urban and one rural. The following is a description of the urban focus group:

> A focus group discussion was held with a Neighborhood Committee. Eight members were present. The members were elected from the families who lived in the neighborhood comprising one street.
>
> My concern was to understand what were perceived as basic educational needs, so that the test instrument and questionnaires we were designing would be consistent with the community's perceptions. In order to focus the discussion, I started with one single "grand tour"

question: "What are the characteristics of a person who cannot survive in this society?" I asked the question in a negative sense deliberately. A positive question may lead the parents to think along publicly announced educational aims and to follow orthodox conceptions of curriculum guidelines.

The responses converged on two points. The interviewees were concerned with "good adaptability" and "good human relations." Good adaptability included adaptation to nature and the changing environment, endurance, persistence, and self-study abilities. Good human relations included relations with family members, relations with peers and workmates, and the management of the self in an organization. Those who cannot socially succeed are those who are unable to cope with the changing environment, those who evade responsibility, those who are incapable of managing their affairs, or those who tend to be isolated. No one mentioned literacy and numeracy, which had been our anticipated answers. Nothing was mentioned in the realms of educational knowledge or skills.

I followed with a number of probing questions related to literacy and numeracy. (For example, "Don't you think a young person should be able to read a road sign?") The informants did not seem to appreciate that these should become part of formal education. "They can always learn from their neighbors or even ask a neighbor to help." "They can always ask for help from passers-by."

The focus group discussion proved extremely illuminating. First, although this information came from only one neighborhood, it demonstrated in a distinctive way that in the parents' minds there are educational goals apart from literacy and numeracy. Second, it showed that the local researchers' insistence on probing beyond literacy and numeracy was necessary in order to understand basic educational concerns in China. This perception from the community subsequently helped us to interpret a large number of research findings that might otherwise have been inexplicable.

Results of the focus group discussions reminded me of writings I had read about Chinese culture. The emphasis on adaptability and human relations is in keeping with findings in other disciplines such as psychology and management studies. There is a cultural tradition in China that plays down the individual self and expects individuals to adapt themselves to the community.[6] There is also an emphasis on "connections" or *guanxi* that is central to any studies about social relations, motivations, and satisfaction in Chinese organizations. These are reflected in Chinese education in its emphasis on moral education, which in the Chinese tradition means learning how to relate to other people in the society.

The importance of moral education in China should not be hard to fathom—it was the basis of the Confucian educational system. This focus has continued to this day in the Chinese "Good in Three" award for students. The award is based upon being "good in conduct,[7] good in learning, good in physical fitness." The award is given to well-rounded students, but the moral component is considered to be the most important one. While most of the students are given this award, it nonetheless reflects a Chinese tradition that values and delineates moral virtue *(de)* from expertise *(cai)*. The Chinese hold that a person who is morally good but poor in expertise is still an acceptable member of society, but a morally bad person is never an acceptable member of society regardless of his or her abilities.

Consequently, our results reconfirmed that literacy and numeracy are not necessarily the core of aims of Chinese education. The local researchers' insistence on including a moral dimension in the test for educational achievement was justified. Thus, the interpretation of the data went well beyond literacy and numeracy. This itself could be an important finding of the study. That is, basic education is not necessarily about achievements in literacy and numeracy, and this conclusion may not confine itself to China alone.

WHY SCHOOLING?

One of the known facts about basic education in China is its relatively high enrollment rate. Although there are still areas where attendance is poor (for example, girls in minority areas), the country, as a whole, tends to show high attendance rates. This phenomenon is of great interest to the international educational community, which is striving to increase attendance rates worldwide. As a consequence, we tried to include in the parents' questionnaire some questions that might provide us with an answer to why such a high percentage of Chinese children go to school. The following describes the process that lead to the final questionnaire:

> We started with a crude questionnaire and spent two days in a rural
> village trying out the questions in order to refine the questionnaire. We

made the assumption in the crude questionnaire that parents' aspirations for education should be related to their hope for their children's future careers. Underlying this assumption was the view that economic motivations would be of paramount concern. Therefore, one item in the questionnaire concerned the parents' desire for a future career for their children. In drafting this section of the questionnaire, census occupational categories were used.[8] In addition, teachers with good knowledge of past graduates helped check this list against all the possible occupations taken up by past primary graduates. The final list of occupations is as follows:

(01)   further studies
(02)   administrator in the village
(03)   professional technician
(04)   skilled worker
(05)   professional farmer
(06)   businessman
(07)   local industrialist
(08)   People's Liberation Army
(09)   teacher
(10)   others

We did not provide the parents in the trial village with this list. We conducted interviews with a few parents in the trial village by asking open-ended questions and providing no answers from our side. The parents were chosen to represent a wide range of educational as well as occupational backgrounds. The interviews I personally did were with three parents: a "professional farmer" (*zhuanyehu,* meaning farmer with technological expertise) who had some junior-secondary schooling, an illiterate female farmer, and a butcher with some primary education. Other local researchers did similar interviews. We gathered during the evening to compare notes and modify the questionnaire accordingly.

We deliberately started the conversation with a "grand tour" question: "Why have you sent your child to school?" Most parents in the rural areas felt puzzled by the question. The most articulate rural parents expressed their bewilderment by retorting "Why not?" or "Why are you asking this?" Some of them even turned to the accompanying teacher and asked for help. Such answers would mean disappointments had the questions been used in other research conventions. In our discussions, however, we came to realize that these responses were valuable data and became excited by these "nonanswers." Obviously, the question being asked was "wrong" because it did not fit into the parents' framework. Since they did not have an answer, we began to question our assumptions and our overall framework about parents' motivations about their children's schooling.

When we felt that the parents' responses to the initial "grand tour" question had been fully explored, we then turned to a more concrete question: "What would you expect your child to do after schooling?" The question did not normally get an immediate answer from the rural parents either. Many parents, particularly those who were illiterate, reacted with doubts and fussed about the question. The following are some such responses:

"How should I know?"

"What do you mean?"

"What do you think I should say?" (Turning to the local teacher)

"I don't know how to answer."

"I have never thought of it!"

We realized that there were parents who actually did not think much about their children's future careers. Such answers, again, could be seen as "nonanswers." Since such responses came largely from illiterate or semiliterate parents, one might easily conclude that a strong correlation exists between parents' level of education and their concern for their children's education. We did not do this. Instead, we regarded these answers as the means to find the real motivation for sending their children to school. With further probing, we were rewarded by the following answers:

"It goes without saying that I wish they could go to universities."

"Of course I want them to get education as high up as possible, but I don't know what they are called."

"I don't mind, as long as they can leave the village eventually."

"I don't mind what they do, as long as they are not doing anything indecent."

In the end, we decided that (1) the questionnaires should be completed by the researchers based upon the answers to our open-ended questions and (2) we should allow answers that we had not previously considered, such as:

"I have never thought of that"

"university study"

"further study, as high as possible"

"leaving the village eventually"

"not doing anything indecent, irrespective of the occupation"

To complement the above interviews, I conducted two long interviews with parents in the city: an engineer and a marginally employed worker from a state enterprise. The engineer was very articulate concerning his motives for his daughter's future and thoughtfully analyzed the general career opportunities available for her. The worker, who had some junior-secondary education, was quite pessimistic about his child's future. Nonetheless, in both cases, a university education was still seen as the top priority.

These interviews implied a number of things. First, there are parents' aspirations for their children that cannot be expressed in terms of a specific occupation. To many of the parents, "education," "more education," or a "university education" are goals in themselves. Second, parents' aspirations for their children might not be realistic. In the trial village, for example, there had never been a single child who went to a university, but parents still took a university education as a prime reason for sending their children to school. Third, parents who wanted more education for their children did not necessarily know the actual path their children had to follow. Thus, "university education," for example, is a notion of an ideal that is not necessarily the same as "further studies."

The actual results of the questionnaire from a sample of 244 parents are seen in Table 2.1.

Table 2.1 Parents' Aspiration: Children's Future Career[9]

Aspirations	Percentage
00 No response	47.5
01 Further study	15.7
02 University	13.3
03 Cadre	1.0
04 Professional	8.6
05 Worker	1.9
06 Farmer	0.4
07 Entrepreneur	0.7
08 Leaving village	4.6
09 Army	1.0
10 Teacher	2.1
11 Decent	2.3
12 Others	1.0

Among the 244 parents, 45.7 percent opted not to respond to this question. Had we not also done the interviews, the answers would likely be seen as invalid. In fact, they reinforced the hypothesis generated by the previous interviews. In the report, I wrote:

> The largest number of parents failed to provide an answer. This merits some attention. When further probed, many of them said they felt [that it was too] difficult to give an answer, or said they had not thought of it. In other words, the parents felt that the question was not a sensible question. This itself was an interesting response. This has to be compared with the fact that parents have little doubt of sending their children to schools. This was evident not only from the high attendance, but also from the interviews done before the questionnaire survey. Parents who send their children to schools do not seem to have [a] calculated rationale for doing so. A sensible interpretation of this is that the importance of schooling has become internalized in the parents' minds [so] that it requires no rational deliberation to support schooling of their children.[10]

Another 29 percent of the parents regarded "further study" or "university" as the goal for their children. This indirectly supports the above assertion, that education per se is seen as a desired goal. As I stated in the report:

> Of those who gave responses, the majority went for "further study as much as possible" or "university study." This seems to reinforce the interpretation . . . that in most parents' minds, schooling was for the sake of schooling. This is in keeping with the cultural tradition which is summarized in the saying "Everything is low, but education is high." . . . As a matter of reality, very few students in the rural schools under study ever went to universities; even study in secondary technical schools (specialized senior-secondary schools) was rare. Yet parents still took university study or further study as a prime goal of schooling. This was the case for urban as well as rural parents.[11]

All in all, "Why have you sent your child to school?" is not a good question to ask Chinese parents. However, from an ethnographic point of view, the nonanswers to this question provide a clue to deeply held cultural views. As LeVine has noted:

> Many ethnographers arrive at the conclusion that what informants find difficult to verbalize is more important, more fundamental, in the cultural organization of ideas than what they can verbalize. They argue that the more fundamental ideas—basic assumptions—are less accessible to verbal formulation because the social consensus in a community protects them from challenge and shifts the focus of discourse to more specific points that are at issue in normal social life.[12]

In other words, "schooling" has become an internalized, taken-for-granted idea. To these parents, schooling is a holistic concept; they are not prepared, nor are they able, to express the goals of education analytically in terms of economic incentives or career prospects. Some economists would argue that in the final analysis, every human being is a rational animal and makes decisions according to cost/benefit analyses; yet this study seems to conclude that this is not the framework that Chinese parents use to conceptualize the role of schooling. Occupational prestige and economic income do not seem to be the reason that Chinese parents support basic education. Using future careers as the basic framework for analyzing this question was a demonstration of the researchers' ignorance of Chinese education. It was only after we had learned this point in the field that we were able to ask sensible questions and deduce what the parents were actually thinking.

Ironically, it could well be this holistic conception of education, when accompanied by the lack of analytic reasoning concerning actual real-world outcomes by Chinese parents, that explains the remarkable level of enrollment in Chinese schools. Clearly, culture plays a major role in how the Chinese perceive the meaning of education. If parents based their decisions solely on an economic calculus, then they might not be as supportive of basic education as they are.

The methodological lesson learned from this episode is important. We might have provided only the original optional answers and forced the parents to choose one. We might well have treated the nonresponses as "others." We might have arrived at a different conclusion by analyzing the data thus obtained, but the most valuable data would have been subsumed under the categories of "no response" or "others." What we would have gotten from our preconceived options would have been, in fact, peripheral to what was really occurring. We would have gotten what we thought the parents thought, but not what they were actually thinking.

This finding could have far-reaching policy implications. In 1993, I was doing research in a developing village in remote Gansu province, talking to parents and local planners.[13] The research was conducted when the Chinese government started to introduce fee-charging for admission to the universities. Parents were very upset. Higher education, which had been perceived as achievable through mere hard work, now carried a monetary burden. If parents lost hope in the possibility of university entrance, then the whole basic education system could collapse. Just how many students eventually were admitted into universities would not be the real concern. The real impact was that parents were abruptly reminded of an economic calculus surrounding further education, and they were suddenly forced to consider the economic costs inherent in a university education. Given what we found concerning Chinese perceptions regarding education, the cost of such a reform clearly outweighs its potential benefits to the state.

BASIC EDUCATION: WHAT FOR?

Another item in the parents' questionnaire pertained to their expectations about what should be learned in schools. That is, it was concerned with what the perceived goals are for basic education. This was designed to be compared with what was discovered from the neighborhood focus-group discussions mentioned earlier. The following is how the relevant item in the questionnaire was framed:

We asked parents: "When your child has completed primary schooling, what do you think he/she should have learned? What should he/she have mastered, and what should he/she have been equipped with?" The original optional responses in the draft questionnaire consisted of two major groups: knowledge and skills. They were:

(01) a good knowledge base
(02) ways of self-learning
(03) skills for independent living
(04) basic skills for economic activities, such as bookkeeping, letter writing, instruction reading

Local researchers insisted that there should be an option dealing with moral education. Therefore we added the fifth item:

(05) a simple and diligent lifestyle

Ethnographic interviews in the trial village, again with open-ended questions, confirmed the necessity of the local researchers' addition. Further, parents also provided responses that are normally associated with human relations: that their children should not fight, that they should not quarrel, and that they should be polite. Other parents said that they did not care what their children learned as long as they were admitted to higher levels of education. There were also parents who responded that they had never thought about this question. When probed with the question "Don't you think schools should also teach some production skills such as farming and accounting skills?," parents in general expressed disapproval. The only exception was a butcher, who said his daughter who was in Grade Four was able to help him with simple bookkeeping.

The modified questionnaire therefore identified ten items as the optional responses:

(01) a good foundation of knowledge
(02) ways of self-learning
(03) promotion to higher levels of study
(04) having a simple and hardworking lifestyle
(05) politeness, shunning fighting and quarreling
(06) specific skills for independent living

- (07)   knowledge of bookkeeping, accounting, correspondence, instruction-reading, and basics for economic activities
- (08)   "I don't expect much—it's only primary school."
- (09)   "I've never thought of it."
- (10)   Others

Table 2.2 shows the responses to the questionnaire from 244 parents. Overall, the most frequently occurring expectation during the interviews was "a good foundation of knowledge"; the second was "promotion to higher levels of education." There was only a slight difference between the various research sites.

Table 2.2 Parents' Expectation of Primary Schooling[14]

Response	Overall Percentage
No Response	**16.0**
Knowledge	30.3
Self-learning	8.2
Further study	24.0
Subtotal: Academic	**62.5**
Good lifestyle	7.2
Human relations	8.4
Subtotal: Relations	**15.6**
Skills for living	1.8
Economic skills	2.9
Subtotal: Skills	**4.7**
Never thought of	0.6
Other responses	0.6
Subtotal: Others	**1.2**

Parents' expectations can be classified largely as dealing with "academic" expectations, social "relations" concerns, or "skills"-related expectations. Subtotals are shown in Table 2.2. A hierarchical pattern of responses is evident in that: (1) the largest percentage included academic expectations (62 percent for "knowledge," "self-learning," and "further studies"); (2) the second highest percentage pertained to human relations

(16 percent for "good lifestyle" and "human relations"); and (3) skill-related expectations were rare (5 percent for "skills for living" and "economic skills"). The "no response" category was dubious because there was no further probing conducted during the interviewing. Had we used the trial interviews as a guide, many of the nonresponses would probably have reflected the notion of "schooling for schooling's sake."

It can be seen from this description that parents' expectations from primary education concerned using the educational system as a means to upward mobility. Also, expectations in regard to personal relations were common, but expectations for using education as a means to acquire work (or life) skills was not given much importance.

These findings are the most salient aspects of the research. First, they confirm the noneconomic motivation for schooling in China. This motivation helps to explain the high attendance and low dropout rates for basic education in China. Second, the findings further support the necessity of including elements beyond literacy and numeracy in studies on Chinese education. Had these elements not been included, the research would have measured only partially what are perceived as the goals of basic education by the Chinese themselves. Third, they question the increasing stress put on vocational education by the government. Chinese parents see education as a goal in itself, with whatever benefits their children may accrue from it lying somewhere in the future. Placing an emphasis on vocational education has the potential of shattering the illusion about the possibility of upward mobility for poor children.

These conclusions are identifiable, however, only through research that was ethnographic in nature. Without an awareness of ethnographic methods, a researcher could conceivably ask questions according to what he or she thinks is important, not what the respondents themselves consider important. Such questions might be concerned with knowledge or skills, since both are desired outcomes in the "goals of education" expressed by many nations. However, such a research regimen would not have revealed that Chinese parents consider the "ability to study further" as a kind of "skill," nor would it have revealed that expectations in the realm of human relations are also considered important aspects of education, because they are not normally perceived as a general educational outcome.

HIGH ACHIEVEMENTS: WHY?

Certain results derived from the Zhejiang project are worthy of note. Despite the obstacles encountered by many Chinese students, most of them achieved the required *basic* standard in literacy and numeracy by the end of Grade Six, and a large percentage of them achieved that standard by the end of Grade Four.[15] This result is not surprising, since Chinese students score highly in international comparisons. For example, Chinese students have scored well in the International Mathematical Olympiad, and they have also fared well against other countries in the International Institute for the Evaluation of Educational Achievements' science and mathematics comparisons. However, the present study was applied across localities with widely divergent socioeconomic levels. The students under study were not the "cream" of the Chinese educational system. Yet the results seem to suggest that high achievement in mathematics is not confined solely to the cities and developed rural areas. The question is, then, How do these students' achievements come about? The study suggests answers at three levels.

First, physical conditions per se do not seem to explain why students achieve. In fact, the project found large disparities among the various research sites. Since the government has decentralized most basic educational policy decisions, the schools themselves reflect the economic conditions of their respective localities. Thus, more wealthy areas are able to pay their teachers more, as well as provide more money per pupil than poorer areas can provide, and once the schools themselves were seen, the perceived disparities between the various schools became even more noticeable. However, the disparity between students' achievements in literacy and numeracy were small: many students from economically stronger areas did not necessarily demonstrate higher ability. Indeed, the disparities within sites were much greater than the disparities between sites. In other words, educational factors were much more influential than economic ones in creating student achievement. This may be partially explicable by taking into account the Chinese value system that rewards sheer effort more than native ability.

Second, China has an existing school culture that is conducive to fostering student achievement. If one accepts the basic premises proposed in the "effective schools" literature, then Chinese schools are very effective.[16] Few disciplinary problems exist as principals play a close supervisory role in the school and the classroom, and hard work from students is expected by both parents and teachers. Thus, all students, regardless of their ability, receive the same curriculum, must meet the same graduation requirements, and are expected to eventually pass the public graduation examination. As a consequence, teaching is target-oriented. That is, a high emphasis is placed upon the mastery of basic knowledge and skills in literacy and numeracy. Since teachers take student achievement as their responsibility, lessons are carefully planned and well taught. The importance of education to the Chinese is seen in their high enrollment figures and by the willingness of parents to donate money generously to the schools. Close home-school relations are further enhanced by frequent home visits by teachers.[17]

Third, it is reasonable to ask: Why have all of these conditions come about in China? The "effective schools" literature is powerful in describing what an effective school is like and why a school is or is not effective, but it is less powerful in prescribing how schools can become effective. As stated, effective schools have high expectations regarding students, but how and why do high expectations occur in some schools and not in others? The answer to this question lies in going beyond what is merely perceived and into the realm of theory.[18]

The Zhejiang project paints a picture of a consistent educational culture in China. This conclusion is based upon noting a consistency across two societal dimensions: (1) an observable consistency within the educational system itself, and (2) a noticeable consistency across social sectors. The five cases in Zhejiang seem to lead to the conclusion that the various "actors" in the educational system—students, teachers, principals, educational bureaucrats, planners, and decision-makers—all share similar values about education and what is expected from students and teachers. Further, there is also a consistency across social sectors. State policies require local governments to give priority to spending local revenues on schools, and there are also policies designed to guarantee continued growth in educational expenditures. These policies seem to be supported by everyone from local farmers to independent entrepreneurs to major enterprises. This support entails everything from actively promoting school policies and practices to financial sponsorships. Thus, there appears to be a consensus regarding educational practices in China at this time.

The observed consensus in regard to the importance of education in China is similar to observations by other researchers studying educational systems in East Asia.[19] Thus, if the various actors in the educational sector share similar values in regard to educational goals and practices, and if the different sectors of the society also share these values, then it can be concluded that these are innate aspects of culture. This conclusion is supported by work from other disciplines as well. The strong emphasis in Chinese education on *efforts* versus *ability*,[20] the reliance on extrinsic motivational practices at the expense of intrinsic motivational practices,[21] and the emphasis on moral education through the extolling of good social relations as the preferred alternative to individualism in Chinese society[22] are all relevant to the findings of the Zhejiang project.

All in all, the Zhejiang project offers some comprehensive empirical evidence of how basic educational practices are carried out in China and how these practices are related to the cultural characteristics of China.

CONCLUDING REMARKS

The Zhejiang project is a useful case study for gaining an understanding of basic educational practices in China and how these practices are related to the cultural characteristics of China. This chapter describes how the study was illuminated by the inclusion of qualitative research methods and touches upon several areas of methodological interest: first, how to handle local researchers who have a specific local research convention; second, how to obtain local perspectives about policy-related issues; and third, how to theorize from empirical descriptions of the educational system.

The use of qualitative methods allowed me to accommodate the local research traditions of Chinese researchers and to better use their capabilities. This permitted me to understand local perspectives about the aims and objectives of education within an alternative intellectual framework that would never have developed if the project had remained purely quantitative in focus. Consequently, this framework made it possible to explain high attendance figures in schools and high achievement expectations within the culture that would have been missed if the research had remained true to the original test instrument.

The Zhejiang project is a case study of only five research sites within one province in China. The findings of the project help raise questions regarding some basic Chinese educational policy decisions. The reluctance of parents and teachers to accept vocational education, and the impact of the implementation of university fees on *primary* school enrollment are two examples of how state educational policies are at odds with cultural perceptions. These findings occurred solely through the use of ethnographic methods. Although I do not claim to be an ethnographer in the strictest sense, I am now aware of the importance of beginning a research project with an understanding of local concerns regarding education, its aims, processes, and outcomes. Hence, it is important to adopt a qualitative focus and to adapt quantitative measures to be in line with local concerns. Even a quantitative researcher should become an "ethno-grapher *sans* ethnography"[23] and conduct quantitative research by means of a qualitative orientation.

NOTES

1. State Education Commission, *Educational Statistical Yearbook of China* (Beijing: Educational Science Press, 1996), 2.

2. For example, see Y. S. Lincoln and E. G. Guba, *Naturalistic Inquiry* (Beverly Hills: Sage, 1985).

3. The project was initiated by the International Institute for Educational Planning, Paris, in 1989, and ended in 1990. The Chinese portion of the study is published as: K. M. Cheng, *The Quality of Primary Education: A Case Study of Zhejiang Province, China* (Paris: UNESCO/International Institute for Educational Planning, 1996). The comparative study is published as G. Carron and N. C. Ta, *The Quality of Primary Schools in Different Development Contexts* (Paris: UNESCO/International Institute for Educational Planning, 1996).

4. The Jomtien, Thailand, conference was concerned with developing and instituting a policy of universal education, and was attended by most international educational organizations.

5. This approach was used in Guinea, where a French team was employed to do the fieldwork and complete the project.

6. For a detailed discussion, see K. M. Cheng, "The Neglected Dimension: Cultural Comparison in Educational Administration," in *Educational Leadership and Change: An International Perspective,* eds. A. K. C. Wong and K. M. Cheng (Hong Kong: Hong Kong University Press, 1994).

7. During the Maoist years, "good in ideology" was used in place of "good in conduct."

8. At the time of the study, no framework existed that delineated occupational prestige in China. With the rapid economic changes that are occurring in China, any such framework would conceivably be obsolete within a short period of time.

9. Simplified from Table 4.4 in Cheng, *Quality,* 56.

10. From Cheng, *Quality,* 1996, 57–58.

11. Ibid.

12. R. A. LeVine, "Properties of Culture: An Ethnographic View," in *Culture Theory: Essays on Mind, Self, and Emotion,* eds. R. A. Shweder and R. A. LeVine (Cambridge: Cambridge University Press, 1984), 66.

13. This was a United Nations Development Project that looked at the "internal efficiency" of basic education. Gansu was one of the three provinces that were studied.

14. Simplified from Table 4.7 in Cheng, *Quality,* 61.

15. The study rated students' attainments as *rudimentary* (having learned something, but not sufficiently to survive in society), *basic* (having met the basic needs, as perceived by the community, sufficiently to survive in the society), and *advanced* (having the capability for admission to the next level of schooling).

16. For a summary of the effective schools literature, see J. J. Herman, *Holistic Quality: Managing, Restructuring, and Empowering Schools* (Newbury Park, Calif.: Corwin Press, 1993).

17. For a more detailed discussion of these points, see Cheng, *Quality.*

18. For an analysis of how one goes about the process of theorizing, see J. P. Goetz and M. D. LeCompte, *Ethnography and Qualitative Design in Educational Research* (Orlando: Academic Press, 1984).

19. For a comparison of these conclusions with Japan, see T. P. Rohlen, *Japan's High Schools* (Berkeley: University of California Press, 1983), or M. White, *The Japanese Educational Challenge: A Commitment to Children* (New York: The Free Press, 1987).

20. See H. W. Stevenson and J. W. Stigler, *The Learning Gap: Why Our Schools Are Failing and What We Can Learn from Japanese and Chinese Education* (New York: Summit Books, 1992).

21. See R. Lynn, *Educational Achievement in Japan: Lessons for the West* (London: Macmillan, 1988).

22. See G. Hofstede, *Culture's Consequences: International Differences in Work-related Values,* abridged edition (Beverly Hills: Sage, 1984).

23. See H. F. Wolcott, "Ethnographers Sans Ethnography: The Evaluation Compromise" in *Ethnography in Educational Evaluation,* ed. D. Fetterman (Beverly Hills: Sage, 1984), 177–210.

CHAPTER 3

National Minority Regions
Studying School Discontinuation

GERARD A. POSTIGLIONE

As the Chinese government defines minority nationalities *(shaoshu minzu,)* they account for about 9 percent of the population. Their population is increasing faster than the majority Han, due in part to a relaxed birth policy in sparsely populated minority areas. The government claims fifty-five national minorities, the largest group having more than fifteen million members and the smallest only about two thousand. The reason these one hundred million people occupy so critical a place in Chinese governmental policies is threefold: (1) They inhabit over one-half of China's land area; (2) 90 percent of the interior border region of China is occupied by minorities; and (3) the area they occupy is rich in mineral deposits, forest reserves, and most of the animals that supply milk, meat, and wool to the country.

Since the founding of the People's Republic, China has been a multi-national unitary state. China currently has 148 autonomous areas, including 5 autonomous regions, 30 autonomous prefectures, and 113 autonomous counties. Together they cover more than 63.7 percent of China's territory.[1] In only one-third of the autonomous regions is the dominant national minority group equal to more than one-half of the population; however, the Law on Regional Autonomy for Minority Nationalities was adopted in May 1984 at the Second Session of the Sixth National People's Congress.[2] It includes provisions for autonomous organizations; rights of self-government organizations; special help from higher-level

I would like to thank Judith Liu, Donald P. Kelly, Regie Stites, and Mark Constas for their useful comments.

organizations; training and assignment of cadres, specialists, and skilled workers among the minority peoples; and the strengthening and developing of socialist relations among nationalities. In short, the policy has been characterized as recognizing one state but many nationalities, with the goal of fostering political integration with cultural diversification.

Given the cultural, regional, and developmental differences between or among China's national minorities, it is virtually impossible to study them as a single entity. Thus, the unified set of national minority policies espoused by the government is intended to be implemented flexibly so as to account for the unique situation faced by each national minority. China's national minorities, referred to as little brothers *(xiongdi)* by the Han majority, can be differentiated according to a number of criteria.[3] These include population size; the nature of group identification held by the minority;[4] the size, location, and terrain of the region they occupy; the proportion of members of the minority group that inhabit an autonomous province, prefecture, or county; their proximity to and relations with other nationalities, including the Han; whether the neighboring Han were migrants or indigenous residents; whether the nationalities are rural or urban groups, agricultural or pastoral groups, border or inland groups, or concentrated or dispersed groups; whether or not they have a strong religious tradition; whether they have a written or spoken language or both; whether members of their nationality also live across the Chinese border in other countries, either as national minorities or as the majority nationality; and, finally, whether they have had a separate tradition of foreign relations with peoples of another region of the world.

The research for this chapter focused on the factors that contribute to minority school attendance (or nonattendance) in three minority regions in China. The objective was to identify how regional, school, and family factors influence school attendance and dropout rates within these regions. Regional factors included population size and density, distance from urban centers, the types of agricultural practices that were engaged in, and the proportion of national minorities to Han Chinese. School factors included school size, teacher qualifications, curriculum, school finance, and the language used for instruction. Family factors included paternal reliance upon children in agriculture and related production and students' perceptions of factors relating to school attendance—with a particular focus on the relevance of schooling to finding employment in the local job market.

The research took place in the Inner Mongolian Autonomous Region, the Guangxi Zhuang Autonomous Region, and Yunnan Province.

While the results from these regions may not be applicable to studies of school discontinuation in all ethnic regions in China, the regions were chosen because of one compelling reason—I was able to arrange access into them. Thus, a proposed fourth area for study in the Xinjiang Uygur Autonomous Region was eliminated because I could not receive official authorization.

Mongols comprise fewer than 20 percent of the population of Inner Mongolia, where the most populous group is the Han. (Their total national population in 1990, while less than five million, was more than in the adjacent country of Mongolia.) The main target county for our research, however, had an almost 80 percent Mongolian population. The Mongols, who ruled China during the Yuan Dynasty (1271–1368), have their own language and written script, as well as a long tradition of support for education and a higher literacy rate than the Han majority.

The Zhuang are the main minority nationality of the Guangxi Zhuang Autonomous Region. Together with eleven other minorities, they comprise 39 percent of the population. The Zhuang are the largest minority in China with over fifteen million people, almost all in Guangxi. In 1957, a standard written version of the spoken Zhuang language and a newly created phonetic writing system were given official status. While a traditional Zhuang language script once existed, by 1957 it was no longer in common use. The Zhuang, however, have a widely accepted spoken language. Only about 20 percent of Zhuang were literate in Zhuang script in 1980 and about one-half could speak their language. The rest used the local Han dialect.[5]

Yunnan province has perhaps the largest number of minority groups, but unlike Inner Mongolia or Guangxi, there is no single, dominant national minority. Research was focused in a Yao and Zhuang minority county. Nearly 4.2 million Yao populate southern China, mostly in Yunnan, Guizhou, Guangxi, Hunan, and Guangdong provinces. They had a spoken but not a written language until one was devised by the new government after 1949, but it is little-used. Nearly 30 percent of the Yao are illiterate or semiliterate in the "national" language *(Putonghua)*.

NATIONAL MINORITIES AND EDUCATIONAL POLICY

The percentage of minority children initially enrolled in primary school (9.2 percent of the total) roughly parallels their proportion in the national population. Several minorities (e.g., Koreans, Uzbeks, and Tartars) even score above the national average on a variety of educational indicators.

Although this is a major achievement, national statistics also reveal that literacy rates for twenty-eight of the fifty-five minorities are below that of the Han;[6] yet students of the Han majority who live in national minority regions fare only slightly better than minority students. This seeming paradox can be partially explained by the fact that schools in national minority regions generally have a lower proportion of qualified teachers. This problem is compounded since national minorities as a whole are underrepresented in completion rates for all levels of schooling, with minority females exhibiting particularly high rates of school discontinuation, resulting in illiteracy rates twice as high as their male counterparts.[7] Moreover, their disproportionately low overall attendance levels, especially at secondary and tertiary levels of the education system, are sure to increase in the coming years because national minority children are the fastest growing school population.

Government policies directed at national minority regions differ from those aimed at the rest of China. Minority areas receive extra resources and financial allocations, part of which can be used for education. In many regions, special minority schools have been established with minority languages used in classroom instruction. School textbooks are printed in minority languages for those nationalities with a written script, and minority students are provided with special advantages in gaining admission to "nationalities universities" and "institutes for nationalities." The main distinction, however, between minority regions and the rest of China is that the former are supposed to be "autonomous." The leaders in such regions (counties, prefectures, provinces) are usually members of minorities. Autonomy is defined by the principle of democratic centralism—the local implementation of national policies. In theory, this permits minorities to enjoy equality of status; however, in reality, their actual autonomy may be severely restricted.[8] Thus, minority groups can run their own schools, but they must abide by all regulations set down by the central government. Minority languages may be used for instruction, though there may not be enough trained teachers who can teach in these languages. Minority history can be taught, but views that differ from the ones specified by the government are not tolerated.

National minority education is still the most difficult area of research within Chinese educational studies. The great diversity that exists between different national minority situations inhibits generalizing about social institutions, including education. Aside from mastering the language and script of the majority Han, it is necessary for the researcher to learn the language of at least one other nationality, something that even few Han do. Even then there are other hurdles. Access to minority areas is often restricted and contacts are usually managed through Han mediators, and therefore one often hears only one side of the story. Moreover, most national minority educational research literature is written by Han researchers, rather than by minority members themselves.

Despite the best governmental efforts to rigorously implement policies under the rubric of democratic centralism, gaps exist between educational policy and practice in China, and these gaps are probably more common in minority regions than elsewhere. However, because of the remoteness and inaccessibility of many regions, these gaps may be harder to discover. There are numerous issues that remain a consistent concern in China's national minority regions, including literacy, basic education, school attendance, teacher qualifications, bilingual education, and opportunities to attend upper-secondary and higher education. Other, more sensitive areas include school autonomy, ethnic integration, and the teaching of minority languages and history. One topic that straddles the gap between educational policy and practice is school discontinuation, because in any multiethnic society, although dropout rates are linked to economic development, they may also reflect the resistance of minorities to the goals and purposes of state-sponsored schooling.

RESEARCH ON MINORITY EDUCATION

Since the mid-1980s, Chinese scholars have begun more extensive research on national minority education. Aside from works that are historical, there are four other types of published research. The first type is general and focuses on national minority educational policies and development;[9] the second type includes collections of articles that describe the development of minority education throughout the country;[10] the third type includes collections of articles on national minority education in specific regions;[11] and the fourth deals with the economic aspects of minority education.[12] The number of articles in academic journals has also increased.[13]

Taken together, this literature has several distinct characteristics. It is descriptive. It places more of an emphasis on policies and their justification than on actual practices. It is almost always written by Han researchers. Fieldwork is usually written in report form, not to make contributions to educational theory. It is ethnographic only in the sense that it describes in great detail various aspects of minority practice, including rituals, clothing, food preparation, and beliefs. It does contain anecdotal stories that constitute useful material for ethnographic information; however, it uses these to support particular educational policy positions or to cite inadequacies in policy implementation. It alerts policymakers to problems ranging from inadequate governmental funding to difficulties in implementing policies caused by the cultural traditions and religious beliefs of some of the minorities. And last, it contains debates on practical matters such as educational finance and instructional techniques.

This situation is changing as the study of education in China is boosted by the introduction of the socialist market economy. Funds for educational research in minority regions have increased as organizations are encouraged to attract outside investment into minority regions. Finally, international development agencies have begun to focus on the educational problems endemic to national minority areas.

ETHNOGRAPHIC RESEARCH ON MINORITY EDUCATION

There are several reasons for the lack of research on minority education, particularly of an ethnographic type, by foreign scholars.[14] First, the academic domain of the researchers is a factor. Although most research on minorities is conducted by anthropologists and is usually ethnographic, researchers had not focused on schooling until the 1990s.[15] Further, comparative education researchers have rarely used ethnographic methods when conducting their studies. Second, there is a view, however misguided, that the results of research on Han majority schooling are more easily generalizable. Each of the fifty-five minorities, by definition, has a unique culture. Because understanding the meaning of education for minorities is an important focus of ethnographic research, the diversity of minority cultures inhibits the prospect of generalizing research findings within China, let alone internationally. Third, given the small number of foreign researchers who study Chinese education, this means an even smaller number will study minorities. While minorities account for almost 10 percent of elementary school enrollments, fewer than one in ten foreign educational researchers who study education in China focus on minorities. Fourth, many researchers began as teachers of English in China. Since English is the third rather than a second language for most minorities, and since minority regions tend to be isolated, contact with minority communities is uncommon for foreign researchers. Fifth, until the mid-1990s, the Chinese educational leadership encouraged the study of Han education more than the study of minority education. Consequently, foreign researchers who speak a minority tongue such as Uygur or Tibetan, rather than any Han dialect, have found it difficult to gain access to minority areas through official channels.

Thus, it is not surprising to find that there has been little ethnographic work by both Chinese nationals and foreign scholars on national minority education. However, both groups of researchers are poised to do more work. Foreign researchers will do more as access increases, and Chinese nationals will do more as they begin to learn and become familiar with internationally accepted research methodologies.

SETTING UP THE CONCEPTUAL PROBLEM

Although some ethnographers may argue against carrying conceptual baggage into a research project, it is nonetheless useful in helping to frame the study of school discontinuation in minority regions of China. As such, four foci for conducting ethnographic research in China are discussed in the following pages. Each of these captures a fundamental problem for China's development of national minority education.[16]

Social Equality

A social equality focus refers to several educational indicators relating to dropping out of school, including rates of literacy, enrollment, attendance, retention, promotion, and graduation, as well as the rate of proportional representation of minorities at all levels of the education system. We can learn a certain amount from the available national statistics, which are now plentiful, if sometimes unreliable. However, this data does not permit us to understand the manner in which minority students and their families come to construct the meaning of schooling. Do minority parents see this construction in the same way as the school authorities? The government? Han parents? Within their own communities? How autonomous were the decisions about attending or dropping out of school? How do minorities view the alternatives to state schooling? Why do national minority children, especially girls, decide to leave school earlier than their Han counterparts?

Economic Considerations

A common view put forth in educational studies is that a shortage of school funds is a major contributing factor to school discontinuation, which, in turn, affects economic development and further school financing. This view oversimplifies the role of economic development.

Because of a lack of resources in certain regions, school places are not always available even for those who would attend. Minority regions get extra subsidies, yet there is an increasing economic gap between the western regions of China, where most minorities reside, and the more populous Han regions. The central government has provided funds for building dormitories for minority students who live long distances from schools, yet students who live at school still must find ways of covering fees for food and clothing, and of overcoming separation anxiety. Major financial responsibility still rests with the localities, and most are short of funds. Families find it difficult to pay school fees, and given the higher birth rate for minority families, this often means fees for more than one child. How willing are minority parents to make the financial sacrifices necessary to keep their children in school? At what point would they consider supporting the decision to discontinue the schooling of their child? Do minority parents prefer *Putonghua* as the medium of instruction since using *Putonghua* increases the economic opportunities available to their children upon graduation?

Cultural Autonomy

Because having a distinct culture is what defines national minorities and because culture is the basis for group identity, the most important focus for educational modernization for national minorities is the maintenance of cultural autonomy. The two main cultural issues confronting Chinese educational policymakers are language and religion. Most minority groups derive the major part of their identity from their language and religion, both of which influence school attendance rates. Can the study of religious texts be used to increase literacy? In what respects is schooling viewed as a support for or threat to the preservation of minority heritage? How much does this conception of the role of schooling play in decisions about attendance and nonattendance? Is school discontinuation a form of resistance to Han cultural hegemony?

National Integration

National integration as a possible research focus is extremely tricky, because it requires a minority group to maintain its separate cultural identity while becoming socialized to accept the state's ruling ideology as a necessary means for the group's integration into the national mainstream. This process is being attempted in several ways, with the various outcomes amenable to study. Admission of minorities to universities gives them higher visibility as they become national models for the younger members of their nationalities. The various nationality schools play a role as well. Although most students in the institutes for nationalities and the nationality universities are minorities, most teachers are Han. How do members of national minorities deal with the identity conflicts that result from their socialization through national institutions? To what degree do schools in minority regions modify their total environment to make it more reflective of the ethnic diversity in the society?

LOOKING BEYOND OFFICIAL POLICIES AND STATISTICS

The reason most often given for why Han children drop out of school is financial difficulties. While this is also true for minorities, they also cite other reasons, such as cultural backwardness, religion, or marriage customs. According to national policy, education in national minority regions is supposed to be organized and implemented flexibly in accordance with the special conditions of the region. Those special conditions usually include taking into account the religion, language, and tradition of minority groups. Thus, some minority girls drop out of school because their parents' religion prohibits coeducational schooling or because of customs that necessitate the preparation of a dowry before marriage. In order to accommodate these special circumstances, single-gender classes can be provided, as well as vocational classes that teach skills for making minority women's clothing. Other minority children drop out because they have difficulty learning *Putonghua*, in which case bilingual education is a partial solution. Because their nomadic lifestyle interferes with school attendance, dormitories have been built so that the children can attend classes. Clearly, this alternative is a double-edged sword for these minority groups. It must also be noted that not all minorities are perceived as having cultural obstacles to school attendance.

Because there is resistance in China to a research problem being defined in terms of a potential social problem, studying school dropout rates might have to be couched in terms of studying school attendance and nonattendance. That is, nonattendance can be viewed as a temporary condition, whereas dropping out can be viewed as a permanent condition that has possible negative social consequences. This dichotomy originally framed the research conducted for this study. However, once the project goals were viewed as having policy implications, it was possible to shift the terminology from attendance and nonattendance *(shangxue, bushangxue)* to terms denoting school discontinuation and dropping out of school *(shixue, liushi, cuoxue).*

During our fieldwork, we received different views concerning the reliability of our statistics, as well as different views as to how diligent teachers were in taking daily attendance. Because attendance figures are related to the amount of governmental resources allocated to a school, it is possible that graduation and attendance rates are manipulated. We heard of some cases where graduates from a poor-quality village primary school who managed to gain entrance to the town's junior-secondary school were sent home with a graduation certificate (available for one *yuan*) partway through their first year of study, because of the teachers' view that these students were unlikely to reach the academic standards necessary for graduation. Presumably, these "sent home" students would be counted as having attended for the length of the junior-secondary school year. Nevertheless, we examined teachers' attendance books during our school visits and most seemed to be doing a very conscientious job. Finally, when asked in one county what was the minimum number of school days that a student had to attend so as not to be counted as a dropout, the answer was one. If such a situation is true in practice, a student could attend a few days per year, year after year, and still be counted as an enrolled pupil.

METHODOLOGY

During our interviews, it became clear that the terms and methods used to measure the progress of basic education in China were designed to put the best possible face on the situation. To emphasize positive accomplishments, official announcements would cite formal enrollment figures, as well as graduation and promotion rates. As noted, however, these figures reflect the number of children who are enrolled but do not necessarily attend school regularly. Likewise, promotion rates into junior-secondary school are based on the number of students who graduated from Grade Six of primary school, not from the total number of students enrolled in Grade Six, since many are unable to meet graduation requirements.

Our study focused on fifteen border counties, five within each of three border provinces of Inner Mongolia, Yunnan, and Guangxi. Field investigations were limited, however, to three border counties, one in each of the three provinces. The objective was to explore the link between dropping out of school and regional, school, and family factors. School principals, students, and county officials filled out questionnaires concerning these factors. These data were supplemented by interviews with county educational officials, school principals, teachers, parents, and students.

Before carrying out the fieldwork, a thorough examination of the related literature on the target national minority counties was undertaken. Knowledge of this background material helped in gaining the confidence of local officials and permitted a more efficient use of the time allotted for gathering data. We found that it was a commonly practiced "rule" that if you knew nothing you would be told nothing, but the more you knew, the more you would be told. Before the fieldwork, I was able to find literature on dropout rates in the target counties. I was able to quote to my hosts the dropout rates for their counties for previous years. With this knowledge, I was thus able to acquire the current figures, and if the difference between the two rates was great, I could inquire as to why. I also realized that provincial and county figures I was given for school dropout rates did little to indicate the situation in particular villages. My literature search identified a minority village within the county I was going to visit that had not graduated a single upper-elementary school student. Although I knew the name of the village I was not taken there. This Yao minority village had five Yao primary school teachers who themselves only had some primary school education. A similar situation existed within another village that had three Yao teachers, but, in this case, the teachers only showed up half of the time, and the students and their parents eventually lost interest in schooling.

Lack of qualified teachers was clearly an issue that contributed to school discontinuation, along with the issue of low salaries paid to teachers. Some teachers were forced to take second jobs; in some cases this meant doing business within the school. One primary school teacher had actually established a shop *(xiaomaibu)* within the school to sell simple products to students, and had earned the title "shopkeeper Huang" *(Huang Laoban)*.

Another contributing factor to school discontinuation was gender-specific. In some cases, minority girl students would not leave their home to attend school unless they were accompanied by another girl. Some girls married at the age of 12 or 13 and would lose interest in schooling after marrying. In these remote minority regions, it is not uncommon to hear that educated women could not find marriage partners easily. Finally, due to "boy bias" *(Zhongnan qingnu),* girls usually do not attend school for more than three years in many minority areas.[17]

A survey questionnaire that focused on how regional, school, and family factors were perceived to influence dropout rates was developed in conjunction with the national research partners. After I identified the research question, we discussed the kinds of questions for inclusion in the survey instrument. This was greatly facilitated by the fact that all discussions and draft questionnaires were in Chinese. Interviews in the field were always conducted in *Putonghua* because our ethnic minority subjects were able to converse in it. This sample bias necessarily skewed our results because we were unable to gather information from ethnic monolinguals.

Handicapped by a research budget that did not permit a preliminary visit to the target counties in order to examine basic conditions, the survey questions we adopted were based upon previous fieldwork experiences in other rural areas of China. Given this methodological disadvantage, we had to be extra cautious about the appropriateness of the survey questions when they were applied to these new rural areas. For example, we asked the distance between home and school, but such answers were not always useful because long distances across the plains in Mongolia would have been faster and easier to transverse than short distances in the mountainous terrain of some villages in southwestern China. In some cases, students had to swim across a river or negotiate a narrow mountain road in the rain in order to get to school, and though the actual distance between home and school may have been short, the dangers for the students were obvious to their parents.

In each county, five schools were selected for the survey questionnaire, including one primary school and one secondary school in the county seat; and three other schools were selected according to their distances (very distant, somewhat distant, and near to the county seat). Principals were asked to randomly select twenty students in each primary school from Grade Five or Six, and in each secondary school from Grade Two or Three. In each county, ten school principals or vice-principals completed a questionnaire. The county information questionnaire was completed by an education department official from each county. Consequently, the information we obtained had already been filtered through layers of educational bureaucrats, and this necessarily affected our final results.

WHY STAY IN SCHOOL? NOTES FROM THE FIELD

This chapter discusses how ethnographic methods can be used to improve the study of national minority education in China. Its focus is on a discussion of considerations for doing research on education in national minority regions and the advantages of ethnographic work over quantitative research, rather than on doing fieldwork itself. Part of the reason it deals less with fieldwork has to do with the nature of research in national minority border regions, which are more sensitive and less accessible than other regions. Nevertheless, the chapter does draw on preliminary fieldwork from a 1993 to 1994 Asian Development Bank–supported study of attendance and nonattendance in national minority regions.[18] Because school dropout rates are most severe in the border regions, the aim of that research was to find out why students drop out of school. Even when the potential problems that faced this project were known, it appeared to be a relatively cut and dried project.

In the field, we soon realized, however, that nothing could be taken for granted. Even basic sampling techniques could not be carried out according to the original research protocol. Though we asked school principals to use random sampling in the distribution of questionnaires to students, it appears that most chose their own method of sampling. We soon discovered this with respect to a survey question concerning parental support for schooling. School principals frequently indicated a lack of support for schooling from families (about one-third of school principals believed that parents are unconcerned about education for their children). According to school principals, this was due to the parents' lack of financial resources, the necessity of having children help with household work, and the low "cultural" levels of the parents, which contributed to their "backwardness" and inability to see the importance of education. While these observations were true to some extent, it also become clear that the lack of relevance of schooling to the everyday life in these minority communities was of equal importance. Schooling failed to make a direct contribution to household income in most cases. Moreover, state schooling was culturally Han in focus, and it tended to ignore the culture(s) indigenous to the region, whether it was Yao or Zhuang in Yunnan, Zhuang in Guangxi, or Mongolian in Inner Mongolia. Thus, the supposed "national culture" *(zhonghua minzu wenhua),* which is promoted as combining Han and minority cultures together, was (and is) more culturally Han than anything else.

We also discovered an apparent contradiction in the student data on a question we interpreted as indicating levels of parental support for schooling. The student questionnaire revealed that 28 percent of parents always helped students with their homework and only 9 percent never helped at all on homework. This occurs within a context in which 40 percent of the fathers and 33 percent of the mothers are illiterate, and the disparity between these numbers suggests that parents are giving more assistance on homework than their educations would seem to make possible. However, the contradiction in response patterns between principals and students may be partially explained on the basis of the student sample selected by the school principals to answer the questionnaire. Almost 30 percent of fathers of children in the sample selected by the school principals had a senior-secondary education or above, far above what one would expect in that part of the country. Thus, a larger number of students—those not in the sample—may be the ones referred to by the school principals in their responses. The students not chosen may live in less fortunate circumstances and thus may get little help from their parents, possibly because of their higher rates of illiteracy.

The fieldwork did, however, make at least two things clear. First, parents who had a senior-secondary education and above were in the minority (though unlikely to be a national minority) in the regions, yet they were overrepresented in the sample. Second, while lack of support for schooling on the part of parents was an important reason given for the dropout problem, there was less agreement between parents and school principals on the reasons for that lack of parental support.

In other fieldwork discussions, the difficulty encountered by minority parents in paying school fees was confirmed. For example, data concerning parents' ability to afford school fees made it apparent that financial difficulties were a constant concern throughout all these regions. Approximately 37 percent of students surveyed indicated that their parents had difficulty paying school fees. We were told by one parent that

> the costs of sending our child to junior-secondary school would be 700 to 800 *yuan* for each year, including meals, books, transportation, and other fees. This is beyond our means. We may not earn this much in a year of work. If the secondary school teacher sends our children back from the school in the first year because they do not do well, we can save much money.

In fact, it was not only the hardship endured by having to pay costly school fees that troubled parents, but the value of the schooling as put forward in the view that "our upper-secondary school students returned home to the home village without a willingness to do the hard physical work." Another parent said, "The upper-secondary school graduates of today were equivalent to the lower-secondary school graduates of ten years ago due to a softened curriculum." Yet the goals of schooling, as perceived by the parents, were frequently minimal at best. Thus, many parents to whom we spoke seemed satisfied if their children were able to learn some simple Chinese characters and calculations.

Our survey data revealed that 26 percent of school principals were not satisfied with the dropout rates in their schools, while 29 percent said they were satisfied with the rates. The rest rated the situation as fair. Quantitative findings such as this are not very illuminating. While the dropout rates varied in different schools, the manner in which school principals arrived at these judgments was unclear and needed further analysis. Well-executed ethnographic methods could certainly have provided more meaning to these figures. Time and access limitations, however, made us rely on quantitative data to satisfy our curiosity regarding the weightings of dropout factors given by school principals to teacher quality, as compared to usefulness of what is learned in school. More school principals attributed dropping out of school to the inappropriateness of what is taught at school to the lives of these minority students (28 percent), than to the qualifications of teachers (8 percent). Moreover, 35 percent indicated that dropping out of school had much to do with "backward thinking" by minority parents. The proportion of Han school principals agreeing with this conclusion was greater than their representation in the sample. This led me to interpret the view of school principals in terms of a possible indication of resistance on the part of minority parents to state schooling. Here again, it would have been advisable to interview Yao parents, for example, within the context of their homes and communities about how they constructed the meaning of state schooling in relation to their ethnicity.

Financial considerations receded into the background as the conversation with teachers turned to the question of language usage. The survey data revealed that only 17 percent of students indicated that they always spoke some dialect of Chinese at home. Approximately 20 percent of the minority students indicated that they never spoke any Han dialect at home, and 8 percent stated that they could not speak *Putonghua* at all. Moreover, 79 percent of students indicated that their teachers used *Putonghua* in teaching, 0.7 percent said their teachers used a minority language, while over 15 percent said their teachers used a bilingual mode of teaching. This information reinforces the obvious assumption that minority languages are still used in many homes, and this may help to explain some of the difficulties minority students encounter in school. Nevertheless, only 2 percent of the school principals thought that the language used in teaching had something to do with students dropping out of school. Teachers viewed this issue with more urgency. From our conversations with minority teachers, language was a major issue. One Yao teacher explained the difficulties of teaching a class of Yao, Miao, Zhuang, and Han students: "First I have to say 'apple' in the local Han dialect, then in *Putonghua*, then in Yao, followed by Zhuang and Miao."

Regardless of the region or minority group, the financial and economic situations were the foremost concern in the minds of parents, as well as teachers, since they did not always get paid on time. In this particular minority area, however, one village was clearly doing better than the others in the county. How did this relative economic success impact the school? The discussions at that school have to be kept within the context of what was going on outside the school. There were opportunities for children to work and earn several *yuan* per day by working outside of the school. As one parent said, "... when that happens, students can't concentrate on their schoolwork." Thus, economic benefits made schooling less favorable than it would have been otherwise. Villagers also doubted the employment benefits of receiving a secondary education, citing that without "connections" *(guanxi),* even high achievement scores in secondary school could not help village children to compete for a job against the urban children who had lower achievement scores. Another parent brought the discourse on schooling down to its most basic level by stating that the goal of schooling is to get a child a job and a residency permit *(hukou);* if it does not accomplish these two goals, then going to school was worthless.

NOTES ON SELECTED DYNAMICS: RESEARCH AND THE RESEARCHER

Who Is the Researcher?

Foreigners, though Chinese-speaking, will usually be at a disadvantage in conducting educational research in China, while "overseas" Chinese (e.g., those from Taiwan or Macau) tend to have easier access. However, this situation may be reversed when dealing with minorities.[19] A foreigner will, at times, be viewed by members of some minority groups as less of an outsider than a Han or an "overseas" Chinese researcher because he or she is also not ethnically Han. Thus, when doing fieldwork in a minority area, a foreign researcher cannot assume that any accompanying Han researcher will be viewed as more of an insider by a minority group *unless* that researcher is acutely aware of the specific interethnic social and cultural relations that have developed in the fieldwork area between the minority group and the resident Han. Consequently, these conditions will influence in some ways the degree to which a foreign researcher can gain access to minority perspectives. But, in the final analysis, Han and foreigner researchers alike both will be handicapped if they do not speak the minority language, and this is a major obstacle to overcome. While it is commonly believed by government and educational policymakers that minorities should speak *Putonghua,* the converse is not true. Thus, in my fieldwork I met only one Han who could speak, read, and write a minority language (Mongolian); in this case, apparently well enough to teach it.

What Is Research?

It is understandably difficult for local education officials, school principals, and parents to understand "research" in the way that many foreign academics have been trained to do. They naturally consider the following questions: What information does the researchers want? Why should we give it to them? How can it possibly help our region? How can their writing an article or book be of any assistance to us? A good reception given by locals to a foreign researcher can be facilitated if the researcher's fees are covered by an international development agency. In this case, local officials may believe that this foreign researcher's findings may be instrumental in determining whether or not their region will receive a grant. While their "willing" assistance may help in conducting the research, it raises new, more difficult problems about the reliability of the data, because the Chinese are notorious for giving answers to questions that either follow the Party's line or correspond to what they think the researcher would like to hear. Cooperating with a foreign researcher is also seen as a way to draw the attention of the State Education Commission so that the region may be identified as in need of special help or, conversely, seen as a model county. In either case, the region would be eligible to receive special funds.

Who Organizes the Research?

Local officials often intervene so as to manage the impressions being given to researchers. On several school visits and in discussions with school principals, teachers, and students, it was not unusual to find that a county official present at the discussions would coach the respondents (in the local dialect) on how to answer the question. I became aware of this situation when I was doing research in Southwestern China, where they spoke a dialect of Chinese that had enough similarities to Cantonese that I could understand what was being said around me. Thus, what I was being told in *Putonghua* was not what the respondent was actually saying in the local dialect.

In the context of discussions with school principals and parents, it was often difficult for educational officials to understand why I was pressing for answers to questions. Though well-meaning, some officials were apparently under the impression that if I visited as many schools as possible, I could make my report look full, and that the content of the visits was only a formality. Given the way that educational research is normally conducted by Chinese researchers, this was not an unreasonable assumption on their part. Further, the pace and timing of the visits limited the depth and breath of the conversations that could be entered during the interviews.

CONCLUSION

The aim of this chapter has been to consider selected aspects for employing ethnographic methods to the study of national minority education. While I have only scratched the surface of this complex subject, I have attempted to emphasize a few critical methodological aspects. First, researchers should anticipate a gap between policy and practice that, although similar in many ways to that in Han rural education, is partly based on the special conditions in minority regions. Furthermore, while educational policies for minority regions are supposed to be applied flexibly, depending on local conditions, how these policies are implemented will differ depending on local conditions. At this level, the innate tension between local autonomy and democratic centralism is put into actual practice.

Second, an awareness of the factors that facilitate the use of ethnographic methods by researchers in China is useful. The socialist market economy will result in expanding access to minority regions for educational researchers; however, there will continue to be a large gulf between the methods employed by foreign researchers and Chinese researchers. Collaboration is one step toward developing better approaches, though this may complicate the dynamics of the research process, especially in sensitive minority regions.

Third, the degree to which one should approach fieldwork with preconceived frameworks is still an open question. Work by sociologists of education on the subject of resistance to state schooling, as well as reproduction theories that are not rigidly Marxist in character, can help to raise useful questions for fieldwork on school dropouts. But employing any theory must fit the conditions actually present in the field. Thus, flexibility on the part of researchers can minimize the influence of irrelevant theories on actual fieldwork experiences.

Fourth, ethnographic methods can be very effective in alerting quantitative researchers to the manner in which survey data are interpreted. They demand that researchers be more conscious of how statistical data are produced in the field. For example, using ethnographic methods helps contextualize the difference between enrollment and attendance figures, as well as the difference between promotion and graduation rates. Ethnographic methods also show the limitations in survey questionnaires and the negotiation that goes on between researchers and subjects. Further, they permit survey researchers to finally grasp the ways in which sampling methods are handled by nonresearchers.

Fifth, without fieldwork interviews, results of survey questions may be misleading, such as those concerning the impact of actual and perceived distance from home to school on school attendance. This point is particularly crucial when dealing with minority regions because of the variations in geographical conditions.

Finally, ethnographic methods can help to clarify survey data concerning the use of minority languages at home and at school, and how language use is so critical to self- as well as ethnic-identity formation.

This chapter is not an argument for one type of research method over another. Used in conjunction with quantitative methods, ethnographic approaches to data collection can help ensure a grounded interpretation of the actual survey data. The reflexive nature of ethnographic research can also ensure that quantitative data can be used effectively to help explain ethnic minority school discontinuation.

NOTES

1. Ma Yin, *China's National Minorities* (Beijing: Foreign Languages Press, 1989), 2.

2. "Autonomy for the National Minorities of China," *China News Analysis* 1391 (August 15, 1989): 3.

3. See Zhou Enlai, "Guanyu woguo minzu zhengce jige wenti" ("A Few Questions Concerning Our Country's Nationality Policy"), in *Zhongguo minzu guanxishi lunwen xuanji (Historical Studies of the*

Relationship Among Nationalities in China) (Gansu: Gansu Nationalities Press, 1983).

4. See Fei Xiaotong, "Ethnic Identification in China," *Social Sciences in China* 1 (1980): 97–107.

5. Yao Shaoyuan, *Guangxi Minzu Guan (A View of Nationalities in Guangxi)* (Nanning: People's Publishing House, 1991), 308.

6. *Educational Atlas of China* (Shanghai: Shanghai Scientific and Technical Publishers, 1995), 12.

7. Ibid., 113.

8. Thomas Heberer, *China and Its National Minorities* (Armonk, N.Y.: M. E. Sharpe, 1989). See also Dru C. Gladney, *Muslim Chinese: Ethnic Nationalism in the People's Republic* (Cambridge: Council of East Asian Studies, 1991).

9. Sun Ruoqiong, Teng Xing, and Wang Meilian, *Zhongguo shaoshu minzu jiaoyu gailun (An Introduction to the Study of National Minority Education in China)* (Beijing: Laodong Press, 1990); Jing Shiqun, *Minzu jiaoyuxue (Nationality Education)* (Gansu: Gansu Education Press, 1991); Xie Qihuang, Sun Ruoqiong, Wang Xihong, and Wang Wenzhang, *Zhongguo minzu jiaoyu fazhan zhanlue jueze (China's National Minority Education Development Strategy)* (Beijing: Central Institute of Nationalities Press, 1991); Wang Lisheng, *Gansu minzu jiaoyu fazhan gailun (The Situation of Nationality Education Development in Gansu Province)* (Gansu: Gansu Nationalities Press, 1988); and Pu Shengyi, *Zhongguo shaoshu minzu fazhan yu zhanwang (China's National Minority Education: Development and Hopes)* (Inner Mongolia Press, 1990).

10. Wang Xihong, *Zhongguo bianjing minzu jiaoyu (National Minority Border Education)* (Beijing: Central Institute of Nationalities Press, 1990).

11. Chen Shou and Wang Xihong, *Guizhou minzu jiaoyu diaocha (A Survey of National Minority Education in Guizhou Province)* (Beijing: Central Institute of Nationalities Press, 1990).

12. Wong Xihong and Wang Wenchang, *Minzu jiaoyu jingjixue (The Economics of National Minority Education)* (Beijing: Knowledge Press, 1990).

13. The journal entitled *Minzu jiaoyu yanjiu (Research in National Minority Education),* published at the Central University of Nationalities in Beijing, is one of the more well-known journals in China in the field.

14. *Foreign* is used here to refer to non-Chinese nationals.

15. See chapters by Dru Gladney, Steven Harrell, Mette Halskow Hansen, and Janet Upton, in *China's National Minority Education:*

Culture, Schooling, and Development, ed. Gerard A. Postiglione (New York: Falmer Press, 1999).

16. Gerard A. Postiglione, "The Implications of Modernization for the Education of China's National Minorities," in *Education and Modernization: The Chinese Experience,* ed. Ruth Hayhoe (London: Pergamon Press, 1992); Gerard A. Postiglione, "National Minorities and Nationalities Policy in China," in *The National Question,* ed. Berch Berberoglu (Philadelphia: Temple University Press, 1995).

17. See Li Qunsheng, "Ningming xian bianjing minzu jiaoyu zhuangkuang" ("The Situation of Ethnic Minority Border Education in Ningming County"), in *Zhongguo bianjing minzu jiaoyu (China's Nationality Border Education),* ed. Wang Xihong (Beijing: Central Institute of Nationalities Press, 1990), 120–126.

18. This study was administered by the International Development Research Center in Singapore, as part of an educational research support program for Asia and the Pacific.

19. This is the case, especially if the foreigner is of a similar ethnic heritage. This group of foreigners includes members of minorities that have settled overseas and returned to China to do field research, as well as ethnic cousins on the other side of the border, including Mongolians, Uzbeks, Koreans, Russians, and others. But these are very few in number. However, the most common foreigner doing research on national minority education would be North American, European, or Japanese.

CHAPTER 4

Juvenile Delinquency and Reformatory Education in China
A Retrospective

IRVING EPSTEIN

In 1983, in the midst of a publicized spiritual pollution campaign, I traveled to China to investigate educational programs for juvenile delinquents in reformatories and work-study schools. Having spent the previous year and a half pursuing language study and comparative research on the same topic in Hong Kong and Taiwan, I understood that it would be difficult under any circumstance to complete a comprehensive study given the sensitive nature of the topic. I was also aware of the limitations placed upon the visitations I conducted: no repeat visits were permitted, public security and reformatory officials were present when questions were asked, and difficult questions remained unanswered due to feigned ignorance on the part of those who were being interviewed. In short, the use of true ethnographic methods was not possible at the time, although this work was definitely qualitative by nature. I still believed that it was beneficial to see with one's own eyes what one had read about in print, and used the visitations as a means of confirming the veracity of published material I had collected. Fifteen years afterwards, I think it is useful to reflect upon the assumptions I made in conducting research on delinquency and reformatory education, and critique those assumptions in light of the changing nature of Chinese education as a field of study. The fact that my research was not explicitly ethnographic in an interesting way highlights issues concerning the strengths and weaknesses of that method in a comparative sense, and it is hoped that this discussion will add to the discourse focusing upon the broader methodological concerns that are expressed throughout this volume.

JUVENILE DELINQUENCY IN CHINA:
THE NATURE OF THE PROBLEM

At first glance, juvenile delinquency in China appears to differ little from its counterparts in other regions of the world. Chinese delinquents are primarily male and engage in deviant behaviors including burglary, theft, murder, rape, arson, and gang activity. Delinquency is primarily an urban phenomenon, although rural violence has increased during the past decade and a half. Female delinquents are more likely to be incarcerated for sexually promiscuous behavior, theft, and activities less violent than those committed by males, contributing to a double standard that occurs internationally. Chinese scholars have described delinquents as being less educated and less intelligent than normal youth; they are more likely to have come from families where parental conflict has been present and have relatives who also have engaged in deviant behavior. Two important behavioral characteristics that have been attributed to delinquents include their plasticity and their eagerness to embrace a "cult of brotherhood." In the former case, they appear to be hardened individuals on the outside, but are emotionally quite fragile and easily shattered. In the latter case, they often commit crimes in groups rather than as individuals and seek peer support common during adolescence.[1]

During the early 1980s, specific attributions made about delinquents could be excessively romantic or often quite harsh and unflattering. They were in various publications depicted as "blossoms in the dust," ignorant *(yumei)*, muddle-headed *(hutu)*, tyrannical *(chengba)*, despicable *(xialu)*, impetuous *(jizao)*, crazy *(feng kuang)*, vain *(xurong)*, conceited *(zifei* or *kuangwang zida)*, reckless *(lumang)*, rotten *(fuxiu)*, and savage or inhuman *(miejue renxing)*. Females, it was noted, were particularly difficult to reform because, once incarcerated, they saw themselves as irreparably ruined, like a vase that once broken could not be put back together *(po guan po shuai)*.[2] Certainly such categorizations reflected a traditional Confucian reluctance to separate an understanding of the nature of deviance with the ethical implications of its occurrence. What was even more striking to the Westerner, though, was the use of unicausality in explaining why delinquency even existed in the People's Republic of China.

Official explanations that sought to account for delinquency's occurrence included the effects of the Cultural Revolution, poor parenting, unsympathetic teaching, unhealthy peer group influences, and susceptibility to the dangerous influences resulting from increased contact with Western media. Certainly the effects of the Cultural Revolution received prominent attention as scholars sought to explain the embarrassing existence of delinquency that remained visible during the post-Mao era. It was commonly pointed out that as a result of the Cultural Revolution, youth born during that time failed to obtain a clear understanding of right and wrong, as authority relationships between children and parents, as well as between citizens and government officials, were easily and regularly compromised. A significant number of youth who later got into trouble had parents who themselves were incarcerated or detained during the Cultural Revolution; certainly the political factionalism that encouraged relatives to inform on one another weakened traditional family ties.[3] But with direct reference to criminal behavior, it is clear that it was the surreptitious reentry of sent-down youth into China's cities in the latter years of the Cultural Revolution, without benefit of residence documentation, that had a significant effect upon increased social dislocation and disorder in the late 1970s.[4]

It should be stressed that it was easy to overemphasize the importance of the Cultural Revolution in contributing to Chinese delinquency, and the political expedience of doing so during the early years of post-Maoism is clear. Scholars in the 1970s and 1980s conveniently forgot or underplayed the fact that waves of delinquency (reported as outbreaks of hooliganism) were reported in the press during the 1950s.[5] It is clear that the eradication of criminal deviance of all types held important political capital for the regime, as evidenced by the publicity given to campaigns aimed at eliminating prostitution in Shanghai and curtailing drug use in Southern China during the early years of the People's Republic.[6] In 1983, although it was no longer possible to deny that the growth of crime generally and juvenile delinquency in particular had become an important social problem, it was imperative that government officials set blame in such a way so as to deny personal culpability; the use of the Cultural Revolution, as an umbrella explanation, served that purpose.

Other explanations for the existence of juvenile delinquency contained important elements of truth but were similarly general and unidimensional. Poor parenting, for example, was attributed to the use of both overly authoritarian and overly indulgent disciplinary methods, although the negative effects of parental socioeconomic disadvantage upon one's ability to adequately perform child-rearing responsibilities were also acknowledged as a contributing factor. In a similar vein, teachers were criticized for their overly harsh disciplinary methods and their emotional distance from youth. One published example told of the inconsiderate teacher who berated the female student in front of the class, comparing her with excrement that deserved to be flushed down a toilet. The incident, it was claimed, provoked the student into committing delinquent acts. In all of these cases, the longstanding Confucian emphasis upon the power of role modeling, whereby the authority figure is normally responsible for shaping the behavior of the underling, is simply assumed as being an operative dimension of social relationships.[7]

The fear of Western "sugar-coated bullets" corrupting Chinese youth was also popularly expressed at this time and was a key issue in the general spiritual pollution campaign. Again, it was reported that when they came in contact with pornographic videos or other media produced in the West, Chinese youth were negatively influenced into conducting the very crimes that the media sensationalized. Beyond the xenophobia that belie such explanations was what many Western scholars have labeled a form of moral panic, whereby a general fear for the future direction of the society in light of de-Maoification was expressed through an ambivalence toward the independence and ethical character of the country's children.[8] The contradiction between viewing delinquents in such negative terms as were previously noted, as opposed to seeing them as powerless innocents, subject to the manipulation of external prurient forces from the West, can best be understood through appreciating the sense of moral panic that characterized the decade.

CULTURAL BAGGAGE BROUGHT TO A STUDY OF CHINESE DELINQUENCY

I, of course, came to my study of juvenile delinquency in China with my own set of assumptions, many of which were grounded in Western views of Chinese society. Deeply influenced by the writings of Whyte (1973), Whyte (1974), Parrish and Whyte (1978), and Whyte and Parrish (1984),[9] I viewed urban Chinese society as consisting of a set of interlocking institutions working to control individual behavior in the neighborhood, workplace, and in schools. The use of informal mechanisms for maintaining social control had its historical origins in the *bao-jia* self-policing system, first established during the twelfth century, but perfected during the Qing dynasty. Thus, the manipulation of local social institutions to informally maintain social control had some historical resonance. Reformatories could logically be categorized as institutions that ideally contributed to social control in a more formal manner, and were to be evaluated on those terms. Having read and been impressed with Etzioni's (1961) categorization of institutions such as prisons and reform schools as being normative-coercive, I viewed my task as one of evaluating the effectiveness of these institutions in light of the ideological shifts that occurred after their initial development.[10] A key question to answer was whether the normative value claims that rationalized coercive treatment of offenders could continue to be effective during the post-Maoist era.

The entire notion of coercion was of obvious interest, and in reading both Donald Munro's view of Mao's belief in the malleability of human character[11] and Bao Ruo Wang's (Jean Pasquale's) description of labor camp life,[12] it became clear to me that the degree to which institutional coercion occurred was often tied to one's participation in the self-criticism process and one's corresponding willingness to confess to wrongdoing. Confession was a necessary precondition to character reformation, but at least there was the theoretical possibility of achieving rehabilitation. Indeed, upon reading *Prisoner of Mao,* it became evident that much of the physical maltreatment that was inflicted upon Chinese prisoners was due to widespread poverty and economic deprivation that affected everyone, rather than an intentional effort to inflict pain on the prisoners. Accounts of life in prisons and labor camps also emphasized the importance of labeling and social stigma, and their effects upon offenders as well as their relatives. The necessity of divorcing one's incarcerated spouse in order to keep one's employment, let alone maintain minimum external social contact, impressed me as being extremely significant. I, of course, understood that issues of stigma, labeling, and coercive institutional practice commonly occurred in the United States and in other Western countries too. But it was the closed nature of Chinese urban life, the lack of privacy, the reliance on connections *(guanxi)* for advancement, and the relatively low degree of mobility that made these issues especially compelling.

CHINESE PENAL INSTITUTIONS

Chinese penal institutions include prisons, reform and reeducation through labor camps, reformatories, work-study schools, and work-study classes. Although the latter institutions were designed specifically for juveniles, offenders can be sent to reform and reeducation through labor camps and prisons too, depending upon the nature of their offense. There is a pecking order throughout the penal system, an institutional hierarchy based upon coercive purpose. Thus, delinquents who are not placed in reformatories are more likely to be sent to labor camps, but within the labor camp system, they are likely to enter reeducation through labor camps that house political prisoners and offenders guilty of moderate offenses rather than those camps that house hardened criminals. By Western standards, any form of incarceration that places juveniles with adult offenders is a violation of children's basic rights. Yet in the Chinese case, it is important to note that the term "youth" refers to those from the age of eighteen up to the age of twenty-five. Juveniles supposedly include those aged fourteen through eighteen, although here, too, clear-cut distinctions between juveniles and youth are often compromised. Juveniles between the ages of fourteen and sixteen who commit serious crimes (homicide, bodily injury, robbery, arson, etc.) bear full criminal responsibility, although the severity of punishment is mitigated and the death penalty is only inflicted upon those aged eighteen and above.[13]

The two institutions that are specifically designed for youthful offenders are reformatories and work-study schools. The former hold relatively large numbers of youth who have been judged guilty of major offenses, and are well-established components of the criminal justice system. Work-study schools, which hold fewer offenders who have committed less severe offenses, were established during the 1950s.[14] They were eliminated during the Cultural Revolution, ostensibly because of their ineffectiveness, but were resurrected during the late 1970s. In 1979, they received widespread publicity as an important solution to combating growing delinquency. A long-held suspicion that remains is that they cater largely to cadre children and children of privilege who have gotten into trouble. Hooper reported that some work-study schools for girls served as little more than homes for pregnant teens.[15] In Guangzhou, two work-study factory classes, gender segregated, were established as local alternatives to the work-study school. Although work-study schools are usually operated under the jurisdiction of the municipal education bureau, these factory classes were operated with the support of the municipal government in conjunction with the public security bureau.

The range of penalties within the criminal justice system can include control *(guanzhi),* criminal detention *(juyi),* fixed-term imprisonment, life imprisonment, and the death penalty. *Guanzhi* refers to public security efforts to control criminal behavior prior to incarceration. In the case of juveniles, they continue to go to school and perform normal functions of everyday behavior, but are required to report to public security regularly and inform upon their actions as well as those of friends. In the case of *juyi* (criminal detention), offenders are actually housed in a confined setting for a period of fifteen days to six months.[16] Juveniles who are sent to work-study schools and factory classes would generally fall under this type of mandate although the length of their incarceration and conditions for their release are quite broad. Offenders given fixed-term imprisonment can be incarcerated from six months to fifteen years and, when combined with multiple offenses, even longer. Generally, offenders housed in reformatories are punished according to this category. One informant told me, though, that some of the offenders I saw at a particular reformatory would simply be transferred to labor camps upon their eighteenth birthday; their chances of ever being released from incarceration were quite slim.

PERSONAL OBSERVATIONS[17]

Upon visiting the principal reformatory serving Guangdong Province and one of the two work-study factory classes in Guangzhou during the spring of 1983, I had the following reactions. The Guangdong Juvenile Reformatory Institute at Shijing housed 520 offenders aged fourteen to eighteen, twenty of whom were female. Briefly closed during the Cultural Revolution and turned into a factory, the facility was reopened in 1972 and had operated continuously since then. Its physical plant, equipment, resources, and so on seemed outstanding, and when I later visited the work-study factory class, officials there apologized for their comparative dearth of resources. The reformatory was a model institution whose affluence was exceptional, but it was, nonetheless, a typically coercive penal institution.

Immediately upon entering, offenders were fingerprinted, issued uniforms, and given haircuts. They were then divided into 150 member groups that were subdivided into cells of ten. Two leaders were elected for each cell; their jobs included leading political study sessions and reporting peer behavior to cadre supervisors. This process, known as collectivist education *(jiti jiaoyu),* played a major part of the offenders' political education. They were pressured into repenting during self-criticism sessions, and insofar as their lack of understanding of appropriate rule-governed behavior was blamed for their willingness to engage in deviance, they were taken to People's Courts and were given lectures by public security officials. At the same time, it was extremely important that they demonstrate publicly their willingness and ability to be rehabilitated. To that end, offenders would be forced into engaging in service activities including construction, street sweeping, and other visible group service activities.

The academic component of the curriculum included instruction in basic skills as well as manual labor in the broadest of terms. Offenders were given four forty-five-minute classes per day with ten-minute intervening rest periods and a two-hour rest period after lunch. The subjects taught included Chinese, mathematics, history, and music (communal singing) with normal class size set at a 50:1 ratio. Some classes were divided into a 20:1 ratio for purposes of remediation, although ability grouping was an exception rather than the rule. The national language *(Putonghua)* was used as the language of instruction as it was noted that the Cantonese youth could at least understand teacher instruction.

Offender manual-labor activities included work in the automotive shop, fishing, growing beans and peanuts, gardening, pursuing flower cultivation and arrangement, and completing construction work. Girls would pursue light manual labor such as sweeping and dusting, but were prohibited from engaging in automotive repair or construction work. These activities are noteworthy for their general rather than technical nature, as well as their collective rather than individual orientation. Since over half of the offenders came from urban environments, the transferability of some of the work conducted at the reformatory to their native settings was questionable. It certainly was unconnected to the institution's academic program.

Offender punishment included forced participation in self-criticism sessions and documentation of repeated offenses for one's permanent record. It was claimed that 5 percent of the offender population left before their sentences were completed but 2 to 3 percent of the offenders had their sentences lengthened. Although it was admitted that incarcerated offenders were subjected to physical punishment during the Cultural Revolution, it was claimed that this no longer occurred, although the use of solitary confinement from one-half to three days in length was acknowledged. Officials were proud of the fact that the facility did not include visible physical structures that would directly impede escape; however, as 1983 progressed, offender escape did become a national issue, penal institutions were criticized for their laxity, and public executions of criminals became a popular alternative to institutional incarceration.

In viewing the Guangdong Reformatory Institute at Shijing, my main reference points included previous visits to similar institutions in Taiwan and Hong Kong. The Guangdong facilities were impressive, but what was most noteworthy was that its institutional rituals did not explicitly condone the coercive treatment of offenders. Such was not the case in Taiwan, where the largest reform school on the island was run by a superintendent who was proud of his military background as a former army officer, where offenders as young as twelve were held in shackles and leg irons, where one's uniform number was displayed prominently, and where the mass haircut was quite visible. Offenders there were required to sit in silence with their hands on their knees for one-half hour after they had completed eating; they regularly marched in unison from building to building. Such rituals, which are supposed to teach internal discipline and self-regulation, have the effect of degrading one's individuality, and were surprisingly absent during my visit to the Guangdong Reformatory. The use of the group for purposes of controlling individual behavior and fostering compliance was much more noticeable though.

The work-study factory class at Fangcun, one of two institutions operating in Guangzhou, served two hundred males. The other institution served females who were charged with theft and prostitution. I was not allowed to visit it because the matter of female delinquency was considered too sensitive for a foreigner to observe and presumably comment upon. The Fangcun institution was first established in 1973 as a series of political and work-study classes for mildly delinquent males. In 1975, its permanent factory component was initiated, and in 1980, it officially became a work-study factory class with an increase in the number of courses and a strengthened education program. Three part-time primary-level-education teachers were contracted from the municipal education bureau to operate the program; other staff came from the factory itself.

Students attending the work-study factory class were between ages fifteen and twenty-five; some were sent from their regular schools, while the others were factory workers or those who were unemployed. The environment could easily accommodate both recalcitrant workers and students, unlike the more restrictive environment of typical work-study schools. Most had previously attended a primary or junior-middle school, but none had attended a senior-middle school. Over 75 percent of the offenders were guilty of theft; other offenses included quarreling, hooliganism, minor gang activity, and gambling—offenses considered too minor for prosecution. Offenders typically stayed at the factory class for six months, but they were allowed to return home on Sundays. Ten percent of the offenders left before their sentence had been completed because of good behavior; 6 percent were required to stay longer because of poor behavior and attitude. Authorities admitted to a 15 percent recidivism rate within one year of release.

Since it was claimed that the purpose of the work-study factory class was to educate rather than punish offenders, a rewards system was instituted to encourage behavioral change. Offenders were assessed marks on a scale of one to ten for their behavioral and academic performance;

upon receipt of eighteen hundred points they were able to leave, and each individual's score was posted on a blackboard outside of the classroom for all to see. Self-criticism sessions occurred on a regular basis, but corporal punishment was no longer used. Authorities noted that there had been seven escapes within the previous eight years; when offenders neglected to return to the facility on Sunday evenings, home visitations were made to ascertain the reasons for truant behavior.

Political education at the work-study factory class included legal and health education, but the teaching of factory discipline was especially emphasized because it was presumed that these students, at best, would be future factory workers. As was true of their counterparts in the Guangdong reformatory, they were taken to public courts and trials to see personally the consequences of criminal behavior. However, as their clothing complemented that worn by regular factory workers and as their haircuts, which were given by teachers or parents, were enforced unsystematically, they were not stigmatized by their appearance and blended in well with their larger external environment. They had access to the factory clinic if they fell ill, and were given a food allotment that included at least one meat and one vegetable dish per day.

The academic program included instruction in *Putonghua* and mathematics, with rudimentary literacy skills along with some history and geography included. The language of instruction was Cantonese as opposed to *Putonghua*; students were divided into primary, lower-middle, and middle school levels, and were grouped by ability within those levels into remedial, average, and above-average categories. Class size was approximately 50:1, and it was claimed that general curricular content paralleled that offered at ordinary public schools.

Vocational training was offered in arc welding, model making, wine making, and photographic machine operation and repair, with factory engineers specifically enlisted to teach the students how to repair electrical equipment. Most of their time, however, was spent engaging in general factory work of a menial nature, ostensibly to teach adherence to factory discipline and a respect for the rhythms of factory work. The parent factory at Fangcun produced diesel engines, though it would be unlikely that a work-study factory-class graduate would obtain employment there. Indeed, it was admitted that 70 percent of the offenders were unemployed after their release.

My impressions of the work-study factory class were positive, as I viewed the facility as a less coercive institution than its reformatory counterpart, which was not surprising since it dealt with offenders who had committed less serious crimes. It was clear that there was some jealousy between officials at the respective institutions, with the work-study class cadres viewing their own institution as lacking in prestige and positive publicity. Thus, my visit as an outside international observer was useful to them in buttressing their stature, and my positive reactions to the facility were reported in an edition of the local newspaper.

Overall, I concluded that juveniles in China faced more conflict outside of institutional walls than within them. The pressures of overcoming social stigma were intense. Indeed, the Chinese national press had reported on a delinquent's suicide as a general case, caused by the offender's despondency over a lack of parental contact while incarcerated. For offenders housed at both the reformatory and work-study factory class, institutional release did not mean starting anew. These youths were regularly required to report to public security officials, to play the role of informant, and to give details of the activities of peers and friends. Thus, their place within the criminal justice system reverted to stage one, *guanzhi,* as it was never expected that they would ever be free of contact with the system. My conclusion was that the use of stigma, negative labeling, and guilt by association, although informally communicated, was nonetheless extremely powerful outside of institutional walls. As essentially Maoist institutions, the juvenile justice facilities themselves communicated quite effectively to offenders the informal terms through which social control was to be exercised in their future lives. Those terms included engaging in manual labor as a means of fostering self-discipline and character reformation, submitting to the authority of the group during self-criticism sessions, publicly displaying remorse for one's actions, and accepting formal authority through a nominal academic routine. The emphasis upon rewarding individual behavior in an effort to promote substantive change was noteworthy, but, overall, the goal of authoritarian collectivism was constantly being reinforced within the institutional settings.

JUVENILE DELINQUENCY IN THE 1980s AND 1990s

Throughout the 1980s and 1990s, juvenile delinquency and youth criminality increased significantly in China. In 1980, for example, 61.2 percent of all criminals were youths and juveniles; by 1989, the percentage had increased to 74.1 percent.[18] This is part of a larger trend where crime increased markedly, from 54 cases per 100,000 filed by public security officials in 1987 to 181 per 100,000 by 1989.[19] The extent of youth and juvenile crime as a percentage of overall crime has become one of the highest in the world. With specific reference to juveniles (as opposed to youths), there has been a significant increase in the number of juvenile criminals and the rate of their criminal activity, although there has been a decline in the absolute number of juvenile criminals relative to other criminals. Still, criminals are getting younger. The total crime committed by fourteen- to eighteen-year-olds increased from 7 percent in 1980 to almost 20 percent in 1989.[20] More and more students are committing crimes while they still are in school, as many attend vocational middle schools and technical/worker schools, institutions with relatively low prestige[21] that are seen as offering no chance for social mobility.

As crime has increased in China, it has grown in urban areas and coastal regions, mirroring the uneven economic development in the country. Juvenile and youth crimes have correspondingly increased with respect to theft, burglary, robbery, hooliganism, rape, and violent criminal activity.[22] The latter category includes bombing, kidnapping, and hijacking as well as homicide, assault, and battery.[23] Crimes are increasingly brutal as firearms become easier to obtain. Gang activity has increased during the 1980s; gangs are larger and more brazen in their activities. Similar to the tongs of old, gangs have become more secretive, better organized, and less spontaneous.[24]

During the 1990s, drug activity increased significantly and has had an impact upon juvenile and youth crime. Drug cases solved by police in Guangzhou in 1994, for example, were three times greater than those of 1981 through 1990 combined, while within Guangdong Province, 80 percent of drug users are under the age of twenty-five.[25] Yunnan Province traditionally has been a source of drug cultivation and smuggling, and its prominence has increased as social and political controls have decreased. As a result, drug trafficking has been accompanied by increases in gun smuggling, child kidnapping, and prostitution, with youth gangs playing a prominent role in these activities.[26] All of these trends have occurred within a general environment that has sanctioned widespread corruption on the part of government officials. From 1988 to 1993, 1.2 million cases of cadre corruption were acknowledged by the Chinese press, with 170,000 cases being reported for 1993 alone.[27]

Authorities have reacted to these trends in a number of ways. They have benefitted from gaining increased access to technology, which has been used to enforce greater social control. Thus, public security bureaus now use automobiles for motor patrol and make better use of telephones and electronic equipment to solve crimes.[28] Other responses have included improving legal education within schools, offering support for mediation, and using residence committees to assist in crime prevention and neighborhood surveillance. With specific reference to reformatories and correctional institutions, efforts have been made to enhance supervision in order to prevent escapes. It was reported that in Shanghai, for example, that inmate escape decreased from 0.05 percent in 1981 to 0.02 percent in 1991.[29] In addition, reward systems have been implemented at a number of facilities (not unlike the system used at the Fangcun work-study class), goal setting and evaluation procedures have been initiated, and some effort has been made to tailor the type of manual work offered to the specific nature of the inmate's offense.[30] At the same time, it should be noted that certain reformatories, as with the larger penal system, continue to force juvenile offenders to make goods that are sold for export in the West, which contributes income to China's prison labor system.[31]

Situ and Liu generally see a shift from reliance upon informal mechanisms of social control to use of professional organizations to maintain social order. Factories and places of employment are now training their own security divisions, and joint defense brigades, whose members come from various work units, patrol recreational areas and public places.[32] This is occurring within a general professionalization of the entire legal system as more lawyers are being trained, along with participants involved in criminal justice.

Still, the ratio of 1 police officer for every 1,400 people remains one of the highest ratios in the world, where the average is 1:50;[33] and the reliance upon the mass campaign to expeditiously identify and punish criminals remains quite strong. Dutton and Lee argue that this type of informal policing allows for flexibility and gives a sense of security to the population. However, in 1996, over one thousand people were executed within a two-month span during China's "*yanda*" (strike hard) campaign, the most violent of its type since 1983. The offenders were quickly tried, convicted, and executed without benefit of appeal. Mass trials attended by up to twenty thousand people were also held, and convicts were paraded in public before being sent off to be shot.[34] It is therefore fair to conclude that in spite of some efforts to professionalize law enforcement generally as well as reformatory education specifically, a reliance upon informal mechanisms for delivering justice remains strong in China.

It is tempting to associate the increase in juvenile delinquency in China during the past two decades with the material affluence that has accompanied swift economic change. However, such an attribution would be excessively simplistic if it failed to take into account increasing urban unemployment rates (officially acknowledged to be about 2.9 percent in 1997), increased urban and coastal migration, diminished control over residential mobility patterns, and structural changes within the educational system. In the latter case, authorities have successfully restricted the number of students with aspirations for attending university, so that in 1997 only 2.84 million high school graduates will take entrance examinations for 1 million available places in the country's colleges and universities.[35] The "cooling out" process begins much earlier, however, toward the end of primary school, when decisions are made as to the type and quality of middle school one can attend. At the senior-secondary level, further stratification occurs as students enter regular academic and "keypoint" high schools, secondary specialized schools, vocational high schools, and technical schools.[36] Although many delinquents do not advance this far through the system, their future aspirations are leveled at increasingly early stages of their development.

Thus, responses to increased youth crime and delinquency can be classified as both progressive and traditional. Progressive responses have contributed to a professionalization of the criminal justice system through the enhanced training and education of corrections officials, as well as through increased data collection and analysis. Chinese authorities joined Interpol in 1984, an event that has encouraged the sharing of information along with enhanced international cooperation, particularly with regard to drug trafficking. Although there is some evidence of professionalization within juvenile correctional institutions, the evidence for a radical change of institutional culture is more mixed; these still are organizations that profess strong ideological beliefs in the redemptive value of manual labor, the importance of character reformation in a general sense, and the need to respect collective authority. Outside of institutional walls, the use of the mass anticrime campaign to address rising crime rates with expediency, swiftness, and harshness continues unabated. And the official response to increased residential mobility and unemployment lies in continued reliance upon residence committees and street offices (whose functions were first formally articulated in 1954) to work with public security and correctional officials in preserving social order and preventing crime.

RECENT WESTERN RESEARCH ON CHINESE DELINQUENCY

Since my own research on delinquency was conducted, scholars have relied upon additional firsthand accounts[37] as well as survey questionnaire research[38] to gain a broader understanding of the topic. Zhang relied upon the assistance of Communist Youth League and public security officials to administer his questionnaires, which were distributed to 369 delinquents housed in reformatories, reeducation-through-labor camps, and prisons, and to 443 youths from the general population. Liu's sample included 403 middle-school students in Shenzhen. In addition, Marvin Wolfgang of the University of Pennsylvania has undertaken a long-term study of a 1973 birth cohort from the Wuchang district of Wuhan, and it is expected that his study will be expanded to include the entire city by the year 2000.[39] Generally, the authors conclude that Western criminological theories are applicable to the Chinese case. Wolfgang's preliminary results indicate delinquent/nondelinquent differences in levels of education, unemployment, susceptibility to school discipline and punishment, dropout rates, and learning attitudes. Others have discovered positive relationships between family deviance and child-rearing practices and delinquency status,[40] and have noted the salience of labeling theory for predicting friendship estrangement but not family ties.[41] There is some disagreement regarding the importance of social control factors over internal personal control factors in explaining delinquency potentiality,[42] but for the most part, all of the research assumes that criminological paradigms refined in the West are operational for the Chinese case. Although the use of survey research in China is a testament to the growing importance of the social sciences there, it should be stressed that the results of these surveys should be treated with caution. Whenever one relies upon the local Communist Youth League director and accompanying correctional officials to administer one's questionnaire (as was the case with Zhang), it is difficult to see how, in spite of pledges of confidentiality, those administering the instruments would be viewed by delinquents as neutral parties. Further, the use of residence committee and school officials to record information while conducting the personal interviews (as pursued by Wolfgang and Liu) presents a similar if less extreme dilemma. Given the nature of their situations, reasonable questions can be raised regarding issues of informed consent and the freedom of delinquents to refrain from participating in such research. Their answers to particularly sensitive questions regarding their attitudes and value orientations must therefore be viewed with skepticism until the political implications of their participation in the research are better understood. Thus, I think that it is at least arguable as to whether the use of quasi-experimental survey research models, postulating cause–effect relationships between various delinquency factors, has been any more valuable in adding to our understanding of Chinese delinquency than the observational research that I and others conducted previously.

A REEVALUATION

When I began my dissertation research, a number of Chinese friends commented that it was strange for one to spend so much time investigating the conditions of youth who obviously would never contribute to society. Given the fact that the educational system had so many problems, in their eyes it would have made more sense for me to investigate policies that might beneficially affect a larger group of individuals who would be in a better position to enhance China's educational development. My response to my friends was twofold. First, I argued that I could better understand the nature of Chinese society by analyzing what was happening to its outcasts. Second, I argued that issues of opportunity and fairness were important in all societies and those issues deserved to be articulated and discussed. There is an arrogance to that response that I believe has colored not only my own research but also that of others pursuing work in Chinese education and Chinese studies generally. Such a response assumes that comparative social and cultural interactions can be understood totalistically. It assumes that observers can unobtrusively use their authority as outsiders to give voice to a group they view as marginalized and impotent. But more important than the naïveté that accompanied these assumptions is their negative impact upon one's ability to grasp the fundamental nature of the research being pursued. In this case, the result was an inability to appreciate the dynamics of social change, a tendency to falsely dichotomize social practices into extreme categories, and a failure to sufficiently control for Western bias in my analysis.

Comprehending the pace and importance of changing social relationships in a foreign context is extremely difficult, particularly when one's research is short-term and significant limitations are placed upon one's access to documents, human subject interviews are conducted while party officials are present, and follow-up visitations to the same facilities subject to initial observation are not possible. Nonetheless, in viewing juvenile correctional institutions as largely closed systems, self-contained organizations expressing their normative-coercive missions in traditionally Maoist terms, I neglected to appreciate either the external or internal pressures that might lead to significant institutional change. It was easy to see how internal and external conflicts might arise. The emphasis upon collectivist education, although a perfectly logical assumption on the part of authorities given the group-based nature of Chinese society, could easily foster gang affiliations that might be openly expressed upon release, since it placed offenders in constant small-group contact. Attempts to maintain contact with offenders themselves after their release, as well as with their street and residence committee officials charged with supervising their behavior and maintaining local order, would have been exceptionally difficult for reformatory officials, given the varied residences and geographical backgrounds of the offenders. Given these actual and potential conflicts, I neglected to comprehend how they would be reconciled or how the pressures for their reconciliation would be addressed. Instead, I viewed these institutions as doctrinaire and inelastic, because that is how I also viewed the ideological principles that governed their operation.

Certainly, I tended to dichotomize the practices I observed into extreme categories. I viewed reformatory education as little more than a form of enforced socialization that legitimized the coercive function of these institutions to the society at large. In so doing, I saw socialization as unidirectional, imposed upon the offenders without their consent, and largely ineffective in changing their value orientations. In truth, it is clear that correctional institutions of all types depend upon their inmates in order to function effectively, given that offender-staff ratios are so large.[43] The question for offenders is not one of their submission or resistance to authority, but how effectively can they minimize institutional constraints and negotiate conflict so as to maximize their individual power and influence. For obvious reasons, I was not in a position to obtain direct information about the actual social dynamics of the offender-guard relationship, but I was certainly remiss in making assumptions about that relationship in the absence of useful information.

A second problem concerned my view of the treatment of released offenders, as I believed that the social stigma offenders confronted upon their release, informally administered, was quite harsh and was of greater long-term consequence than the treatment they received within institutional walls. Here, too, the dichotomies of formal (institutional) versus informal offender treatment were simplistically constructed. In the West, for example, issues of offender stigma certainly are evident in spite of efforts to professionalize probation and after-care treatments. Unemployment rates remain high, as do recidivism rates. Recent Western efforts that rely upon community approaches to policing and emphasize informal preventative intervention strategies, which are implemented before delinquent behavior becomes severe, further blur the distinction between formal and informal approaches to crime prevention and the eventual disposition of criminal cases.

With regard to the Chinese case, in focusing upon the importance of social labeling as a function of social control, expressed through the activities of informal organizations such as mediation, street, and residence committees, I again failed to comprehend the internal dynamics of those organizations. Impressed with the importance of group affiliation and the lack of individual privacy that was afforded individuals living in urban China, I neglected to appreciate how individuals were able to maximize their status not only within group settings, which was a traditional pattern, but above and beyond them as well. In short, the use of *guanxi* to maximize one's interests implied a reciprocity with respect to individual relationships on a one-to-one basis that I had underestimated. Released delinquents, I believed, without access to strong group support lost the personal ties necessary to successfully reintegrate within the society, and as a result, their stigma was informally codified. What has occurred over the past two decades, though, has been an erosion of group loyalty throughout many aspects of urban Chinese life due to increased individual entrepreneurship, residential migration, and a tolerance for higher unemployment levels generally, as the government has retreated from its traditional paternalism. Instead, one sees a decrease in the social stigma of having engaged in illegal or quasi-legal activity and a significant increase in corruption on an individual basis at all social levels. My analysis failed to foresee this trend.

I previously noted that I viewed the Maoist ideological principles that played an important role in the articulated mission of reformatories and correctional institutions to be doctrinaire and inflexibly administered. Insofar as I viewed ideology as performing only a conservative rather than a progressive function, I believe that I allowed Western bias to color my perspective. Certainly, I failed to challenge the ideological assumptions of carceral bureaucracies such as those in prisons or other coercive institutions, as they have evolved in the West; nor did I critique the notions of professionalism that these institutions promote. In truth, ideology can be transformatory as well as restrictive, and in the Chinese case, its Maoist variant served many by giving a sense of direction to the future without renouncing the collective past. For all of the abuses and excesses that occurred within and beyond reformatory walls in the name of ideology, it is certainly arguable as to whether Chinese delinquents are better off today in a less overtly politicized environment, or whether delinquents in Western environments have ever fared better than their Chinese counterparts did two decades ago.

The basic question that remains unresolved is whether such weaknesses are indicative of the limitations of more general research patterns, and, if so, whether ethnographic approaches have the potential for redressing these weaknesses in ways that other research methods fail to achieve. Certainly, we see the growth of collaborative research and the use of survey research in the study of Chinese delinquency and criminology over the past two decades, and these trends are representative of what has occurred within Chinese studies generally. It is arguable, however, whether those advances in themselves help in our understanding of Chinese society. If I erred in my own work, through emphasizing the cultural uniqueness of Chinese social interaction with respect to social control and labeling practices—depicting them totalistically and in dichotomous terms—more recent studies of delinquency have denied the importance of cultural context completely, and have instead attempted to use the Chinese case as evidence for the viability of their preconceived Western theories. Neither perspective does justice to the subjects of cross-cultural investigation.

Can the use of ethnographic methods make a difference? I believe that it can under certain conditions. To the extent that critical ethnography employs a reflexivity that calls into question the fundamental nature of the subject (researcher)-object relationship, the tendency to totalize the foreign in the name of cultural distinctiveness or use the foreign to superficially reaffirm the primacy of Western paradigms can be checked. At the same time, a critical ethnographic approach holds the possibility of our exploring more honestly the ramifications of the politics of access and the use or censorship of information to control social behavior, issues that have traditionally confronted scholars pursuing social research in China. It is doubtful, for example, that foreigners or natives would ever be granted the access necessary to complete a full-bodied ethnographic study of a Chinese correctional institution because to Chinese officials, the political sensitivity of the environment would outweigh the usefulness of any information that might be gathered and shared through intensive observation and analysis. But in examining the operations of schools and their relationships to family, work, and neighborhood, the critical ethnographer has the opportunity to gain insight into the nature of normalcy and deviance, personal motivation and leveled aspiration, self-interest and collective loyalty, open and closed opportunity structures—in short, the fundamental conflicts that characterize so many aspects of Chinese life on a daily basis for those who are successful, as well as for those who are marginalized and dispossessed.

Chinese educational and correctional facilities share more than the most common of institutional characteristics. If correctional institutions rely upon very basic educational programs to legitimize their coercive practices, coercion, even if its appearance is less overtly visible, is regularly used within educational settings to enforce school policies as well. As Foucault so convincingly argued, the relationship between curricular discipline and the formal as well as symbolic exercise of power upon the individual has had strong historical resonance in the West,[44] and there is no reason to think that a similar relationship does not exist in contemporary China. Indeed, when the operation of work-study schools and factory classes for delinquent youths has been assigned to municipal education bureaus, such a relationship has been made more explicit and more formalized for those judged mildly delinquent. Traditional views of mainstream schools highlight their reliance upon remunerative characteristics (such as the distribution of grades and other symbolic rewards) that are supported by a modest degree of coercion (enforcement of compulsory attendance). For the Chinese case, however, the relationship between normative, remunerative, and coercive institutional goals is complex and in a state of flux, particularly as larger numbers of students have become increasingly disenfranchised, due to the imposition of rigid status hierarchies among and within schools, and their corresponding culling-out policies. The necessity of reevaluating the nature of authority patterns within schools is clear. And if such a reevaluation were to occur, the relationships between teachers, students, parents, administrators, and community members would be analyzed in terms that did justice to their complexity. Scholars would do more than simply identify the extent to which common practice corresponded to official policy. Instead, they would begin to investigate the ways in which instructors use various pedagogies in their efforts to assume control over students' private space and physical movement, while concurrently asserting authority over knowledge dissemination and production. Although the terms through which such authority is expressed are more harsh and visible within correctional institutional settings, they are no less salient to the culture of educational institutions and deserve to be scrutinized.

The usefulness of applying Basil Bernstein's notions of strong and weak framing systems (pedagogical relations between teacher and student) and classification codes (collection of curricular material on the basis of disciplinary boundaries) to Chinese educational settings has been noted by Western scholars.[45] But because the reformatory and work-study factory class cases highlight how strong framing systems and weak classification codes can coexist in unexpected and contradictory ways, it is even more imperative that scholars investigate the pedagogical and curricular similarities and differences that exist in more traditional educational settings. Certainly, delinquency studies highlight the importance of examining the nature of peer interaction within and outside of school boundaries more intensively; and this, too, is an area that has been neglected by mainstream Chinese educational scholars.

Nonetheless, the pursuit of ethnographic research in educational domains holds particular promise because the terms of the discourse easily transcend cultural boundaries and are inherently familiar and personal to all of us. It is because our educational experiences have been crucial to the formation of our own identities that we understand that the terms through which those experiences are expressed in cross-cultural situations are so important. Although it is arguable whether critical ethnographic approaches to the study of Chinese education have to this point fulfilled their ultimate promise, researchers committed to the method are asking the appropriate questions, a necessary precondition to enhancing our understanding of Chinese society.

NOTES

1. Irving Epstein, "Psychological and Behavioral Attributes of Juvenile Delinquents in the People's Republic of China," *Asian Thought and Society* 12 (1987): 267–269.

2. Ibid., 268, 271–272.

3. Ibid., 267.

4. Thomas Bernstein, *Up to the Mountains and Down to the Village* (New Haven: Yale University Press, 1977), 93, 261, 313–314.

5. "Rascals and Juvenile Delinquents Rampant in Shanghai," *Survey of China Mainland Press* 1576 (July 24, 1957): 30–31; "Don't Overlook the Work Concerning Teenagers," *Survey of China Mainland Press,* 2675 (February 9, 1962): 18–19; "Don't Let Your Children Do Small Business," *Supplement to the Survey of China Mainland Press* 105 (March 14, 1963): 44–45.

6. Xiong Bo, "Jiefang chu Shanghai liumang gaizao jilue" ["Introduction to Remoulding Shanghai's Hoodlums during the Initial Post-Liberation Period"], *Shehui* 2 (1982): 29; Zhou Yinjun, Yang Jiezeng, and Xue Suzhen, "Xin shehui bagui bien chengren: Yi Shanghai gaizao changzi shihua" ["The New Society Turns Ghosts into Human Beings: A Talk on the History of Reforming Prostitutes in Shanghai"], *Shehui* 1 (1981): 46–51.

7. Epstein, "Psychological," 268–270.

8. Heidi Ross, "The 'Crisis' in Chinese Secondary Schooling," in *Chinese Education: Problems, Policies and Prospects,* ed. Irving Epstein (New York: Garland, 1991), 109–144; Delia Davin, "The Early Childhood Education of the Only Child Generation in Urban China," in *Chinese Education: Problems, Policies, and Prospects,* ed. Irving Epstein (New York: Garland, 1991), 42–65.

9. Martin K. Whyte, "Corrective Labor Camps in China," *Asian Survey* 13 (1973): 253–269; Martin K. Whyte, *Small Groups and Political Rituals in China* (Berkeley: University of California Press, 1974); William Parish and Martin K. Whyte, *Village and Family Life in Contemporary China* (Chicago: University of Chicago Press, 1978); Martin K. Whyte and William L. Parish, *Urban Life in Contemporary China* (Chicago: University of Chicago Press, 1984).

10. Amatai Etzioni, *A Comparative Analysis of Complex Organizations* (Glencoe, Ill.: Free Press, 1961).

11. Donald Munro, *The Concept of Man in Contemporary China* (Ann Arbor: University of Michigan Press, 1977).

12. Bao Ruo Wang, *Prisoner of Mao* (New York: Coward, McCann and Geoglican, 1973).

13. Guo Jianan et al., *World Factbook of Criminal Justice Systems: China* (Washington, D.C.: U. S. Department of Justice, Bureau of Justice Statistics, www.ojp.usdoj.gov/bjs//abstract/wfcj.htm, 1993).

14. Daniel J. Curran and Sandra Cook, "Growing Fears, Rising Crime: Juveniles and China's Justice System," *Crime and Delinquency* 39 (1993): 309–310.

15. Beverly Hooper, *Youth in China* (Victoria, Australia: Penguin, 1985).

16. Guo et al., *World Factbook,* 1993.

17. The following information comes from Irving Epstein, "Juvenile Delinquency and Reformatory Education in Chinese Society," (Ph.D. diss., University of California, Los Angeles, 1984); Irving Epstein, "Children's Rights and Juvenile Correctional Institutions in the People's Republic of China," *Comparative Education Review* 30 (1986): 359–372; Irving Epstein, "Reformatory Education in Chinese Society," *International Journal of Offender Therapy and Comparative Criminology* 30 (1986): 87–100.

18. Hang Hangwei, "Jinnian lai woguo qingshaonian fanzui de jiben zhuangkuang he tedian," *Qingshanian fanzui yanjiu* [1991], trans. as "The Basic Conditions and Characteristics of Youth and Juvenile Crimes

in Our Country in the Last Five Years," *Chinese Education and Society* 26 (1993): 88; Curran and Cook, "Growing," 300–301.

19. Situ Yingyi and Liu Weizheng, "Comprehensive Treatment to Social Order: A Chinese Approach to Crime," *International Journal of Comparative and Applied Criminology* 20 (1996): 97.

20. Curran and Cook, "Growing," 301.

21. Hang, "Basic," 97–99.

22. Ibid., 92.

23. Ibid., 93.

24. Ibid., 96–98.

25. Liu Weizheng and Situ Yingyi, "The Causes, Control, and Treatment of Illegal Drugs," *CJ International Online* 12, no. 5, www.acsp.uic.edu/OIJC/PUBS/Cji205 htm (1996).

26. Michael Dutton, "Translation: The Basic Character of Crime in Contemporary Cina," *China Quarterly* 149 (1997): 161–177.

27. Joe C. B. Leung and Richard C. Nann, *Authority Benevolence: Social Welfare in China* (Hong Kong: Chinese University Press, 1995), 161.

28. Situ and Liu, "Comprehensive," 106–107.

29. Ibid., 104.

30. Ibid.

31. D. Lee, R. Neff, and J. Barnathan, "China's Ugly Export Secret: Prison Labor," *Business Week* (April 22, 1991), 42–43, 46.

32. Situ and Liu, "Comprehensive," 105.

33. Michael Dutton and Tianfu Lee, "Missing the Target? Political Strategies in the Period of Economic Reform," *Crime and Delinquency* 39 (1993): 327.

34. Amnesty International, "China: One Thousand Executed in 'Strike Hard' Campaign Against Crime," *Amnesty International Homepage,* www.amnesty.org (July 5, 1996).

35. "Competition Rate 3 to 1 in College Entrance Exams," *China News Digest-Global GL 97–099* (July 14, 1997): 3.

36. C. Montgomery Broaded and Chongshun Liu, "Family Background, Gender, and Educational Attainment in Urban China," *China Quarterly* 134 (1996): 53–86.

37. Curran and Cook, "Growing."

38. Zhang Lening, "Peers' Rejection as a Possible Consequence of Official Reaction to Delinquency in Chinese Society," *Criminal Justice and Behavior* 21 (1994): 387–402; Zhang Lening, "Consequences of Official Reactions to Delinquency in Chinese Society," (Ph.D. diss., State

University of New York at Albany, 1995); Zhang Lening and Steven F. Messner, "Family Deviance and Delinquency in China," *Criminology* 33 (1995): 359–387; Zhang Lening and Steven F. Messner, "School Attachment and Official Delinquency Status in the People's Republic of China," *Sociological Forum* 11 (1996): 285–303; Liu Weizheng, "Perceptions of Delinquency Among Junior High School Students in Shenzhen City of the People's Republic of China: A Control Theory Perspective," (Ph.D. diss., Indiana University of Pennsylvania, 1994).

39. National Institute of Justice, "Delinquency in China: Study of a Birth Cohort: A Summary of a Presentation by Marvin Wolfgang," Research Preview, http://www.ncjrs.org/txtfiles/china.txt (May 1996).

40. Zhang and Messner, "Family."

41. Zhang, "Peers' Rejection" ; and Zhang and Messner, "School Attachment."

42. For example, Zhang and Messner (1996) argue in favor of the importance of school attachment while Liu (1994) emphasizes value orientation and socialization.

43. Finn-Aage Esbensen, "Participant Observation in a County Jail," *International Journal of Offender Therapy and Comparative Criminology* 30 (1986): 166.

44. Michel Foucault, *Discipline and Punish: The Birth of the Prison* (New York: Pantheon, 1977).

45. Irving Epstein, "Critical Pedagogy and Chinese Pedagogy," *Journal of Curriculum Theorizing* 9 (1989): 69–98; Ruth Hayhoe, *China's Universities and the Open Door* (New York: M. E. Sharpe, 1989).

CHAPTER 5

Rural Chinese Education
Observing from the Margin

LYNN PAINE AND BRIAN DeLANY

OVERVIEW

Most education in China is rural. Yet discourse about education, both from outside observers and Chinese researchers, tends to put rural schooling at the margins. The education of China's rural children and youth, although ritually noted as important to China's future, is most often ignored or quickly characterized as problematic and hence in need of major reform. In this chapter, we consider the problem of marginality—in terms of the focus given rural education within official education discourses, in terms of educational practice in a particular rural community, and in terms of how our position as foreign researchers affects the way meaning is constructed.

This chapter begins a conversation that highlights challenges facing rural education, as well as dilemmas facing ethnographic researchers. To this end, three small pieces are discussed. First, we present the ways in which rural Chinese education is viewed. Second, we focus on one school in rural Shandong, describing patterns of interaction, pedagogical practice, and the enactment of commitments as a way of considering the meaning of school life for students, parents, and teachers in this community. The portrait painted, however, raises questions for us as researchers collecting data, interpreting that data, and writing about it. The final section of this chapter considers some of these questions and explores how our locations, histories, and stances as researchers affect the work we do and the meanings we construct.

We appreciate the support of the Committee for Scholarly Communication with the People's Republic of China, the Spencer Foundation, and Michigan State University's Asian Studies Center for their financial support of this project. We are very grateful to Judith Liu and Donald P. Kelly for their thoughtful feedback on versions of this chapter. We also want to thank Jian Wang and Naihua Zhang for their assistance in transcribing tapes of classroom observations and interviews.

LOCATING CHINESE RURAL EDUCATION WITHIN
AN ACADEMIC DISCOURSE

Considering the proportion of China's educational energies and human resources that are engaged in the countryside, it is ironic that rural schooling has so often been treated as an afterthought, examined unreflectively and unsystematically, and otherwise left at the margins of thoughtful educational debate. In sheer numbers, rural schooling comprises the vast majority of basic educational activity.[1] In 1990, 91 percent of all primary schools, 95 percent of primary teaching sites,[2] 78.4 percent of primary pupils, and 76.4 percent of primary teachers were located in rural areas.[3] Even at the junior-high level, where urban areas and towns account for a disproportionate share of schooling, 66.3 percent of students and 62.7 percent of teachers were in rural schools in 1990.[4] In terms of numbers, rural schooling should be at the center of Chinese education.

Despite considerable research on educational practice or its reform, there has been remarkably little discussion of rural schooling. Research by Chinese scholars on rural education has a brief and rather undeveloped history: "From the perspective of educational research, little is done to study rural education since 1949. . . . Rural education does not have a place in the entire science of educational research."[5] Certainly the same argument, if only stronger, can be made for research conducted by foreigners on Chinese education.

Both Chinese- and foreign-initiated research that does include rural schooling tends to marginalize much of the work, thoughts, and interactions of those who define rural schooling through their daily practice: rural teachers, school administrators, and students and their families. In academic and policy discourse, issues related to rural schooling are most often analyzed in macroscopic terms, at the level of systems analysis or organizational analysis, with policy issues dominating the discussions. Educational discourse has tended to be shaped overwhelmingly by quantitative analyses, with local-level data typically included only to illustrate a point about generalized national patterns. When rural education has received any attention, it is most often cast in economic terms, with human capital and developmentalist assumptions shaping definitions and interpretations of educational "problems" and phenomena. In their survey of Chinese- and English-language literature, Cheng and Paine found that the following topics predominated: (1) the interaction between education and the economy; (2) dropouts and school repeaters; (3) vocational education and the reshaping of rural curricula to meet the needs of rural economies; (4) coordinated (or "holistic") reforms designed to integrate changes in and the development of educational, scientific, and agricultural sectors; (5) economic concerns and how they will impact the various regions; (6) teacher-training issues dealing with shortages, professional preparation and status, and norms of practice; and (7) educational planning questions.[6]

While this is a long and impressive list, there is, in fact, relatively little discourse that addresses daily educational practice in rural areas and particularly scanty attention to life beyond the school entrance gate or the principal's office. Classroom interaction, the experiences and thoughts of students and teachers, and pedagogical concerns all tend to be discussed indirectly. Ethnographic work in this context is particularly valuable, as it lets researchers explore lived experiences and the meanings constructed by rural community members, not just the official policies aimed at them.

When one considers how the texts of educational discourse are generated and who is involved in the production of such texts, it is not surprising that rural education is marginalized. The relative neglect of rural education generally and of classroom-based studies of rural schools specifically can be explained for both Chinese and foreign researchers. The organization of research production in China and the close ties between academic research and centers of policymaking make physical distance a major barrier to researchers' access to rural school life; the most influential or widely published researchers tend to live in large urban areas, cut off from daily rural life. Because academic researchers, who tend to come from urban areas, shape their projects in terms defined explicitly or implicitly by policymakers' needs and agendas, it is not surprising that so much of the discussion on rural education is policy-oriented, considering schools from an economic perspective and striving to develop a national or provincial picture so as to help with policymakers' planning needs. Considering local conditions, taking time to let questions or analytical categories emerge, and relying on local participants to define themselves and their stories—all elements typically seen as significant for ethnographic research—do not fit well either with these epistemological traditions or with the need to meet policy deadlines, the impetus that drives much of China's academic research.[7] Finally, since research is oriented toward developing exemplary models for dissemination to the rest of the country, it has a powerful effect on which rural sites get studied and how they are investigated.

Foreign academic researchers often arrive in China with a different set of epistemological traditions that shape their work. They may not be looking for exemplars; their work is often less directly policy-linked and hence not as constrained in scope or in time. However, the problems of "distance" that are encountered by Chinese scholars are magnified (and distorted) by the very "otherness" of the foreign researcher. Locating sites to study, negotiating access to them, and drawing up a research protocol tend to make the foreigner's experience of Chinese rural schooling one that must be mediated through the urban Chinese experience.

Thus, there is an ironic and problematic situation in understanding rural Chinese schooling. While the majority of basic education is rural, discussions about education tend to place rural schools at the margins; to describe their roles in flat, unidimensional, and numerical ways; and to make invisible the daily experiences of teaching and learning. That the dominant discourse of education does this raises significant problems for researchers who hope to get some insights into daily life in rural schools. As we turn now to the story of one school, we hope to illustrate this point, and to suggest the value of an ethnographic approach to studying rural education.

THE MEANING OF SCHOOLING AT BURNTWOOD TOWNSHIP CENTRAL SCHOOL[8]

As you turn off the dirt road, the gate announces that you are entering Burntwood Central Junior High School (BCJHS) and the Burntwood Township Education Commission office. A large cement circle holds a small garden of flowers off to the left as you enter the school grounds, and beyond that and off to the right are two rows of red brick, single-story buildings. The front buildings house the school office (on the left) and the Commission office (on the right), and behind these are four classroom buildings on the right and teachers' offices, storage areas, and teachers' apartments on the left. Far in the back is the single-story girls' dormitory. The boys who board at school are housed off the school grounds, just across the street. On the far left is the playground, an open dirt field with basketball hoops erected at either end of one section. It is the site of frequent formal and informal games in which students and teachers alike participate and speak about with pride. The toilets and kitchens ring the far periphery of the campus.

The outsider notices quickly the efforts at orderliness. Despite the ubiquitous dust, small teams of students from each class *(ban)* share brooms and straw baskets as they sweep areas of the campus each morning as the school day begins. Large blackboards, one for praising and one for criticizing students or entire classes, are located on the ends of the front buildings. The boards, like the classroom buildings, are arranged to reinforce the significance of grade groupings and the *ban* structure within grades.

Although the buildings and activities speak of order, there are also abundant symbols of change. Amidst all the busy activity of school life, carpenters live in small quarters on the right side of the campus and are noisily at work each day constructing new classroom buildings. While we are there observing, the teachers vacate their office to allow the first-year students to use their space as a temporary classroom. Administrators enthusiastically report that a multistoried teaching building will soon be built as a symbol of Burntwood's commitment to educational progress.

BCJHS, like its architectural plan, captures many of the changes occurring within Zouping County and the country as a whole. As a "central" *(zhongxin)* school, it is regarded as the best school in the township, one of seventeen townships in the county. Despite the improving conditions, Burntwood's facilities pale in comparison to the "keypoint," "experimental," and normal schools housed in the county seat. Yet, even at this level, education is considered important since it is seen, realistically or otherwise, as a means to escape agricultural life. The school offers the best chance of leaving village life permanently for work in the county seat or other places. Thus, students are willing to walk or bike from neighboring villages, or, for the lucky few, to board on campus in order to receive an education there. Consequently, immense pressures are placed on students to "make the grade," and the school manifests the tensions characteristic of rapid economic and social transformation.

Located in Shandong, a coastal province considered economically well-developed and educationally progressive (owing in part to its honor as being the birthplace of Confucius), Zouping is a landlocked county with a population of about 670,000. Provincial officials describe it as in the upper-middle ranks of counties for Shandong in terms of economic and educational development. Zouping shows great topographical variation as well as great disparities in economic development. Encompassing both flat plains and mountainous areas, it historically has relied on its wheat, cotton, and corn production. In recent years, county leaders have moved aggressively to exploit Zouping's natural resources and to try to develop an industrial sphere. Thus, a textile factory, a brewery, mineral-water bottling plant, and a copper mine with refinery and smelter have been built. Since the mid-1980s, Zouping has experienced tremendous growth. Yet the uneven distribution of natural resources, combined with differences in local leadership, have resulted in some townships flourishing, while others have not.

Although Burntwood began to industrialize rather late, it has fared reasonably well even though 70 percent of its income still comes from agriculture. Burntwood is not the wealthiest or largest of the county's townships; its thirty-six thousand people live in forty-one villages and had a reported per capita income of five hundred *yuan* in the year 1989 to 1990, making it tied for number nine among the other townships.[9] Burntwood is rather distinguished in the county in education, ranking typically near the top in terms of educational attainment. By the late 1980s, Burntwood elementary schools attained a 98 percent graduation rate, and between 1981 and 1990 the township had gone from having 66 percent of its elementary graduates continuing on into junior high school to 99 percent. In terms of promotion from junior high to any form of senior-secondary schooling, the township in 1990 had a 15.6 percent rate of promotion. As in all aspects of its work, BCJHS's promotion rate is higher; in 1989 it was 37.5 percent and for the graduating class of 1991 it was 27 percent. Similarly, the school's teachers were more qualified than their counterparts at the other two junior highs in the township. Thus, in many ways the school is better than average in the township and in the county, yet not among the few elite schools in Zouping County.

We began studying BCJHS in 1990. Data reported here come from two field trips, one in 1990 and another in 1991. We are aware of the limitations and constraints in this ongoing work, but we are struck, nonetheless, by questions about the meaning of education for students, teachers, and parents in Burntwood, and wonder about the implication of these questions for thinking about China's rural education.

Initial field research consisted of two trips that totaled nine weeks. The first focused on interviewing and document collection. In addition to time in Burntwood and in a village served by BCJHS, we interviewed in the county seat and in five other townships. Interviews were conducted at the county-level bureaus of education, finance, and labor; with the vice-magistrates and officials in charge of general education and vocational education; with members of the education commissions for seven of the county's seventeen townships; and with school principals and teachers at thirty-four schools that are representative of the range of the county's schools.[10] With this information providing an overview of rural education, Lynn returned in 1991 to explore the everyday practices in schools as a way of learning about the educational experience of students and teachers and, in particular, to examine the many kinds of knowledge and opportunities for learning that are available to students. The majority of fieldwork time was spent at BCJHS, primarily with one *ban* of students. Lynn attended the classes of a graduating year's *ban* and during free times talked informally with students and teachers. She also observed the school's other *ban* and in the evenings visited families in a nearby village to talk with parents. Classroom interactions were videotaped or audiotaped to allow for further analysis. Further, historical records of the school's resources, staffing, student population, and promotion rates were collected, as well as a complete set of textbooks for the graduating year and samples of student writing on their views of knowledge. In addition to time at BCJHS, Lynn conducted similar but shorter observations and interviews at six other schools in the county.[11]

Many symbols suggested significant changes for Burntwood, and for the role and practice of education in this county. The daily hammering and sawing for the new classrooms, the plans to build a multistoried modern teaching facility, the recent consolidation of the township's five junior highs into three and the attendant movement in faculty and students that came to Burntwood, and the introduction of a new labor-skills course to better serve the needs of Burntwood's economic construction—all speak of an image of modern schooling, efficiently distributed, that both connects rural students to cosmopolitan practices and strengthens the ability of school graduates to serve their local communities. It is an image familiar to readers of human capital theory, of rational planning, of school planners who argue for the powerful role of schools in national development and modernization.

While analyzing our interviews, studying the discourse of classroom lessons, and reviewing student writing and school and county documents, we noted patterns that suggest alternative ways of viewing schooling in Burntwood. Our analysis points to how Burntwood's rhythms, despite its apparent breaks with tradition, seem steeped in powerful, long-standing social and cultural patterns of stratification, privilege, and marginalization.[12]

Investments and Sacrifices

Schooling at BCJHS is a labor-intensive activity. Students described their day as starting at 6:00 in the morning and going until after 10:00 at night. The official school schedule for summer term (the opening term of the school year) expects students to be out of bed by 6:10 and to have completed their morning exercises and be studying by 6:45. Even though the first period class does not begin until 8:40, students are expected to be in their seats and working long before that. Various students interviewed—both dormitory and commuter students—reported rising early and arriving at school by 6:00 A.M. Evening study hall, with two periods, lasts until 9:45 P.M.

The fifteen and a half hours of the school day are carefully scripted for each class. Although several hours are allotted for study hall and occasional class periods for individual study, students and teachers reported that these periods are most often used for direct instruction. County bureau officials complained that rural schools used too much of the day for instruction, trying to "cram in" too much information.[13] Both students and teachers at BCJHS seem to believe that future success is directly related to the number of hours spent studying.[14] This view is so ingrained in their psyches that it has become the only way to conceive of schooling.

BCJHS students described using their free time strategically, choosing either to do homework or, as one put it, "rest for half an hour, so I have full energy for classes in the afternoon." In contrast, students interviewed at the county's keypoint secondary school boasted about the amount of free time they were able to spend outside of school. As one boy scornfully replied, when Lynn asked him if what he read at home was related to schoolwork: "Definitely not classwork. I finish all my lessons at school. The books I read at home are not part of the school curriculum." BCJHS students' days extend well beyond the evening study hall and the school gates. Many parents and students reported that even after school students spend more time studying, whether they lived in the dormitories or at home. Even students in the second-year group, who admit to less pressure than third-year (graduating) students, limit their nonacademic activity after school. As one said: "I only watch TV on Saturday night." Even this option is not available for the graduating class, who attend school seven days a week. Consequently, these students are unable to help their parents with the fall harvest, which other students are able to do. Thus, attending school represents a major investment to graduating students in terms of time and lost labor; yet it was a sacrifice to a goal they and their parents see as worthy.

Most parents of BCJHS students agreed that their children's school work was demanding and exhausting. They talked about how their children could not afford the time to come home for meals, but would, instead, stay at school and eat only steamed bread *(mantou)* and water. Yet all these village parents expressed tremendous support for their child's effort and their own sacrifices, which they regarded as necessary for helping secure their child's future educational and occupational goals.

One father's story exemplified this theme of sacrifice and commitment. The father, who is a farmer, explained how he often goes to see the teachers "to understand my son's situation." With the boy in school all day, the father felt that "the school knows better how he is doing." The teachers persuaded the father that

> given how hard the third-year students have to work, the family needs to make sure he gets enough nutrition. Not everyone has the economic conditions necessary for this, but we'll do as much as we can. We only have two children, so our finances aren't too strained. So now I don't allow him to come home at lunch. . . . It's not worth it to race home and eat, not get much rest, and go back. It takes energy just coming and going. Better to stay at school, do some homework, stay cool.

In such simple and deliberate acts, parents showed their support: they accommodated to their children's schedules, they went without their help, and they made special provisions for them. Support also meant that parents pushed their children to make sacrifices. Thus, as this father explained, going to school meant that he would not allow his son to come home during school hours. This was not easy on the boy because "Sometimes at night it's dark. You know country roads aren't well-lighted, and [my son] gets scared coming home. But there isn't dorm space available."

That BCJHS students spend so much time at school is understandable since their parents, many of whom are illiterate, "can't help" them with their homework because the parents "can't understand it." Nonetheless, parents stressed the importance of a junior-high education for their children. "I can't say he likes to study," one father said of his son, "but it's the only way out."

These peasant families are sophisticated consumers who strategically try to plan the goals for their children's schooling. While they described various ways to leave the village—through studying or enlisting in the army—"the main road is school." A mother echoed those thoughts: "Only through education can rural kids make their way *(chulu).*" To help their children succeed, parents, too, make sacrifices. Parents reported spending at least 160 *yuan* or more a year on their child's junior-high schooling. A mother said that "we can do without him" as labor in the fields, and that she and her husband would do whatever was necessary to support their son in his studies. If parents make sacrifices for their children, these acts do not go unnoticed by the child, who "feels guilty and obligated towards the parents."

It is ironic that these peasants, many of whom are illiterate and most of whom have less than a complete elementary education, are sophisticated enough consumers in the educational market to be actively engaged in trying to improve their child's chances. Even if parents were unable to help their child with homework, they would nevertheless ask "How's the homework?" as a way of checking on their child's progress. Parents who could afford the time reported that they would go to Burntwood, a few kilometers away, to meet with teachers and to get advice on how to help their child. All the parents were aware of the ability-grouping practices used by the school and where their child and other village children stood, and why. They were also aware of their child's chances of testing into the next level of schooling. They could quote comparative exam scores by school, analyze their child's *ban,* and compare how that *ban* fared with the others.

While state policies are increasingly stressing the need for vocational secondary education, these policies are in conflict with the aspirations of parents who know that a hierarchy of schooling exists in China. Success means reaching the top of this hierarchy. Parents would consider vocational education for their child only if other higher-status educational opportunities were blocked or were unattainable for their child. Parents suggested that schooling remains an important avenue for social mobility.

While parents want the best for their children, students and teachers know by the second semester of the second year who is likely to go on in school and calculate their school strategies accordingly. As one BCJHS teacher noted, this knowledge "influences students' studying. . . . Those who know they have no hope are unlikely to be motivated. At the same time, parents still hope they can go on, so this is also a factor."

Parents may wish for their children to continue in school, but at BCJHS, only one-quarter of the graduating class can reasonably hope to attend senior-secondary schooling. Consequently, competition becomes acute and is symbolized in some rather unpredictable ways. For example, girls in the third year all had short hair. This marked a change from the girls in the first or second year, who wore bows in their long hair. When we inquired about this transformation, the girls explained, quite naturally, that by graduation year they had no time to fuss with their hair. For these girls, such subtle adjustments are regarded as worthwhile if it increases their chances for success. Interestingly, in a nearby "ordinary" junior high school, where only one in two hundred students had gone on to senior schooling in the previous year, girls in the graduating class had long hair and wore bows and jewelry. Perhaps for them, sacrificing notions of appropriate femininity to the goal of higher education was pointless.

While these vignettes are impressionistic, they serve to remind us of three things: the role of sacrifice, the differential need to sacrifice, and the relationship of sacrifice to marginalization. When asked about their futures, most of the students we interviewed said that they would "keep studying."[15] "Studying" per se comes to represent not just an action but access to life outside the village. Consequently, the act of studying becomes associated with changing one's life. As junior-high students progress, pursuing their studies will take them to schools farther from their homes. Thus, studying begins and consolidates the process of distancing them, mentally and physically, from their present lives.

Studying takes its toll. However, as one homesick student living in the dorm explained, "You get used to it." For these students, school is serious business. Even extracurricular activities reinforce this message. When students in the graduating *ban* were asked about the previous evening's class meeting, they stated: "We talked about how to use our time well for studying . . . about study methods . . . and study attitudes." School takes work. It takes deliberate effort. It takes sacrifice.[16]

For BCJHS students, dedicating themselves wholly to a regiment created by the school separates them from family, from individual choices, and—for the girls—from local cultural norms. The process of sacrifice, while an act of commitment, can also be seen as a process of marginalization, as the choices of students and parents reinforce the distance between their present lives and some desired alternative life that exists outside of the village.

The Lesson of Classroom Interactions

Across all subject areas, BCJHS's Year 3 Class 2 students received highly traditional, teacher-led instruction. While some subjects (such as English, geometry, or algebra) provided more opportunities for students to practice or to drill, the structure of the lessons, their pace, and the nature of questioning were all determined by the teachers, who controlled the nature of classroom interactions. Even when students were most engaged verbally, teachers carefully orchestrated the interaction by relying almost totally on a "call and response" approach. In this approach, the teacher begins a sentence, pauses very slightly, and waits for the class in unison to complete the sentence. Apart from participating through this teacher-directed, classwide pattern of verbally "filling in the blanks," the most common experience for students was to go through the forty-five minute period without talking, being called on individually, or asking a question out loud. In fact, classroom observations reveal that, on average, only nine of the sixty students would be individually involved during a single lesson; the other fifty-one students would be silent during a lesson, except for their participation as members of the entire group's responses. Since English classes, in particular, tended to increase this average, given the drill and practice techniques used by the teacher, it was not uncommon in other classes that no single student or at most two or three would be verbally engaged during a lesson. An important socialization process is subtly going on here. It appears that students are being taught that important knowledge comes from teachers and textbooks; that learning involves listening, thinking, and silent practice; and that the knowledge espoused by the teachers and the textbooks is not to be challenged.

The didactic orientation of the lessons also suggests further messages about knowledge. Many classes involved constructing a lesson outline, and rarely was there more than one possible explanation for the content of the outline. This instills a belief that the knowledge taught in the curriculum is always fixed and logical; consequently, outlining was used to find the most efficient way to organize the knowledge embodied in the text.

Certain individual lessons stand out as emblematic of the broader patterns we observed about teaching and learning at BCJHS. Lesson content was dictated by the textbook (which was produced in the provincial capital) and by impending exams. The curriculum content was aimed at inculcating certain types of knowledge and privileging that knowledge (and its source) over other types. This message was consistent across all subjects: Important knowledge was academic knowledge—but only if it was socially and politically approved.

Events in a third-year students' politics course dealing with Chinese socialist construction help illustrate this point. During the period of our observation in 1991, the former Soviet Union disintegrated following an aborted coup. While it is understandable why the instructor chose not to discuss this event in class and chose instead to rigidly adhere to a curriculum content that would be tested, his silence concerning this tumultuous event, one that could affect China directly and one that was receiving significant press coverage, was noteworthy.

More striking to us, however, was the similar lack of connection between course material and the immediate lives of the students. The teacher methodically marched through the textbook's sections on the socialist construction of political reform, with an emphasis on the development and the accomplishments of rural economic reform. For several days the class listened to the recent history of rural economic reform, and why it needed to occur. In their own villages, they and their families had been active participants in this reform process. Yet listening to the lessons one would never know that we were in a rural school, that students might have some direct experience of the content of the lesson, or that their experience might shape their understanding of the lesson. Rather, the teacher referred directly to the book, read aloud large sections of the chapter, asked students to read passages from the book, and directed students to find answers to questions by quoting the book. In an exchange that typified the centrality that the orthodox interpretation presented by the text played, the teacher called on a student to answer a question, which prompted the student to read the answer directly from the book. To reaffirm the correctness of the answer, the teacher then reread the passage from the book, giving the students a second chance to hear it.

At one point in the lesson, the teacher drew the students' attention to a cartoon in the chapter. The drawing, alluding to a classic tale, shows three monks sitting with an empty water bucket and has the caption "Three monks with no water to drink." The teacher remarked, "Some classmates say they don't know what this picture means." Rather than allowing the class the chance to produce various interpretations of the drawing or to consider a range of ways the story might apply to the broader theme of the chapter section (on the weaknesses of the prereform system), the teacher was quick to point out the meaning of the cartoon as an illustration of the problems of egalitarianism. The teacher moved immediately from stating that some students were confused to saying, "This is three monks not having water to drink. Everybody take a look. Three monks have no water to drink. What about when there is one monk, and when there are two monks?" A student answered, "When there is one monk, he picks up the water himself." The teacher continued, without inviting further discussion of the student's response, "When there are two monks?" and another student replied, "Two carry the water." The teacher then repeated what the student said and forged ahead to make his argument:

> Two carry the water. What about three? With three there is no water to
> drink. A picture like this expressively tells us a truth. It says when a
> person has no one else to rely on, he picks up the water, and when there

are two people, he picks up the pole with the other man and carries the water, but when there are three people . . . this picture tells us a truth, that is, there were many shortcomings in the economic structure of the past that were obstacles to the development of productivity, like egalitarianism, the iron rice bowl. So now we need to reform.

In talking about his teaching, the politics teacher explained that it is "easy for these students to understand rural reform" but that ease does not occasion any opportunity for him to deviate from or to supplement the text. He sees his course as important because "students need to understand national policies so they can work within the law." He acknowledged that "many students feel this knowledge is no use if they return home" to work in the fields. But that concern does not deter him from meticulously following the text.[17]

In an English class, the teacher seemed even less willing to consider the paradox between what students are taught and how little it corresponds with their probable future lives. Newly arrived at the school, the teacher was assigned to teach first-year junior-secondary students. As evidenced by one lesson, she was clearly unable to fit prescribed course content to the level of the students. For the first twenty-eight minutes of a class, she drilled the students on variations of basic sentences concerning an object and its color. ("It is a Jeep." "Is it a Jeep?" "Is it green?" "It is green.") Despite extensive repetition, students were unable to change "It is green" into a question. She called on one student, who could not do it, and then told him how to do it. Throughout the lesson, she called only on students who raised their hands, but given the difficulty most students were having with the lesson, not many hands were raised. Time and again she asked, "Who wants to read?" and no one volunteered. Consequently, the class reverted to call and response, with the teacher reading out sentences and the class trying, but not succeeding, to repeat them. As the class proceeded, the teacher appeared increasingly frustrated, criticizing one student who read badly and saying rather harshly, "Look at each word carefully," and to another student who failed to produce the sentence she wanted, "In class you need to listen carefully."

After the lesson, Lynn talked with her. The teacher was obviously dissatisfied with the lesson, but saw the students as responsible for the failure. Pointing to their peasant backgrounds, she saw them as lacking a critical knowledge base, as not working hard, and, therefore, as doomed to fail. As we talked about her own professional teacher preparation, it became clear that no institutional support existed to help her deal with students who literally do not know the English alphabet, and she had no experience in teaching beginners. Yet she firmly believed that the students were the problem. Even though they came with no prior background and had little chance of ever using English outside of school, she saw no reason to try an alternative approach to teaching the specified curriculum.

This vignette from the English class illustrates our point on the paradox between course content and the projected life experiences of students from BCJHS. Both the formal curriculum and the hidden curriculum, as well as the pedagogical techniques used by teachers, tell students that the important work of school is learning knowledge that comes from a cosmopolitan, political center, one that is far removed from their villages and their daily experiences. A Chinese-language teacher complained that "the problem is that the policy calls for moral, intellectual, and physical development, but actually the pressure is for promotion and the teaching is still chiefly the duck-stuffing method."

Ironically, the one place in the curriculum that might have offered a practical learning alternative for these students failed to challenge the hegemony of the national curriculum. BCJHS, like all the junior highs in the county, was engaged in introducing a labor-skills class, a course that the government designed to infuse some vocational content into the curriculum as a recognition that basic education is, in fact, terminal education for the majority of students. However, the teacher chosen to teach the course had no practical knowledge about vocational education. In one class we observed, his actual teaching time was quite short; he stopped class rather abruptly, and let students work (as it turned out later, on a range of unrelated things). It was clear he knew little about the content of the lesson—when to water and fertilize particular crops—and suggested that students should elicit the information from their parents. An education official observing the class was shocked because, as he put it, telling students that parents can be a source of knowledge means that there is no reason to learn this subject through formal schooling. The time, organization, and pedagogical decisions made about this course suggested that practical knowledge is subordinate to theoretical knowledge and that junior-secondary schooling is unconcerned with preparing students to work for or even to contribute to the betterment of the local community.

While vocational education was being poorly received at BCJHS, the county Bureau of Education was actively trying to raise its educational status by making it more "academic." As one official explained: "The Bureau of Education is trying to lead people to give it [labor skills] more importance by including it on the senior high entrance examination." Students, however, seemed to see through this effort to make them value what was universally regarded as inferior knowledge. While teachers sometimes referred to labor skills as a course students like (saying, as one did, that "anything applied that can be put to use, they like"), no student we interviewed ever nominated labor skills as a course they liked or considered important. Students' answers varied on what courses they valued, but those courses were always academic, and never practical, in content.

In short, the labor-skills course, by being a caricature of an academic course, reinforced a sense of division that separated the practical knowledge that guided their parents' lives and the academic knowledge that the students were being taught. In other words, labor-skills knowledge, despite government attempts to elevate its status, was seen as a parody of "true" knowledge. This experience confirmed what attendance in academic classes had implied—that, as rural students, their social position was marginal in the society and that if they were smart, they should try to distance themselves from rural life.

Whose Knowledge?

We asked students in Year 3 Class 2 to write briefly about what they thought knowledge is, where it comes from, how it is created, and who "creates" it. While responses from the sixty students differed, there was a strong consensus about who "creates" knowledge. The most common response was that the "great laboring masses" are the source of knowledge. Others mentioned "all people," "humanity," or "people who work diligently and make great sacrifices." While these choices may be reminiscent of Communist Party slogans, it was striking that, for all the references to the "great laboring masses," only one student included themselves in this category by writing: "We are the new life youth of the 1990s. We are the creators of knowledge, but we shouldn't ignore that ancient people were creators of abundant knowledge and we believe people in the future will also abundantly create knowledge." For the others, knowledge is constructed, defined, and redefined by others far from their daily experience. Thus, education at BCJHS contributes significantly to their feelings of marginality.

Despite engendering these feelings of marginality, it also appears that BCJHS is actively constructing possible futures for some of its students that will take them far from their villages. With the goal of a brighter future leading them, successful (or hopeful) students seem willing to commit themselves to an educational process that privileges a knowledge base that is foreign to their rural, agrarian lives. That is, schooling at BCJHS delineates differences between the self, as a resident of a rural community, and some valued, distant "other." In defining this "other" as a product of "modern" schooling and by linking it to an image of the "modern" Chinese citizen, rural schooling supports a conception of knowledge that is promoted by authorities located in urban, cosmopolitan centers. If students (and their parents) accept the validity of this knowledge and strive for academic success, then success means abandoning their villages. Consequently, the entire practice of Chinese education marginalizes the significance of practical, rural knowledge.

AS OBSERVERS AT THE MARGIN

Thus far we have portrayed the marginality of schooling in rural China in a variety of ways. First, while rural education defines Chinese education, it typically appears in discussions on education as a residual category since most studies deal solely with urban education. Thus, while rural schooling may be at the center of educational activity, it remains outside the focus of academic and policy discourse. Second, the "distance" that separates rural schools, students, and teachers from "legitimate" and valued curricular knowledge is reinforced on a daily basis in classroom activities. Rural lives are typically marginalized when compared to the modern conditions highlighted in urban-based school texts, tests, and teacher training.

We have described the ways schools contribute to this marginalization, but it is also important to recognize that as outsiders, we, too, function at the margins. While we hope our stories of Zouping provide the reader with a sense of authenticity, nonetheless, it is important to place these stories in the context of our research, and to explore how this research becomes part of these stories and influences their construction. Thus, we consider how our position affects our research and examine the ways in which text and audience shape our understanding and interpretations of events.

Position: How Who We Are Affected Our Research

Neither of us arrived in Zouping County as a generic outsider; rather we brought with us a particular set of opinions, abilities, and objectives that would frame our research. Our initial access to Burntwood was made possible by our connections to a variety of Chinese and American scholars and officials, and using these connections affected how the people in Burntwood came to view us. While we both were viewed as foreigners, our genders, ages, language facility, interviewing styles, understanding of the culture, experience in school settings, and prior research interests gave us differing perspectives on the research and differing interactional experiences in Burntwood. Moreover, whether we appeared for interviews together or as individuals also affected our research experience. In short, who we are and were had a powerful effect on what we were able to learn.

For example, Lynn's strong Chinese-language skills, broad knowledge of Chinese culture, and extensive interview experience in China provided texture and nuance to the discussions in which we both participated. With this background, Lynn had an intuitive sense of what would or would not be considered appropriate questioning by Chinese educators. Brian, on the other hand, with only minor Chinese-language skills, lacked such intuition. Despite earlier interviews in urban settings in 1986, 1987, and 1990, the rural Chinese cultural context seemed arbitrary to him. Only a running subtext from Lynn provided him a structure for behaving appropriately in social situations.

Each of us, though, had something different to contribute to the interviews and social events. In the midst of interviews a newcomer is invariably granted the "grace of ignorance," and thus Brian could ask questions, through Lynn, that she could never ask herself. Brian could be expected to take on the onerous tasks of toasting and drinking in social gatherings, a feature of rural social interaction that dwarfed similar gatherings previously encountered in the cities. Happily, we found that our social interactions, especially around drinking, reinforced the locally practiced patriarchal notions of gender and perhaps encouraged our official hosts (all male) to see Lynn as nonthreatening.

Chinese conceptions of gender problematized Lynn's position as a researcher. To the men of Zouping, however, Lynn could be excused from the evil of "careerism" by virtue of having arrived with Brian, her husband. Ironically, to the women of Zouping, Lynn's status as a researcher was seen as a sign of commendable independence, something several women spoke about with good-natured approval. Further, this status made it possible for Lynn to interview older women administrators. Once credible with both groups, Lynn was able to conduct her research freely. In the end, Lynn conducted all of the classroom observations on her own as well as the majority of the interviews.

While Brian lacked a thorough understanding of Chinese culture, his experience as a public school classroom teacher and department head gave him a cachet with Chinese educators. Thus, his knowledge of the many routines and roles in the daily mundane activities required to keep a school functioning established a rapport between him and Zouping's educators. A common discourse on the daily life in schools often allowed the trading of stories of what it is like to work in the schools in either the United States or China. Within the context of normal school roles, rules, and responsibilities (scheduling, making a budget, evaluating teachers, testing pupils, working within a bureaucracy), educators were quite willing to discuss what can often appear, in other contexts, as privileged information. While Brian had to rely on Lynn for the Chinese translation, his far lengthier experience in the daily life of schools, teachers, and administrators brought an authenticity and a sense of mutuality that helped tremendously in establishing early, good relations with some key educators in the county.

Talking about his own experiences in American schools, Brian showed a genuine interest in the trivia of the daily hassles, schedules, and challenges encountered by Zouping's school administrators. What emerged from these conversations was their concern about how resources are managed and their efforts to generate new sources of income. In the end, however, everyone agreed that students were the crucial resource in maintaining a school's reputation and income stream.

This interest in resource issues affected Lynn's questioning of policy issues related to the finance and governance of schools. In starting her work in Burntwood, Lynn wanted to continue the line of questioning that Brian had initiated. Rather than just focusing on classroom observations, she wanted to know how a school's environment affects classroom activities. Consequently, our research evolved into a close examination of classroom life with a commitment to understanding the organizational context of the school and its community. Whether in terms of the attention a student received from the teacher, the content of school texts, or the school's admission policy, we increasingly saw school life as involving the construction and management of opportunities and resources.

Our work in Zouping surprised us. Our foreignness was an indelible feature of our research. Even while working in an urban setting, we recognized that it was pointless to try to pretend to be other than outsiders, but moving into a rural setting doubly reminded us of our "otherness." Whatever familiarity Lynn may have had with Chinese educational discourse was now shaken not only by a hard-to-follow local accent, but also, more importantly, by local terms, assumptions, and expectations based on rural patterns of life. Simple things like the school calendar reflected the rhythms of an agricultural community in ways we had not anticipated. Our inability to chat convincingly about crops in our own community made it difficult for us to initiate conversations, even with school people. The difficulty of bridging the gap between our being foreign urban researchers and our subjects being rural Chinese teachers, students, and parents influenced our data collection methods. We were so worried that our "otherness" would limit our ability to keep accurate fieldnotes of what was being said or done that we chose to use videotape and audiotape whenever possible.

Our work in Zouping showed us how limited our overall understanding of Chinese education actually was. The way we looked at Chinese educational issues, the words we chose to use in interviews, and our frames of reference were all powerfully shaped by urban Chinese colleagues. By shifting contexts, we realized, albeit slowly, that we needed to reassess the meaning of our research and our understanding of schooling. Like Bateson's notion of peripheral vision, we came to realize that being forced to shift our research focus to the countryside created new insights on the scope of Chinese education.[18]

We began this project with an understanding that ethnographic methods would have to be employed if we were going to understand school and community life in Zouping. Ethnographic research would allow us to go beyond mere statistical measures. Given the tendency of statistics to flatten the texture of social life such that commonly used descriptors—like "dropout," "successful school," or "academic course"— may not mean the same thing in different contexts, using ethnographic methods became important to us. And given what we have already said about our foreignness, our urbanness, and related features of our "otherness," we needed to find ways to bring to the surface subtle social and cultural nuances that might otherwise have eluded us.

To paint an overall picture of education in Zouping, we collected a range of statistical data about education and life, and systematically interviewed school people in a range of schools in the county. However, we needed ethnographic work to help us understand both the texture behind the sketches these numbers and interviews produced and to raise questions and even doubts about their reliability. By relying on ethnographic methods, we gained an inkling about the opportunities and resources schools do construct, and we could begin to get some sense of what that process of construction entailed. Quite literally, it was only by spending long, hot days in the dusty schoolyard and in the crowded classrooms that the complex meanings and attendant paradoxes inherent in such catch phrases as "making schools modern" or "educational construction" began to make sense. Listening to a droning lecture in a Chinese literature class over the constant intrusion of hammers and saws helped Lynn think in new ways about both the deep commitments associated with school expansion (and modernization) and the real burdens it puts on those who experience it. We had to feel the heat of those long days to experience the pressure that schooling exerts upon Burntwood's young people. Mere statistics cannot convey the nuances of this social milieu in the same way that sitting next to a young student, who has been sweating at the same desk for several hours and still has many more to go, can do. Seeing a whole day in the classroom unfold, and a week turn into multiple weeks, helped provide a hint of what school life might be in a way that cross-sectional survey data would never allow. Being able to spend time in the schools, however briefly, provided an important insight on how schooling affects the lives of students, their families, and their community.

As foreign researchers, our experiences may be unique. For example, our ordeal with Zouping's summer heat may have been burned in our imagination in a way that goes unnoticed by local school children. This example helps explain why it is important to consider who we are, what we brought to our experience, and why we needed to find ways to document the voices of teachers and students in order to record their experiences directly. The videotaping and audiotaping of classroom interactions gave us a literal text of student-teacher interaction. This text was supplemented by an interpretive one derived from our fieldnotes. Thus, we have both the facts derived from the classroom and our interpretations of them. Neither by itself tells the entire story.[19]

Text. The textual construction of our research is undergirded by normative assumptions about what constitutes legitimate research on China, as discussed in DeLany and Paine (1991).[20] The West's conception of China has changed over the last decades from one of cultural and political uniformity to one of cultural and political diversity. This shift from Maoist egalitarianism to the socialist market economy has left researchers searching for an understanding of how educational policies are and will be implemented. Moving from more macroviews of schooling, educational researchers are increasingly studying what occurs in schools, classrooms, and family-school relations; and shifting from descriptive macroviews of policy processes, researchers are now also concerned with how those policies are generated, implemented, and deflected in actual school practices. In short, a text about Chinese rural schooling shows, in microcosm, the broader changes affecting Chinese educational discourse and occurring in Chinese educational practices.

In conceptualizing our text, we are acutely aware that how we interpret the data is often at variance with what our hosts may want or expect. That we should want to look at everyday events, to focus on ordinary schools, to ask the same questions of many people, to spend day after day in the same classroom was baffling and at times disturbing to our hosts. As the work developed on this project, we spent a lot of time justifying and altering our approach. As such, the research process required constant negotiation and was, consequently, a time-consuming process that involved resolving misunderstandings.

Misunderstandings arise because ethnographic research is inherently multivocal. Further, as participant-observers we could not help but be interlopers in and interpreters of other people's lives. Our choice of research questions was determined by who we are and were as researchers, how we "entered the field," and who those educators were with whom we had associated. In contrast to this complex of factors that framed the research, the choice of words and ideas that make their way onto the page is ours alone. We have tried to remain faithful translators of the text of our respondents' lives, but like all translators we must choose the words for the text ourselves.

Finally, in relation to text there is always the question of audience. How much do the readers of this chapter know about China, how do they think about research as a process, and what experiences do they have in conducting or understanding research in China? To what extent have the readers thought about ethnomethodological considerations? Clearly any text on education on China would be received differently by an American audience than by a Chinese one. Consequently, it is important to recognize the constructive aspect of writing, to affirm the belief that we are telling accurate stories. While our stories reflect what we have been able to see and what we make of our observations, we also recognize that these are not just the stories of life in and around BCJHS, but our stories as well.

Research for whom? With no audience, there is seldom a play. Researchers like ourselves make use of opportunities such as those provided in Zouping to make careers, generate texts, and find new worlds to interpret. At the same time, those being interviewed have their positions to consider. For both parties in an interview there is always an unspoken subtext involving power differentials at play. Those selected to be interviewed have their importance, position, and status both inside and outside their organization reinforced. Thus, the Zouping project confirmed that both parties—researcher and subject—enter into the dialogue with idiosyncratic goals and with the hope of achieving those goals.

In Zouping, the challenge was to find some common ground. We were accustomed to dealing with urban educators, individuals whose stories about schools were something to which we could easily relate. This was not the case in Zouping. We had little in common with village and country life where educated persons are rare and where someone with a post-secondary education is found only in a position of authority. This meant that our "natural" counterparts were nowhere to be found except in positions of power. This exaggerated the power differentials present in the various research situations and influenced how we conducted and reflected upon the research. Given our status as educators, we were able to find common ground with the educators of Zouping. This commonality, however, separated us from the very people the schools primarily serve—peasant families and their children. The common bond of practice that allowed us to talk more easily with teachers and school administrators only reinforced the power differentials that separated us from the students and parents we had hoped to study.

Because of this separation from the people we wanted to study, we often felt on the margins in our work at Zouping, but we realize nonetheless that these margins are a powerful place to be. Our location gave us ready access to multiple sources of data that are normally hidden, to a different variety of frames available for interpretation, and to new audiences for reading the story we are writing. Despite the difficulties that we encountered, the results of our work at BCJHS can only expand the core of knowledge available concerning rural education in China.

NOTES

1. Basic education here refers to all education that falls under the Compulsory Education Act, which includes primary and junior-secondary education.
2. The disparity between the number of schools and the number of sites occurs because the remoteness and the lack of population in some areas precludes the building of schools, but not the holding of classes.

The term "teaching sites" includes educational settings that fail to meet local standards for a school—that is, there is a lack of trained teachers in the school and grading procedures are lax—but that nevertheless offer instruction.

3. For a definition of rural and related terms, see Kai-ming Cheng and Lynn Paine, "Research on Education in Rural China" (paper presented at the conference on Chinese Education for the 21st Century, Honolulu, Hawaii, November 19–22, 1991).

4. *Zhongguo Jiaoyu Tongji Nianjian [Educational Statistics Yearbook of China, 1991/1992]* (Beijing: State Education Commission, Department of Planning and Construction, 1992).

5. C. Teng and T. X. Zou, eds., *Xiang de jingji yu jiaoyu de diaocha [Study of the Economy and Education of Counties]* (Beijing: Educational Science Press, 1989), 1; cited in Cheng and Paine, "Research." As Cheng and Paine argue, research related to educational planning may be an exception to excluding rural education from the discourse, but we cannot give much credence to the results of these planning studies because so little research is actually conducted in the countryside.

6. See Cheng and Paine, "Research."

7. We were struck in our first visit to Zouping by an encounter we had with a group of young researchers from one of the provincial capital's major research centers. They came to do a few days' research and to carry out their institute's expectation that they should have contact with the "grassroots." Over our first meal together we listened to them speak quite openly about their attitudes toward the village and the countryside. Their remarks were startling by the fact that they made no effort to hide their scorn for the local accent, were dismayed at the local standard of living, and held extremely paternalistic attitudes toward the locals. While only a single anecdote, it resonates with comments we have heard from many of our urban colleagues over the years and perhaps serves as an indication of the marginality of rural education.

8. Burntwood Township, as well as all other proper names used here, are pseudonyms for schools, townships, villages, and people living in Zouping County.

9. Township officials told us that the actual income was closer to 800 *yuan,* but that the 500 *yuan* figure represented what gets officially reported to the state for tax purposes.

10. Zouping County had eight senior-high-level schools (including keypoint and nonkeypoint academic, vocational, and technical), twelve

junior high schools (keypoint, central, and ordinary), and fourteen elementary schools (central and ordinary).

11. These included a village feeder elementary school for BCJHS, an elite elementary school, an ordinary junior high, two elite junior highs, and two senior-secondary schools.

12. While we write here in the language of images, we do not mean to imply that what follows are impressionistic reactions. Rather, they are emblematic of the larger patterns that systematic analysis of interviews, observations, and documents revealed.

13. Yet even these officials spoke of "a contradiction that can't be resolved" between trying to raise educational quality while trying to lighten the students' work loads.

14. Thus, teachers acknowledged, for example, that they taught longer hours and gave more homework than official policy recommended.

15. This response was not universal; however, as one highly reflective student stated, when asked about his desired future, "What can you do but go home and work?"

16. Interestingly, while parents and students either explicitly or implicitly made clear the great sacrifice students at BCJHS made, more than once teachers described the current generation of students as different from earlier cohorts. One administrator said today's students are "less able to 'eat bitterness' [endure hardship]." Now students ate steamed buns (*mantou*) made from white flour. "When we were students, we ate cornmeal *wowotou* [a coarser-grained bun] and sweet potatoes for our main dish." A male math teacher echoed this sentiment: "Students now are a little different from when we were here [as students]," as he suggested today's pupils are not as tough as previous ones. At the same time, administrators and teachers throughout the interviews also acknowledged students now have a "heavy burden" of school work.

17. Similarly, while the substance of his class focused on reform, his pedagogical techniques (and the subtle messages associated with it) remained traditional.

18. Mary Catherine Bateson, *Peripheral Visions: Learning Along the Way* (New York: HarperCollins, 1994).

19. We find Wolf's multiple rendering of an event in Taiwan particularly helpful in reminding us about the complexity of the ethnographer's task. Just as she realized that certain key actors in her story have their voices muted, despite the multiple versions of the story she tells, we note

that the voices of students that we present here are not as loud or as elaborated as those of parents and teachers because students spoke with us in shorter bursts and with seemingly more constraints upon them than adults. See Margery Wolf, *A Thrice-Told Tale: Feminism, Postmodernism, and Ethnographic Responsibility* (Stanford: Stanford University Press, 1992).

20. Brian DeLany and Lynn Paine, "Shifting Patterns of Authority in Chinese Schools," *Comparative Education Review* 35 (1991): 23–43.

CHAPTER 6

In the Moment—Discourses of Power, Narratives of Relationship
Framing Ethnography of Chinese Schooling, 1981–1997

HEIDI A. ROSS

> **October 5, 1981.** I'm stuck on the surface. A flailing fly. An accepting fly. NO ONE is telling me what's going on. Nothing seems real. You can't be a fly on the wall as a teacher or as a researcher. The students smile, so willing. The teachers smile, so supportive. NO ONE is talking WITH me except the custodian. Perhaps this whole trip is a bad idea. Said the big fly.

I have chosen four "moments" between the years of 1981 and 1997 to evoke changes I have seen in Chinese schooling since the fumbling attempts at understanding I so pitifully recorded in my first research journal. My roles during these moments, as teacher-researcher, narrator, collaborator, and consultant, raise different questions regarding the nature of field research and what constitutes ethnographic data and ethnographic writing; the shifting sociopolitical contexts that influence these definitions; and the complex personal obligations that shape the negotiation of research outcomes. In succession, these moments also reveal a gradual but spectacular decline within China of totalizing state and communist discourses on educational authority and public purpose, and a concomitant emergence of multiple, locally inspired narratives of schooling for private interest and representation.

I would like to thank Judith Liu and Donald Kelly for their insightful comments on this chapter, and my colleague Jing Lin of McGill University for her creative and unfailing contributions to our collaborative field endeavors. I am also grateful to the Spencer Foundation, Colgate University, and the Pacific Basin Research Center for their generous research support.

The official surface of Chinese schooling, which seemed to me so unyielding, so predictable, and so intractable when I taught in a Shanghai middle school in the early 1980s, was, of course, a fiction. In retrospect, its foundation—shored up by an illusion of consensus created through state teaching outlines and Maoist slogans about moral, physical, and intellectual cultivation—was already eroding.

Over the next decade, scholarship on Chinese society and schooling tracked and revealed this erosion in a number of ways. Monolithic portraits of Chinese education (drawn in an era when research was limited to "data" gleaned from the official stories of state education policy) were replaced by studies that began to reflect schools shaped by, if not responsive to, the interests and social clout of local communities and economies. Likewise, the 1949-centered axis of Chinese history, which had functioned to promote a belief in the uniqueness of communist achievement in China's destiny, destabilized. Continuity across the 1949 divide is now a predominant theme in histories of China's educational development.[1] As part of this process, even May Fourth Movement (1915–1921) nationalism—claimed and interpreted by the communist state to support the legitimacy of its revolution—has been revealed as "a great creator of stereotypes."[2] As the official stories of state discourse are challenged by the unofficial stories of daily life, once unthinkable interpretations of Chinese history—that nationalism and socialism might be problematic for women and "minorities," for example—emerge. And scholars seek an understanding of Chinese education "that encompasses both the articulated, moralized, rationalized ideas and the ones that had to be expressed in more fragmented and ambiguous ways."[3]

Coupled with the tremendous educational reforms associated with market socialism, this deconstruction of China's "mnemonic edifice of national unity"[4] has dramatically altered Chinese schools and our understanding of them. Schools have become less completely state agencies as "public" and "private" activities and interests have been recognized as "not hermetically sealed spheres, but interlinked, sometimes indistinguishable, fields of power."[5] In this context of sometimes overlapping, sometimes colliding state and local interests, it has became not only possible but imperative to write about school life as a realm deeper and more contentious than state policy, inhabited by ambitious parents, bored and engaged students and teachers, and the encroaching market.

I realize that the tension I highlight in this chapter between top-down, moralized, and rationalized discourses on Chinese education and fragmented, local, ambiguous narratives of individuals finding meaning in the processes of schooling may create a false dichotomy. Official and unofficial stories of schooling are in constant interaction. Nevertheless, I make the distinction to document changes in my efforts to understand the connection between how people live their daily lives and the public stories, or narratives, they come to tell about what gives their lives meaning and importance.

This chapter is organized against the backdrop of a displacement of state discourse with narrative. It is also an artifact of the influence of postmodernism on—sometimes referred to as the "literaturization of"—the human sciences.[6] While I do not agree that cultural analysis is merely textual strategy or discursive practice, I have come to conceptualize the "field" of fieldwork as more than geographical location. The field is also a field of obligations in which the researcher's identity and understanding develops as a process of negotiation. From this perspective, my approach to ethnographic marginality, for example—an "ambiguous status of belonging simultaneously to more than one collective entity"[7]—rests upon a certain optimism about our abilities to learn through collaboration, which in turn enables "us to make our way as researchers without a fully orchestrated score."[8]

I am optimistic, as well, about the insights derived from such an unpredictable, incomplete practice,[9] even though the title of this chapter reflects my ambivalence about it.[10] My ambivalence emerges here in two ways, first in relationship to the "ethnographic moment" that has troubled cultural anthropologists and critical educators for the last fifteen years. My ambivalence is also evident in my reflections on the significance of ethnographic methodologies to our understanding of Chinese schooling. Thickly described portraits of classroom settings can reveal with startling clarity students and teachers as actors who "practice" culture. At their best, ethnographies illuminate how that practice is shaped by larger social patterns, bringing the everyday into relation with history. Ethnographic methodologies also allow researchers to simultaneously "discover the trace of the other in the self,"[11] question their own "uninnocent positions" in the field, and produce multivocal texts that present teachers and students in their own words. Whether ethnographic studies of Chinese schools can or should meet the demand by critical ethnographers that they serve as a proxy for agency and democratic action is less clear to me, and remains one of the fundamental but unanswered questions in this chapter and in my thinking.

THE FIRST MOMENT: POWER AND IDENTITY IN CRITICAL ETHNOGRAPHY, 1982–1987

Writing in a Field of Obligations

November 13, 1982. My twelve open-ended interview questions have been "approved" by the principal, but hardly in the manner I expected. I want to talk with fifteen language teachers in our two offices about all these questions—their reflections on teaching purpose and methodology, their lives as secondary school teachers, their feelings about their profession and their students. Surely, after a year this would be a comfortable conversation for us. We discuss these issues continually in our offices, over lunch, even while someone is washing her hair over the coal burner. "Well, no, this is no problem at all, a splendid idea," says the principal. "I'll arrange schedules, talk with the staff." Today I received a list of times when I am supposed to meet with my colleagues. Their names are listed opposite the question or two they are "most qualified" to answer!

When I taught in a Chinese secondary school from 1981 to 1983, I was protectively housed, as were many of the 120 foreign teachers working in Shanghai at the time, in the Jing Jiang Hotel, the "panda palace" originally built as the Cathay Mansions in the French Concession by Sir Victor Sassoon. From within our isolated gate, China seemed "a country where social reality was explained in terms of a shared public morality expressed in ideological form."[12] Chinese schools, too, appeared as highly functional, consistent message systems, in which teachers, symbolic mediators of the state, built predictable structures of persuasion for their students.[13]

This vision of schooling jibed unevenly with the theories of critical ethnography in which I had been schooled and which were being interpreted by comparative educators as significant to the cross-cultural study of schooling.[14] I arrived in China consumed by the structure-agency debate, assuming that all societies were patterned by the unequal distribution of power; that all schools both reflect and shape these inequities; and that educational research, implicated in the distribution of power, had the potential for transforming the structures of schooling. Agency complicated my thinking about just whose interests my research in China might serve, and, I hoped, would also enable me to envision schools as instruments of national policy *and* sites for constructing social alternatives. Finally, and ironically, I believed the concept of agency could also help me avoid an unintended consequence of much naturalistic research—that it "affirms a social world that is meant to be *gazed upon but not challenged or transformed.*"[15]

In fact, I was astounded that my colleagues purposefully denied neutrality in pedagogy yet deprived themselves of a critical vocabulary for describing the outcomes of teaching. For my part, I never believed my dissertation would represent an "objective" reproduction of Chinese school life. As a teacher, I willfully altered the pedagogy I hoped to understand. I was even prepared for an assault on my identity. In the field I carried around a file on which I had printed from a source long forgotten: "Good ethnography is an intellectual exorcism in which we are wrenched out of our self." Yet, despite my definition of teaching as a dialogical process, I was not prepared for the extent to which my colleagues believed that transforming my teaching practice, at which they became expert, was their responsibility.

I am indebted to their caring tutelage for a number of reasons, not the least of which being that I learned about the fluidity of power in field relationships. Although my dependency on my colleagues first alarmed me, in retrospect, I am surprised that my role as "acceptable incompetent" bothered me at all. I am also chagrined that it took me so long to realize that "in our concern over colonial luggage, we tend to forget the complex power negotiations that also go on among individuals."[16]

My inability to communicate to my principal why it was I wanted to record my colleagues' multiple perspectives on education indicates how hard it was for me to fold my research assumptions into the teaching practice that provided me with legitimacy in the eyes of my colleagues and superiors. It also indicates that I failed to see how firmly my colleagues' views of research were anchored in the evaluative nature of Chinese society. Far from preventing me from freely sharing ideas with other members of the teaching staff (which I did on a daily basis as we prepared common lesson plans and examinations), the principal spent a long evening, she told me the following morning, carefully identifying which colleagues could provide "the best answers" to my questions. She knew I would be grateful, engaged as I was with such a full teaching load, for this efficiency. In response, I tactfully explained that I wished to ask *all* of my colleagues *all* of the questions on my list—for comparative purposes. (Actually, I mumbled something about building a rich portrait of the teaching staff.) My principal could not fathom why I should take such a circuitous route to wisdom, believing as she did that "the role of researchers is to help report the merits of the meritorious."[17]

It was not until I returned to the United States that I realized how strongly the field of obligations and assumptions about teaching and learning that I had left in China would and should extend into the writing process. In the absence of my colleagues, and the longer I wrote, the more my fieldnotes became "headnotes," a term Simon Ottenberg has used to describe how the artifacts and lessons of the field are transformed, sometimes beyond recognition, by an individual scholar's search for meaning. The farther I felt "the field" recede from these headnotes, the more I worried about what Ruth Behar has called "the privilege of my pen."[18]

Furthermore, just as I could not take for granted that my research assumptions would retain validity in a Chinese context, neither could I count upon my graduate institution's understanding that my research methods had bent to a Chinese context, something that at one point nearly cost me my graduate school career. When Chinese officials politely refused to complete the human subjects research paperwork required by my university, they told me in warm confidence, "Of course, you understand we approve; it's all fine; we just can't say so. Let's just write a quick letter explaining this to someone."

Such negotiations fundamentally altered my perspective on the aims, processes, and consequences of ethnography—and of comparative education. When I began my fieldwork as a graduate student I did so intent upon sharing with a North American audience what is important in the school lives of Chinese educators and students. I hoped to make accessible those distant experiences, believing that increased familiarity could enrich our "own" educational dialogue. I am now more cautious about the concept of culture, which, when cast as intrinsic and coherent, constructs, as well as explains, difference. I am convinced that our understanding of school systems is enhanced by recognizing the ways in which they are connected within one educational world, and that we benefit from attempts "to write about lives so as to constitute others as less other."[19]

Meeting this challenge raises a number of the questions that have fueled recent debates about ethnography, which I summarize later. Foremost among these questions is what happens to ethnographic authority and audience when the so-called "objects of analysis are also analyzing subjects."[20] If I needed reminding of how perspicacious some of these subjects can be, I was in 1996, when fifteen years after my first teaching experience in a Chinese secondary school I reunited for dinner with my former students in the Shanghai Sheraton. Our group of twelve included eleven graduate degrees, three cellular phones, and two children. The "students" hilariously recounted the ways in which I had inadvertently introduced them to "McWorld": their first Coca Cola, their first pop music, their first discussion class, Christmas tree, *Seventeen* magazine. I cringed at their stories. They laughed at how far we had all strayed from our "cozy one voice, one school, one nation."[21]

I had brought to our reunion my book about their school. The subtext, which they immediately recognized, was printed on the jacket cover beneath the title and could be understood only by those able to read Chinese characters: "Make foreign things serve China." The admonition alluded to the political slogan that directed foreign-language training in China after 1949. I presented the ethnography to one of the students who figured most prominently in it. She eyed the cover shrewdly, then nodded at me. "It's you," she said, with a grin. "It's also you." "What?" I asked, confused. "You," she replied. "You're the foreign thing."

Framing the Ethnographic Moment

Six years before this reunion, I attended an international symposium, held at Nanjing Normal University, on the history of Chinese Christian colleges. After a mainland scholar presented his paper on "campus culture," an American English-language teacher in the audience suggested that he extend the research by adopting an "ethnographic" approach. *No one* at this conference of bilingual, internationally trained scholars could suggest a suitable translation for what his suggestion might mean. The Chinese word being used for ethnography was "ethnology," *renzhong xue,* a term which could connote none of the debates among scholars in the human sciences about how the postmodern "predicament" of research purpose and method has complicated central concepts like "others" and "cultures." Our inability to communicate to each other what ethnography might mean provoked no more than a brief flurry of interest. The lack of authentically collaborative contacts between scholarly research cultures, and the lack of common assumptions about methodology and vocabulary, simply halted discussion.

The moment crystallized for me how the politics of ethnographic practice and the texts produced from that practice are to be found as much within the cultures of academia as in the patterns of inequality that structure and sometimes separate the worlds in which we conduct research. Some anthropologists claim that ethnography is "the one vehicle above all others" that can help us toward a more reflexive practice and theory.[22] They are joined by educational theorists who likewise see in ethnography "a fruitful site for learning about strategies of a post-modern praxis."[23] Other scholars, however, are skeptical about generating theory and policy from ethnographic insights, precisely because those insights have become so contingent upon the local contexts from which they derived.[24]

The "crisis" in ethnographic representation to which each of the scholars previously mentioned alludes can be seen as a response across the disciplines to a profound uncertainty about what constitutes an adequate depiction of social reality.[25] It is also the product of working in a world "marked by borrowing and lending across porous national and cultural boundaries that are saturated with inequality, power, and domination."[26] In such a world, writing, too, becomes an enactment of power relations, even a hostile assertion of authority.

As an educator, I view with both relief and apprehension this reinvention of ethnography for an era that has rejected the master narrative of modernity. I feel special reluctance at giving up some of the progressive "no longers" of postmodernism—particularly modernity's "vision of worldwide progress through scientific enlightenment, personal liberation, and voluntary cooperation based on mutually perceived self-interests."[27] I acknowledge that we can write only at the limits of ourselves, that the knowledge we construct will never be adequate to its object.[28] Yet it is precisely such awareness that allows us "the possibility to choose alternative ways of knowing," and helps us recognize the necessity for dialectical fearlessness.[29] And it is through such fearlessness that we may imagine fields and texts "that would contain only subjects: no spectators, only actors, all similarly compromised."[30]

Conceptualizing researchers and subjects as compromised actors rests upon the assumption that ethnographic selves are historically contingent and, if written about elsewhere, subject to local reappropriation. Disturbing ethnographic identity in this manner requires that authors redress what has been called their "absent presence" in ethnographic texts. Because we cannot avoid political and ethical decisions in methodological choices, we clearly should not erase these decisions from the research account. Yet the confessional tone that prompts some writers to declare, "I am my fieldnotes"[31] has rightly, in my opinion, been countered by those who remind us that "If classic ethnography's vice was the slippage from the ideal of detachment to actual indifference, that of present-day reflexivity is the tendency for the self-absorbed Self to lose sight altogether of the culturally different Other."[32]

With positions, texts, and identities fluid, negotiated, and contested, how shall we evaluate the validity of ethnography? While some scholars answer this question by radically redefining validity as a *process* negotiated through dialogue, most researchers acknowledge that although ethnographic texts are "seriously compromised" fictions that inscribe and legitimate particular worldviews, they are still fictions that at least anthropologists "cannot yet do without."[33]

One conclusion to be drawn from the previous reflections is the need for ethnographers who "cannot help but narrate" to subscribe to what Gayatri Spivak calls a "radical acceptance of vulnerability."[34] "Under what conditions and to what ends do we enter into relations of cooperation, mutuality, and reciprocity with those whom we research?"[35]

Such a question might sound naïve, impertinent, even neo-imperialist in the context of China, where missionaries, revolutionaries, and spies have at best exhausted us with their wild-eyed praxis. As Marilyn Young once reflected to Robert Bellah, "China was the last revolutionary redeemer state that I'm going to back. . . . An alienated cosmopolitan is just what I want to be."[36] I eschew alienated cosmopolitanism, in part because I believe we all live local lives. In addition, I retain hope in the subversive challenge of "morally engaged" research, because it forces us to confront "questions of power and conflict that disrupt a comfortable academic world still heavily influenced by the myths of harmony and meritocracy."[37]

Like each of the postmodern debates discussed above, this claim presents serious challenges to researchers who engage in ethnographic analysis in Chinese schools. Postmodern research and its vocabulary clash with how the purposes and aims of social science are defined by mainland Chinese scholars, whose disciplinary and methodological claims remain guided by a faith in modernity, with its core belief that human beings can progressively shape themselves and their worlds. Furthermore, the critical posture adopted by scholars who see themselves and their work as implicated in power relationships is often at odds with how Chinese teachers and administrators, like my principal, view the purpose of research, which is to identify, even celebrate, "good" educational practice. Finally, while it is common for "periphery" scholars to chide their Chinese counterparts for a lack of an ironic or critical stance toward Western theories,[38] my research colleagues often laugh at what they see as a fundamental misunderstanding of their critical absorption of "what is good and bad about the West." They find unpersuasive comments about power, and reply to my equivocations about position: "You are just too sensitive about these criticisms. Just say what you think."

THE SECOND MOMENT: NARRATIVE AND THE HISTORICAL ETHNOGRAPHY: THE SHANGHAI McTYEIRE SCHOOL FOR GIRLS, 1988–1995

September 28, 1991. I was looking for a seat on the train from New York City to Utica when I ran into a colleague who also taught at Colgate. I told him that I had been in Manhattan conducting interviews for a research project. He asked, surprised, "Don't you work in China?" I explained that I was interviewing alumnae of a Shanghai school, and that I had stayed at the home of a graduate whose husband's export business had taken her to a lovely apartment near the World Trade Center. I excitedly recounted my research routine of teas, informal conversations, dinners, a wedding. His face suggested growing skepticism. I continued with a story about how several of us wept together after an especially poignant interview with a graduate of the class of 1921, who after ending a brilliant career as a lawyer was dying in a cramped flat, isolated from friends and family. When I'd finished the sad tale, he looked at me for awhile and finally said, "That's interesting, but it's not research."

I noted previously that one of the most important lessons I learned during my first moment in the field of Chinese schooling was that "cultural" explanations of social processes, including teaching and learning, construct, as well as explain, difference. The moment I realized this need to write against as well as with culture, I also began to question scholarship that essentialized culture and forgot history.[39] Good school ethnography must situate careful, honest portrayals of the daily, "cultural" lives of individuals within history. This lesson came to define my approach to ethnography (which I call historical ethnography) and inspired my interest in the use of narratives to understand and construct portraits of schooling and identity.

Sympathetic to my interests in the historical development of Shanghai secondary schools, my principal in 1982 suggested that I take a day off from teaching to visit the Shanghai Number Three Girls' Middle School (#3). She had been a chemistry teacher at the school years before, and assured me that I would find the visit fascinating. Accustomed to the dusty, noisy compactness of Shanghai schools, I wandered in appreciation one afternoon along sweeping lawns, clusters of female students gathered about a lotus pond, stately dormitories, marble floors, and golden stained glass.

It would be over six years before I returned to the campus to study the historical development of #3, from its illustrious establishment as the McTyeire School for Girls, arguably Republican China's most prestigious girls' secondary school.[40] Southern Methodist missionaries founded McTyeire in 1892 to provide a Christian education to Chinese daughters of "the well-to-do classes." McTyeire lost its religious affiliation in 1952 and was renamed the Shanghai #3 Girls' School. As China's only all-female key school, #3 has become a national model for public and private girls' schools founded by educators and parents eager to provide appropriate educational opportunities for their daughters.

I spent five weeks in the winter of 1989 visiting classrooms, talking with students and teachers, and combing through school archives. I stayed in a dormitory room, and the girls who boarded at the school crept along the hallway to talk long into the night about their dreams. Occasionally, I visited my colleagues at the language school where I had once taught, sipping tea in their new apartments, which had been supplied by the school and which they could lease or buy. Unfortunately for the school's next generation of students, many of my colleagues had left teaching for more lucrative careers, or were moonlighting in the evenings with little time to attend to their day students' needs. Their conversations exuded both anxiety and a new lease on life. In this homecoming of high-rises and easy laughter, I could think of nothing except how much easier it now was to conduct research in China. When I left for the United States in February, I looked forward to my return in June.

This return was abruptly delayed by the Chinese government's brutal suppression of the Democracy Movement on June 4, 1989. Misinterpreting a frantic telephone call from the #3 librarian on June 6 to mean that I should postpone my field trip, I was surprised a week later to receive a reassuring phone message: "We all want you to come and carry out your work. You should come now. You never know what the future will bring."

The summer of 1989 was a painful time to be in Shanghai. Pupils from #3 who in May had marched in solidarity protest with their college-level counterparts were being asked to reevaluate their thinking. Teachers wept in despair. I was stunned by the gentle openness and self-reflection of their conversations. Emotions, especially sadness and anger, were very close to the surface. As the summer—and the tenth-grade students' mandatory military training—drew to a close, their army officers, participating teachers, and I attended a farewell banquet. The banquet ended in drunken, open regret at what the awful beginning of the summer had wrought.

The goal of my research at #3 and certainly my position as researcher were transformed that summer when I began conducting oral histories of McTyeire and #3 teachers, students, and alumnae. In three years the school would celebrate its centennial anniversary, and I had agreed to transcribe and edit a collection of memories and life stories of McTyeirean alumnae.

What followed was a journey from gracious homes to nursing homes, from reunions to weddings, in search of McTyeire and #3's past. With each conversation, the "scruffy edges of memory"[41] gave shape and weight to this past. As stories piled up, were placed in juxtaposition, and argued over by classmates, I became intrigued by how McTyeire's "official" history was being rewritten by its graduates through their efforts at coming to terms with their own histories. Vera Schwarz has noted that "locked away in the heart, the remembered past grows stale and sour, while official history becomes bloated with convenient myths. If allowed to be aired side by side, memory and history grown more vigorous."[42] Witnessing the enlivening bond between McTyeirean memory and history, I began to conceptualize research as storytelling and McTyeirean narratives as a method of inscribing practical, caring power in the present. I also began to differentiate between coherence, which I tried desperately to find, and consistency, which I knew I never could. Coherence, I realized, "allows for many kinds of connectedness, including associations of ideas and feelings, intimations of resemblance, conflicts and tensions."[43]

My growing appreciation of the power of memory and narrative to construct a coherent identity across exceptional geographical, generational, and ideological distances has prompted me to explore recent methodological writings by phenomenologists. What I have perceived in the past to be a neglect of structural considerations in this literature still concerns me. However, the admirable attention phenomenologists direct toward the principle of intentionality—that we "question the way we experience the world"—helps me conceptualize how research might be conceived of as a caring act.[44]

This possibility convinced me, once and for all, to replace "discourse" (those dominant stories ossified by the state as they move across and define fields of power) with "narrative" as my concept for identifying how meaning is created through the relationships that sustain the research process. Likewise, it convinced me that "the use of narrative and dialogue can serve as a model for teaching and learning across the boundaries of disciplines, professions, and cultures."[45]

In recording McTyeirean stories, I became the narrator within the story, indebted to and liable for others' memories, in such a way that my professional and personal loyalties were impossible to disentangle. As we became "mediums for each other's stories,"[46] my familiar ethnographic question regarding the power of the writer to select "which stories will be told and which suppressed"[47] gave way to the different concern about what to do with the multiple accountabilities that shaped my relationship with the McTyeire story. Margery Wolf has suggested that "if there is any crisis in ethnography, it is a growing uncertainty about our dual responsibility to our audiences and our informants."[48] This uncertainty became urgent to me, as my audience and my informants, with whom I had developed a very personal relationship, were one and the same.

Toni Morrison has written that memory "is not an effort to find out the way it really was—that is research."[49] Wedged between the "facts" of history and the poignancy of that history transfigured through personal memory and commitment, I remain vexed by my role in this project. If it is true that ethnography and history normally help us encounter others with safety, with retrospection, and with a clarity that at the time simply did not exist, then this endeavor is not exactly either. Yet no other project has made so clear to me how much "writing is about history coursing its way through us."[50]

THE THIRD MOMENT: CULTURAL COLLABORATORS IN THE MATERIAL SCHOOL, 1996–1997

August 13, 1997. We have just finished shopping at the bookstore and try every possible restaurant looking for an empty table. Finally, a place with air-conditioning and empty seats where we can spread out. I can't believe that the quietest place we've found to put our presentation together is the Shenzhen Hard Rock Café!

A significant consequence of my turn toward narrative (and research as relationship) in the McTyeire and #3 project was that it convinced me never to conduct an ethnographic project that was not explicitly collaborative. Thus, my research collaborator and I found ourselves, after a day in Shenzhen, sitting in the cool darkness of the Hard Rock Café, finalizing the details of a workshop on qualitative research that we would be presenting at an international conference on Chinese education in Hong Kong.

While ethnographic approaches are still rare in the methodological repertoires of mainland educational researchers, Chinese educators at major normal universities are often familiar with the *Handbook of Qualitative Research*.[51] It is with informed opinion that they reject postmodernist vocabulary that seems unseemly, if not alien, in the context of their overheated economy and visions for the future. Foreigners conducting ethnographic fieldwork in China are numerous, however, and they pull from their experiences all sorts of advice on the "101 ways to knock on your subject's doors."[52]

The collaborative project I am now engaged in examines how educators and parents form, invest, and reinvest "social capital" through the processes of senior-secondary education.[53] In particular, my colleague and I seek to understand how the educational abilities and needs of students of various social class backgrounds (especially of daughters of a group we call the "latent middle class") are reacted to and converted into academic achievement, educational opportunities, and ultimately social identity and community trust.

Our work in numerous schools along China's eastern coast convinces us that educational disparity poses a serious challenge to the future of equality of educational opportunity in China, and, by extension, social cohesion and stability. As the socialist narrative of public good is replaced by a market narrative of private interest and initiative, just what "common good" means in the Chinese context is contested, and schools are increasingly perceived as institutions for enhancing individual capacities and life chances.[54] These are the processes that give dual meaning to our "material school" designation: the centrality of schooling to individual and community health and stability, and its inexorable incorporation into the commodifying hold of market socialism.[55]

As the economic and social conditions of China's communities become more diverse, so do their schools,[56] and the rapid but not uncontroversial expansion since the early 1990s of private and all-girls' schools reflects most distinctively the increasing plurality of Chinese schooling. Girls' schools offer public, private, academic, and vocational options for pupils from advantaged and poor and minority families, and their missions and curricula vary dramatically. Some principals state proudly that they train girls for jobs "suited to the special characteristics of Chinese women." Girls being trained as service personnel for the hotel industry, for example, spend hours in the classroom tucking in sheets and pouring drinks with graceful composure. Other schools explicitly counter what they perceive as the "Japanization" of Chinese femininity and require students to take drivers' training and martial arts.

No summary is adequate to the divergent experiences of girls within these schools, which, in any case, vary across ethnicity, region, and social class. Girls do share in common, however, the tendency to express in open-ended interviews outrage at being "silenced" by parents and teachers. Their willingness to talk, something I have noted of #3 students as well, is striking, and their firm understanding, even by their early teens, that market socialism has had a mixed impact on the career and life options of women belies the urgent pronouncements of Chinese officials, who like their development counterparts worldwide, have embraced female education as an immediate priority, a linchpin, even the silver bullet of development.[57]

Despite their sensationalist portrayal in the press as havens for the little emperors and empresses of China's newly affluent families, private schools also vary tremendously in quality, curriculum, and intent. Some take crass advantage of parental anxiety that children need to "make it" in China's market-oriented society. Some are established by philanthropic organizations and individuals as acts of social service or glory in the hometown. Annual tuitions range from six hundred Chinese *yuan* to well over ten thousand American dollars. The best private schools provide sites of innovation in teaching in the arts and recognition of students' rights, and are not uniformly contributing to educational stratification, precisely because they close educational gaps left by a state unable or unwilling to provide sufficient schooling for the Chinese population.

Market socialism has indeed changed the face of Chinese schools, and doing research within them, in countless ways. Interviews with principals are interspersed with whether *The Bridges of Madison County* was a convincing film. Students stage fashion shows with music cuts taped from MTV blaring in the background. In a private school with exorbitant tuition and an approach to knowledge we can only dub "depoliticized humanism," we listened to a group of young educators discussing how to develop a curriculum around Howard Gardner's notion of multiple intelligences. That the two of us—one born and raised in China and now a Canadian citizen, one of Northern European background and an American citizen—are now involved in a joint project to understand this pervious, exceptionally vital, and contradictory world further complicates the hybrid nature of our encounters.

My collaborator, accustomed to moving about Chinese schools un-inhibited by foreignness, is shocked (as I am mortified on her behalf) by the unpredictable disruptions of my presence. Sometimes onlookers assume she is my interpreter, a story that is both handy and condescending. At other times, my body is a nuisance or worse, as pedicab drivers express their infuriation that my colleague, again assumed to be some sort of handler or guide, "doesn't let me" ride in the direction they wish to take me. Once a video camera that in my colleague's hands was perceived as innocuous was seen as a threat when placed in mine, because a nervous administrator feared that my interest in Chinese institutions could somehow be associated with the Shanghai orphanage scandal.

Such moments are cause for sober reflection about marginality, eth-nicity, and how our bodies become repositories for and inscriptions of difference. How our physicality signals meaning has prompted me to re-think what I do and what I become when I am *traveling in the field*. My understanding of the consequences of field travel in this sense has been influenced by postmodern literary and cultural critics, such as Edward Said,[58] who locate cross-cultural theorizing, or "traveling theory," in the "postmodern moment of destabilized nation-states, cultural and eco-nomic diasporas, and increasing disparities of wealth and power."[59] Trav-eling theory has provided me with a useful vocabulary for critical reflection upon what happens to our selves, our positions of authority, and our scholarship as we move about this porous world—especially as it underscores who benefits from so fundamentally disturbing identity.[60]

My colleague is not so enamored of "traveling theory," or its as-sumptions regarding the problems of shifting positionality, for that mat-ter. She shares with many Chinese colleagues to whom I referred earlier the opinion that I am simply *"way* too concerned about these issues of power! You're too apologetic about being a foreigner!" While she agrees that we cannot just shed our skin and become interchangeable scholars irrespective of ethnicity and background, she prefers to see travel as engaging in the deepest sense of the word, necessitating a certain unpre-dictability and loss of control, as well as an enlargement of perspective— the recognition that our work will always demand a diverse range of commitments.

In our lighter moments we give in to the metaphor of field research as adventure, accepting the role (problematic for me, exhilarating for her) of "tourist claiming the community on a global scale."[61] Successful adventures do indeed include guides who obtain access and acceptance, as adventurers tend to take unusual routes—the most challenging and exciting of which appear unexpectedly, when bridges are built between strangers through genuine communication. Such bridges are precariously sustained by treading delicate political lines, the transgression of which is avoided only when the adventurer develops a sharp sense of local context. Ethnography, of course, is indispensable to adventurers, because "it offers the opportunity to develop a sense of locally significant questions and the strategies for answering them within the context of the field experience."[62]

Our experimentation with various metaphors for understanding our positions within collaborative research has reminded us time and again how crucial to our work is the central commitment of qualitative research to the study of human experience from the ground up.[63] First, our desire to understand schools from Chinese points of view can be achieved only in interaction with Chinese teachers, parents, students, and administrators. Second, the research methods associated with qualitative fieldwork facilitate the construction of a multivocal portrait of schooling, in which the positions of researchers in dialogue with subjects are continually reevaluated. The emphasis we place upon capturing the diversity of Chinese school experiences; our conviction that gender and social class intersect to create multiple perspectives on these issues; and our concern that our research conclusions create opportunities for collaboration between Chinese and foreign scholars—all demand that we incorporate into both research design and final interpretation multiple responses to our questions.

THE FOURTH MOMENT:
PBS MEETS THE MATERIAL SCHOOL, 1997–1998

May 29, 1997. We are over an hour late on our second day of filming. The vice-principal, who was upset that we showed up early and for all practical purposes unannounced yesterday, is now shaking with fury. He has been standing outside to greet us. We are nothing but trouble with our cameras and our demands. He stands close to me, his face inches from mine. This is absolutely unacceptable behavior, he screams. Classes have been rearranged for filming. You can't do this to us, to our teachers. I do not know how to be apologetic enough in the face of his venom. I know in many ways he is correct. This is the difference between the tight time frame and script of journalism and the cautious, painfully, slowly negotiated work of ethnography. There is

no time here for the presentation of self through the tending of relationship. I feel deflated, ashamed at the wake of disarray and hurt feelings
our careless speed has churned up.

The commitment to multiple perspectives I have tried to bring to my
research is suddenly an unaffordable luxury—and a nuisance. I have
come to Shanghai as a consultant to a filming project on the relationships
among educational innovation, employment opportunities, corporate
ideology, and the global economy.[64] How Shanghai's educators are ad-
justing their schools' curricula and cultures to the demands of market socialism will serve in this PBS special as a counterpoint to portraits of
educational reform in the United States. In one breathless week we film
scores of hours of tape in two secondary schools struggling to provide an
excellent education to junior and senior high school students. I am at
once delighted and mortified at the remarkable extent to which we probe
and intrude into the daily lives of administrators, teachers, and students. I
am also astonished that our producer feels satisfied when he can retrieve
from a grueling twelve-hour day of filming two to three minutes of on-air
time. My desire to dwell on the contradictions of teaching practice, to
take time to care for prickly human relationships as we focus those contradictions through the unforgiving lens of the camera, is crushed by the
compressed time frame in which we must create convincing portraits of
Chinese schooling. I wonder at how I did not anticipate the intense im-
mediacy of filming at breakneck speed. When I later recount my role in
this enterprise to Gerry Postiglione, he informs me that this must be my
fifteen minutes of fame. If so, I want it back. Feeling more like a "vulnerable observer" than talking head, I don't know which team to root for, the
furious vice-principal or the film makers with an elegantly crafted
story.[65] Clearly, the worlds of journalism and research represent distinct
cultures, and what is deemed appropriate and successful in one may be
quite destructive in the other.

"Education for Success"

Filming begins in Zhabei District #8 Junior Middle School. The early
morning haze lifts above seventh and eighth graders, dressed in sky-blue
uniforms, milling about the school's cement courtyard. A jumble of tene-
ments, fluttering laundry, and half-completed skyscrapers bear down on
the cramped campus. Students jostle into rows for a perfunctory flag-
raising ceremony, the Chinese national anthem broadcast above a throb-
bing moan of construction.

We are greeted by Zhabei #8's principal, Mr. Liu Jinghai, who guides us up a damp flight of stairs. The school's drab interior is typical of public schools throughout the city—dim hallways enlivened by black-boards covered with intricate student drawings, colorful admonitions against smoking, tedious final examination schedules. A full-length mir-ror is strategically positioned at the base of the stairwell as a symbolic re-minder to students to be mindful of proper decorum.

In Mr. Liu's greeting room, we settle onto a low leather couch. Something of a quiet visionary, Mr. Liu describes how he has received national recognition for his philosophy of "education for success," ap-proved by the State Education Commission as one of three methodolo-gies for improving basic education. Mr. Liu's definition of success was profoundly influenced by his experiences during the Cultural Revolu-tion. He credits his appreciation for "two of the key elements of success-ful education—the power of self-learning and critical thinking" to five years spent in the countryside, when he became convinced that all pupils could achieve academically, provided they had self-confidence and op-portunities to succeed.

> The first priority in education is not academic excellence. It is confi-dence. Low examination marks do not indicate lack of ability, but rather a lack of confidence and, consequently, motivation. . . . The most important starting point for good teaching is to have faith in stu-dent potential. There are three points to my philosophy: belief that each student has the desire to learn; belief that every student can learn; and belief that all students can and will achieve. Teachers have to over-come their own lack of faith in poor children. The parents of our stu-dents are primarily from lower-working-class families. Crime, low educational attainment and aspirations—these are prevalent in this dis-trict. It is our responsibility to compensate for problems by providing students with opportunities to succeed.

The extension to local schools of greater curricular, financial, and staffing autonomy has allowed Mr. Liu to recruit teachers from every re-gion of China, "bringing diversity to the school, so that we have many philosophies and approaches, providing our students with rich re-sources." Mr. Liu's progressive conviction that academic success must be grounded in self-confidence is echoed by a mathematics instructor, who describes student achievement as his responsibility: "To believe in the students' abilities, to instill that belief in them, to work out different approaches to problems. The desire to learn is ever-present in all students, no matter how deeply buried, and it is the teacher's role to bring that desire to the surface."

These thoughtful comments seem sincere to me, nonformulaic. I am likewise struck by the angry impatience of an English teacher who is asked "why she bothers" spending so much time on working-class students who will not attend college.

> Why!? These students will become the builders in the future of our country! We have to help them to learn, to build their abilities, to be a useful person! You see, too, everyone is important. We have large classes. Fifty-three students. Yet in each student's family, they are the only child. The parents want them to have a good job, a brighter future. So we pay attention to each child, for the development of each child, for the sake of their families, for the sake of this district.

For the past four years, all of Zhabei #8's graduates have continued their studies in high school, and two-thirds have gained entrance into selective academic and technical-vocational schools. The irony that such conventionally narrow markers of educational success have enhanced his national reputation is not lost on Mr. Liu. He freely admits that a five million *yuan* investment (from a Hong Kong executive) that has guaranteed the completion of a new school campus would have been unlikely without them. Nevertheless, Mr. Liu's passion to help students in need makes me hopeful that more of Shanghai's educators might be pressed to address the increasing disparity in educational quality and opportunity that has accompanied market socialism.

> Working-class children all have the desire, the instinct, to succeed. But these have been submerged in past failures. We revive their desire. We don't add this to children. We recover, revitalize their potentials. Education is a basic human right. This right is not just for the individual but for the development of the entire nation. The crux of educational reform lies in viewing education as more than just the teaching of subjects. It is the development of the whole child—and ultimately of society. This is the whole meaning of lifelong learning. Education succeeds when students realize their potentials, develop these, make use of these, and contribute to society.

In Step with the Market: Yifu Vocational and Polytechnic School

Mr. Zhang Jianping, the principal of Yifu Vocational and Polytechnic High School, steers his red motor scooter from a torrent of traffic and glides to a stop in the courtyard of the newly constructed Jing An District Children's Palace. Children's Day, June 1, is a scant three days away, and the second-year students from Yifu's film animation program are rushing to complete a mural of Shanghai on the sprawling walls surrounding the Palace. They smear dripping gobs of primary colors across a sea of white, creating jaunty, smiling planes and ships. A banner, flapping from the tale of one grinning vessel, reads, "Wow! This is our own children's center!"

When I ask, with some skepticism, if they'll complete the project on time, they laugh, confidently explaining, "We do these community service things all the time." Mr. Zhang later tells me that they engage in such activities once a month. A large part of their education is devoted to "hands-on" experiences, capped by a fourth-year internship at a local office or enterprise. I praise the mural's design, assuming it has been a class creation, until I am corrected by a boy who points to the teacher who drew the mural's outline. "We're just filling it in," he said with an easy smile.

Mr. Zhang, like his pupils, exudes an upbeat confidence and optimism that is characteristic of teachers and students at elite urban technical high schools, whose up-to-date training in computer animation and fashion, graphic, and architectural design is funded by contributions from government bodies and work units, and culminates in increasingly lucrative job placements throughout the city. The popularity of such institutions in metropolitan China sometimes outpaces that of the most highly selective academic preparatory schools, even among professional parents, who believe that their children will find high-paying, stable, hometown careers upon graduation.

While the patterns of school life at Yifu and Zhabei #8 are similar—students lined up outside school gates to greet teachers, daily exercise routines, rigorous reviews for examinations—Yifu's facilities are much more extensive and its educational mission much more pragmatic. Yifu's privileged funding (some of which comes from the central government) and specialized goal of training mid-level professionals are evident in state-of-the-art computer labs, elaborate design rooms, and constant reference by Mr. Zhang and his teaching staff to the importance of cultivating students for the market economy.

During our stay, a visiting architect delivers a lecture to fourth-year students on postmodern design. Third-year students produce a fashion show, modeling the funky clothes that designate their committed and locally re-creative membership in global youth culture. They saunter down a runway to the blaring beat of pop music, a choreographed stream of black leather and chenille, the girls sporting on their bared shoulders the popular Southwest China "ethnic look" of body tattooing.

Mr. Zhang stresses that in serving the individual career aspirations of these pupils he is serving society. Service, in the context of Yifu, has come to mean the development of commercial market forces. It is from this perspective that Mr. Zhang shares with Principal Liu a highly critical view of "traditional" teaching, which, he explains, "encourages rote learning for tests, with students stuck within the closed walls of schools. Even updated knowledge is not enough. Students need opportunities to practice what they learn." The Director of the International Exchange Division of the Shanghai Education Bureau praises Yifu for being "in step with the market," a model for education's crucial role in China's future.

> The goal must not be high scores. Now we have competency-based education. All the teaching methods and the curricula have to be revamped, schools retooled. . . . The competitive market and society requires students with a different orientation. The old fighting with exams is not the kind of fighting students will have to do. There are over twelve million people in Shanghai and, including college students, over two million pupils. One out of every six people in Shanghai is studying. Students can't be too narrowly trained in such an environment; they need a broad and firm foundation in the basic subjects. This is lifelong learning, but geared to the market. In the last ten years Shanghai has graduated four hundred thousand students from vocational and technical schools, and over 60 percent of all high school students are in vocational and technical programs. . . . We've had to work hard to influence parents away from college preparatory schools. Our schools must satisfy both parents and the enterprises. The mentality that a child will be a dragon is deeply rooted in China, and education is seen as the key to a better future. You know that China has 20 percent of the world's students trained with just 3 percent of the world's educational expenditures. Everyone wants a better life, and the government wants to make opportunities for higher living standards. That's it—the crux of it all. Capital and technology may be borrowed from abroad,

but the labor force must be trained from the inside. Education is the absolute key to China's future.

As our filming at Yifu Polytechnic draws to a close, members of the production team express astonishment at the energy and rhythm of Chinese schooling. They are impressed by the classroom's careful orchestration, the single-minded concentration of students, the scheduled naps, the melodic cadence of the eye exercise chant, the caring exchange of high expectations between students and teachers—always in hallways that simply roar with voices. The producer shakes his head as we move onto the streets and the din of ten thousand construction sites. He tells me he has never filmed in an environment with so much white noise.

Neither the noise nor the grammar of Chinese schooling—its family metaphor, the prevalence of performance models of teaching and learning, the ideology that hard work brings success, the assumption that all children can learn—has changed so much in the last fifteen years. What has changed is that while debates over educational and social goals seem to have become impoverished or at least restricted in the United States, in China they have widened.[66]

This divergent trend, however, is not leading the two systems in opposite directions. Thomas Rohlen has called the present an age of "collective intelligence," forcing societies to consider and reflect upon themselves collectively.[67] In fact, the educational reforms we have witnessed could serve as a counterpoint, as it did in the film narrative, to our own concern that as "the belief system that undergirds public education has fragmented," we must "negotiate a common ground of purpose sufficiently generous, compelling, and plausible that it can unify citizens in support of public schooling."[68]

CONCLUSION: THE CHALLENGE OF ETHNOGRAPHIC AGENCY AND DEMOCRACY IN CHINESE SCHOOLING

The role of education in a world of uncertainty and ambiguity is not just to produce well-socialized people. It is to produce people who are conscious of the process through which they and others are being socialized. This is not just a nicety of democratic principles. It is a necessity of education in a modern multicultural age.[69]

I believe that the message of the centrality of public schooling to social well-being is as important for China as it is for the United States. As China pursues a course of educational diversification, greater commitment to vocational training with direct business linkages, and continued devolution of school funding and authority, schools become localized, commercially driven, anxious institutions. As stratified schools are required to secure an ever-increasing proportion of funding from local resources, they become more tightly linked to the needs and desires of local constituencies, and are perceived as institutions serving private interests rather than public good.

Prestigious schools like #3 and Yifu Polytechnic, recognized for their ability to prepare carefully selected students for college-level training or high-paying jobs in China and abroad, are securely positioned to take advantage of local material and cultural resources, many of which derive from the social and professional networks of students' parents. In fact, such schools have begun to "advertize" this advantage at recruitment fairs and in flashy brochures. Less prestigious vocational and rural schools, having less political, intellectual, and economic "capital" upon which to draw, are increasingly disadvantaged, a fact that their students realize with brutal clarity.

When I began my study on the relationship in China between educational and social stratification two years ago, the contribution to total educational expenditures in China on the part of the central government had dropped to a mere 11 percent. The fact of the matter is, China's spectacular mobilization of local resources for education (which has been so controversial that nearly one-half of China's provinces at one point called for a reversal of educational devolution) has had the effect of making schools much more community than state institutions.[70] Accompanying this trend, practice at all levels of Chinese schooling runs well, if sometimes chaotically, in advance of national, provincial, county, and local educational policy, law, and mechanisms for evaluation and accreditation.

That communities and individuals are usurping social functions of education previously monopolized by the state is, to me, the most intriguing, and most significant, outcome of the conjuncture between market and educational reforms. As the state loosens (albeit unevenly and certainly not always with public approval) its powerful hold on schools, schools have relocated along a spectrum of authorization and control that is characterized at one end by the school as state agency, at the other end by the school as constituted within the market. In between, a more ambiguous but also more autonomous, negotiated space is constructed by individual educators, community groups, parents, and students themselves.

It is in this in-between, more autonomous space that I (cautiously) suggest democratic educational experimentation is proceeding, a process that renews my optimism about the possibility of critical ethnography within China. Admittedly, I am reminded by many educational theorists that schools, and the symbolic systems they help construct and reproduce, are clear instruments of power. I am likewise advised about the dangers of appropriating the vocabulary of civil society for twentieth-century China.[71] Yet the rich associational life of some of China's best schools may be creating a space suggestive of a different conception of power—what Hannah Arendt once called the human ability to act in concert. While the opportunity to construct such a space in the schools of any modern school system is rare, I am more hopeful today than I was a decade ago that Chinese teachers and students may do so.

Most particularly, this space seems to be prompting Chinese scholars to develop a critical vocabulary for evaluating the educational and social consequences of rapid development—a trend that has created an important avenue for collaboration among international scholars. Chinese educators have much to contribute to worldwide debates about schooling and social equality. They have lived through some of the twentieth century's most radical experiments with redistribution of human and material resources, paradoxically carried out alongside some of this century's most violent economic, political, and social polarization. Even though Chinese socialism has fallen far short of empowering Chinese citizens to become the principal agents of history, it has nevertheless left a strong legacy among Chinese educators that the school, first among all public institutions, must be a space for reflection upon public responsibility and social equality. How that legacy is being reenvisioned will not only tell us much about social stratification and schooling in China but also provide a vivid portrait of how global patterns of economic and political reform influence the ways schools reinforce social inequality.

It may not be surprising, given my stake in comparative education, that I have come to understand that what is involved in ethnographic work is similar to what is involved in the development of more democratic schooling. Both endeavors involve learning how to listen and to confront power, and how to talk across differences. Both endeavors also involve realizing that our behavior—including the ways we teach and conduct research—is a cultural product. Engaging Chinese education provides us with a unique opportunity to understand how our work as educators and academics, at home and abroad, might "promote a process of critical yet respectful participation in which both communal and global ends can emerge. When this process includes local symbols amplifying their meanings for other cultures and for different groups, and when it explores international connections in terms of justice as well as wealth, then such an education is democratic."[72]

NOTES

1. One of the most recent examples is Suzanne Pepper's comprehensive history, *Radicalism and Education Reform in 20th-Century China: The Search for an Ideal Development Model* (New York: Cambridge University Press, 1996).

2. Tao Tao Liu and David Raure, eds., *Unity and Diversity: Local Cultures and Identities in China* (Hong Kong: Hong Kong University Press, 1996).

3. Patricia Ebrey, *The Inner Quarters: Marriage and the Lives of Chinese Women in the Sung Period* (Berkeley: University of California Press, 1993), 271.

4. Vincent Crapanzano, "The Postmodern Crisis: Discourse, Parody, Memory," in *Rereading Cultural Anthropology,* ed. George E. Marcus (Durham, N.C.: Duke University Press, 1992), 72.

5. Gail Hershatter et al., eds., *Remapping China: Fissures in Historical Terrain* (Stanford: Stanford University Press, 1996), 3.

6. This trend is explored in detail in the now classic volume edited by James Clifford and George E. Marcus, *Writing Culture: The Poetics and Politics of Ethnography* (Berkeley: University of California Press, 1986) and the feminist response and reevaluation edited by Ruth Behar and Deborah A. Gordon, *Women Writing Culture* (Berkeley: University of California Press, 1995).

7. Cho-yun Hsu, "A Reflection on Marginality," in *The Living Tree: The Changing Meaning of Being Chinese Today,* ed. Wei-ming Tu (Stanford: Stanford University Press, 1994), 239–240.

8. Penny Oldfather and Jane West, "Qualitative Research as Jazz," *Educational Researcher* 23, no. 8 (1994): 22.

9. Because I believe that just what ethnographic research entails can only be answered in the context of specific research projects, I use the term *ethnography* broadly to encompass a number of qualitative research approaches.

10. The dual meaning of *framing* in this sense was suggested to me by Michelle Fine's ethnographic study of high school dropouts in New York City, *Framing Dropouts* (Albany: State University of New York Press, 1990).

11. Deborah A. Gordon, "Border Work: Feminist Ethnography and the Dissemination of Literacy," in *Women Writing Culture,* eds. Ruth Behar and Deborah A. Gordon (Berkeley: University of California Press, 1995), 382.

12. Sulamith Heins Potter and Jack M. Potter, *China's Peasants: the Anthropology of a Revolution* (New York: Cambridge University Press, 1990), xii.

13. See Heidi Ross, *China Learns English: Language Teaching and Social Change in the People's Republic* (New Haven: Yale University Press, 1993) for the study that resulted from this experience.

14. See Vandra Lea Masemann, "Critical Ethnography in the Study of Comparative Education," in *New Approaches to Comparative Education,* eds. Philip Altbach and Gail Kelly (Chicago: Chicago University Press, 1986), 11–25.

15. Leslie Roman and Michael Apple, "Is Naturalism a Move Away from Positivism? Materialist and Feminist Approaches to Subjectivity in Ethnographic Research," in *Qualitative Inquiry in Education: The Continuing Debate,* eds. Elliot Eisner and Alan Peshkin (New York: Teachers College Press, 1990), 53.

16. Margery Wolf, *A Thrice-told Tale, Feminism, Postmodernism, and Ethnographic Responsibility* (Stanford: Stanford University Press, 1992), 134.

17. Martin Schoenhals, *The Paradox of Power in a People's Republic of China Middle School* (Armonk, N.Y.: M. E. Sharpe, 1993), 36.

18. See Ruth Behar, *Translated Woman: Crossing the Border with Esperanza's Story* (Boston: Beacon Press, 1993).

19. Lila Abu-Lughod, "Writing Against Culture," in *Recapturing Anthropology: Working in the Present,* ed. Richard Fox (Santa Fe: School of American Research Press, 1991), 149.

20. Renato Rosaldo, *Culture and Truth: The Remaking of Social Analysis* (Boston: Beacon Press, 1989), 21.

21. Throughout this chapter, I include quotations for taped or directly transcribed comments, made in the context of formal and informal interviews and conversations. This statement was pronounced with a decidedly ironic tone by a student who loved, even in his high school days, to mock political slogans with those of his own making.

22. Joan Vincent, "Engaging Historicism," in *Recapturing Anthropology: Working in the Present,* ed. Richard Fox (Santa Fe: School of American Research Press, 1991), 47.

23. Patti Lather, *Getting Smart: Feminist Research and Pedagogy with/in the Postmodern* (New York: Routledge, 1991), 15.

24. For example, see Martyn Hammersley, *What's Wrong with Ethnography* (New York: Routledge, 1992).

25. See Lather, *Getting Smart.*

26. Rosaldo, *Culture,* 217.

27. Robert N. Bellah et al., *The Good Society* (New York: Knopf, 1991), 217.

28. See Gayatri Chakravorty Spivak, *The Post-Colonial Critic: Interviews, Strategies, Dialogues* (New York: Routledge, 1990).

29. See Donald A. Schon, *The Reflective Turn: Case Studies in and on Educational Practice* (New York: Teachers College Press, 1991).

30. Spivak, *Post-Colonial,* 84.

31. See Roger Sanjek, ed., *Fieldnotes: The Making of Anthropology* (Cornell: Cornell University Press, 1990).

32. Rosaldo, *Culture,* 7.

33. James Clifford, *The Predicament of Culture: Twentieth Century Ethnography, Literature and Art* (Cambridge, Mass.: Harvard University Press, 1988), 10.

34. Spivak, *Post-Colonial,* 18.

35. Lather, *Getting Smart,* 303.

36. Bellah, et al. *Good Society,* 241.

37. Nelly Stromquist, "Encyclopedic Knowledge and the Case of the Missing Women," *Comparative Education Review,* 34, no. 4 (1990): 574.

38. For example, see Crapanzano, "Postmodern Crisis."

39. Margot Badran makes this point particularly well in her study *Feminisims, Islam, and Nation: Gender and the Making of Modern Egypt* (Princeton: Princeton University Press, 1995).

40. A brief history of the school is available in Heidi Ross, " ' Cradle of Female Talent': The McTyeire Home and School for Girls, 1892–1937," in *Christianity in China: From the Eighteenth Century to the Present,* ed. Daniel H. Bays (Stanford: Stanford University Press, 1996), 209–227.

41. Vera Schwarz, "How to Make Time Real: From Intellectual History to Embodied Memory," in *Remapping China,* eds. Gail Hershatter et al. (Stanford: Stanford University Press, 1996), 13.

42. Ibid., 24.

43. Margaret Buchmann and Robert E. Floden, "Coherence, the Rebel Angel," *Educational Researcher* 21, no. 9 (1992): 4.

44. Max Van Manen, *Researching Lived Experience: Human Science for an Action Sensitive Pedagogy* (Albany: State University of New York Press, 1990), 5.

45. Carol Witherell and Nel Noddings, *Stories Lives Tell: Narrative and Dialogue in Education* (New York: Teachers College Press, 1991), 2.

46. Behar, *Translated Woman*, 14.

47. Witherell and Noddings, *Stories*, 1.

48. Wolf, *Thrice-told Tale*, 137.

49. Toni Morrison, "Memory, Creation, and Writing," *Thought* 59 (1984): 385.

50. Deborah A. Gordon, "Culture Writing Women: Inscribing Feminist Anthropology," in *Women Writing Culture*, eds. Ruth Behar and Deborah A. Gordon (Berkeley: University of California Press, 1995), 429.

51. Norman K. Denzin and Yvonna S. Lincoln, *Handbook of Qualitative Research* (Thousand Oaks, Calif.: Sage Publications, 1994).

52. Mary Scoggin, "Gaining Entree: 101 Ways to Knock on Your Subject's Door," *China Exchange News* 22, no. 3 (1994): 22.

53. This research project, conducted with Professor Jing Lin of McGill University, is supported by the Pacific Basin Research Center.

54. See Jing Lin and Heidi Ross, "The Potentials and Problems of Diversity in Chinese Education," *McGill Journal of Education* 33, no. 1 (1998): 31-49.

55. We borrow "material" in this sense from Merry White's book, *The Material Child* (Berkeley: University of California Press, 1993).

56. See Kai-ming Cheng, "A Decade's Reform in China's Education: Social Consequences and Implications for Research" (Keynote address presented at the Fifth Conference on Chinese Education for the 21st Century, Hong Kong, August 1997).

57. See Heidi Ross, "Growing Up in a Chinese Secondary School for Girls," *Journal of Women and Gender Studies* 4, no. 1 (1993): 111–136.

58. Edward Said, *The World, the Text, and the Critic* (Cambridge, Mass.: Harvard University Press, 1983).

59. Caren Kaplan, *Questions of Travel: Postmodern Discourses of Displacement* (Durham, N.C.: Duke University Press, 1996), xi.

60. For an example of traveling theory applied to educational fieldwork, see Peter McLaren, "Collisions with Otherness: 'Traveling' Theory,

Post-colonial Criticism, and the Politics of Ethnographic Practice—The Mission of the Wounded Ethnographer," *Qualitative Studies in Education* 5, no. 1 (1992): 77–92.

61. Kaplan, *Questions,* 7.

62. Andrew B. Kipnis, *Producing Guanxi: Sentiment, Self, and Subculture in a North China Village* (Durham, N.C.: Duke University Press, 1997), 19.

63. See Denzin and Lincoln, *Handbook.*

64. See "Learning to Survive," part three of the four-part Public Broadcasting Service series, "Surviving the Bottomline with Hedrick Smith."

65. I borrow the term "vulnerable observer" from Ruth Behar, *The Vulnerable Observer: Anthropology That Breaks Your Heart* (Boston: Beacon Press, 1996).

66. For discussions of the impoverishment of discourse on American education, see David Tyack and Larry Cuban, *Tinkering toward Utopia: A Century of Public School Reform* (Cambridge, Mass.: Harvard University Press, 1995) and Neil Postman, *The End of Education: Redefining the Value of Education* (New York: Knopf, 1995).

67. Thomas Rohlen and Gerald LeTendre, eds., *Teaching and Learning in Japan* (New York: Cambridge University Press, 1996), 1.

68. Tyack and Cuban, *Tinkering,* 140.

69. Walter Feinberg, *Japan and the Pursuit of a New American Identity: Work and Education in a Multicultural Age* (New York: Routledge, 1993), 133.

70. See Cheng, "Decade's Reform."

71. See Bryna Goodman, "Creating Civic Ground: Public Maneuverings and the State in the Nanjing Decade," in *Remapping China,* eds. Gail Hershatter et al. (Stanford: Stanford University Press, 1996), 164–177; Frederick Wakeman, Jr., "The Civil Society and Public Sphere Debate: Western Reflections on Chinese Political Culture," *Modern China* 19, no. 2 (1993): 108–138; and Gordon White, Judo Howell, and Shangha Xiaoyuan, *In Search of Civil Society: Market Reform and Social Change in Contemporary China* (New York: Oxford University Press, 1996).

72. Feinberg, *Japan,* 194.

CHAPTER 7

Reconstructing the Past
Reminiscences of Missionary School Days

JUDITH LIU

> When I first saw her, I thought to myself, "This young girl who comes
> from the West, can she understand our way of thinking? Can she un-
> derstand our point of view? I have my doubts. Will she have any points
> of agreement with us?" That was the first thing. The second thing, I
> was afraid that she would think, "You are all antiques; people from the
> past. I am so much more advanced compared to you." If she wants to
> hear about my background and my life story, if I tell her about myself
> will she think, "Oh, this old lady, who is she?" That is what I feared.
> That is why I kept watching you yesterday. That is why I kept running
> in and out to see what you had to say to the others.[1]

This trenchant remark by "Auntie" Liang goes right to the heart of the
methodological problem that underlies conducting ethnographic research. Dialogic ethnographies seek to create texts that weave the various threads of a subject's story and the researcher's analysis into a
lifelike tapestry that both the subject and the researcher can regard as a
"truthful representation" of the subject's story. Yet this very process is
determined by any number of variables such as power, age, class, status,
and an understanding or knowledge of the culture of the person being interviewed (or for that matter, who the "other" in ethnographic research
really is)—the same elements that made "Auntie" Liang question the
value of doing our proposed interview. Consequently, these elements

I wish to thank Donald P. Kelly for his creative comments, illuminating insights,
and care with detail in this chapter.

have the potential to undermine each interview and, with it, the ethnographic enterprise itself. This did not happen with "Auntie" Liang because she finally concluded through *her* observations of *me* that she felt "very close to this little girl" who was "just like a young girl who had been born and raised [in China]."

The following study of a cohort of women who attended St. Hilda's School for Girls, an American Episcopalian missionary school in Wuchang, Hubei Province in the 1920s and 1930s, was more the result of serendipity than it was the product of intent. I stumbled onto the subject in 1982 while I was conducting research for my dissertation in the People's Republic of China. My mother accompanied me on this nine-month sojourn, and in virtually every city we visited, I met pseudomaternal women, "Aunties" who were none other than my mother's classmates and schoolmates. The strength of the affective ties between and among these women was so great that despite the fact that some of them had not seen each other in almost fifty years, time and distance melted away whenever they gathered to reminisce about their lives. In the enigmatic world of ethnographic research, it turned out that the arrival of my mother and me in a given city gave cause for elaborate banquets organized in our honor and was used as an excuse for the women to meet. As such, my interviews were of secondary importance to these women, and they were tolerated in deference to my mother.

Because of my mother, I was given entree into this group of women and given a cachet that most ethnographers must struggle to gain. In theory, this cachet helped establish my credentials as a serious researcher with these women as well as gain rapport with them; however, in practice it necessitated the creation of a three-tiered interview format, with my mother serving as a nondisinterested interlocutor between the woman being interviewed and me. This format permitted her to ask questions on my behalf that I could never have asked, because in Chinese culture, decorum "dictates" that respect for elders on my part must be maintained at all cost. Although my mother's role as an interlocutor had the potential for creating tension within the interview—how can the respondent be candid in the presence of a nondisinterested third party?—this did not happen. My mother's position as an insider— as an accepted peer—made it possible to create a multivocal situation through collaboration and negotiation as to how the interview was going to proceed and as to what topics were going to be covered. Thus, when I could no longer elicit more information during an interview, my mother could:

Judy: What other special impressions do you have of St. Hilda's?

Auntie Huang: I can't think of anything special at this time because most of the time I don't think of these things.

Mom Liu: I consider the eating arrangements at St. Hilda's very special.

Auntie Huang: Right, right. We used to serve portions to each person. The system of eating was very good. Each table had a leader. Every person received a plate full of food. Each person was given a plate. The system of eating was very good. Also, the system of eating desserts was equally good. We were not permitted to eat recklessly.

Because the research was historical, some methodological problems arose. The subject of my dissertation dealt with the impact of the Cultural Revolution on the daily lives of "ordinary" Chinese citizens, and, consequently, I primarily studied the workers in a paper mill in Beijing. Studying the impact of missionary education did not occur to me at that time, and I was initially unprepared to do that type of research. Consequently, the sociology of education was not a subdiscipline with which I was particularly familiar, and the same could be said for missiology. Further, I was fairly ignorant of Chinese history prior to the founding of the People's Republic in 1949. The respondents thus were dealing with events and times of which I was not a part, but of which my mother was a part. As someone who lived through the events at the school, my mother was able to facilitate in the re-creating of shared experiences by building the bridge that linked the living voices of these women to me and joining the past to the present in the historical sweep that spans their lives. The affective ties that bound these women together at St. Hilda's were recalled as a means to restrengthen those ties:

Mom Liu: And what about your impressions [of St. Hilda's]?

Auntie Xiang: I thought the environment was very good. And all of the students were encouraged to help one another, and we all got along very well. Right? And the older students were always concerned and caring about the younger students. And then there were your classmates. We were all good to one another and very good about helping one another.

Judy: And look at the St. Hilda's classmates!

Auntie Margaret Wang: Exactly. We're just like family. We're always [enjoying each other's company]. Therefore, while I was living at the school, even though I wasn't able to go home, our daily lives were filled with people mutually helping one another. People caring for one another—that's something I believe came from our education there.

Using my mother as an interlocutor also had the effect of showing how much the biographies of these women were so intertwined that they were well aware of each other's personal histories as well as amused by each other's foibles:

Auntie Yi: We returned to my family's old home in Hunan, Huayong County. I went to live with my uncle and aunt.

Mom Liu: That was your older brother!

Auntie Yi: Right. With my older brother and his wife because my uncle and aunt were not there. I lived with my older brother and his wife. Seventh brother and his wife.

Auntie Fu: Do you remember that during Sundays we all had to take afternoon naps?

Mom Liu: Only sick people had to take afternoon naps.

Auntie Fu: It wasn't just those who were sick. You've forgotten. The entire school had to take an afternoon nap. We had to sleep until a certain time before we could get up. During afternoon naps, you weren't allowed to read novels, not allowed to knit. (Laughs)

Mom Liu: I couldn't remember because I was always reading novels and knitting. (Laughs)

In performing ethnographic work that is historical in nature, the possibility of multivocality is further increased through extant texts. Since St. Hilda's was a missionary school, information regarding its goals, why it was established, and what went on there as perceived by the teachers and administrators is available in the Episcopal archives in Austin, Texas. Thus, I am privy to a level of knowledge that the respondents themselves do not have.

From the Episcopal archives, I discovered that St. Hilda's began in 1875 as "the Jane Bohlen School for Girls at Wuchang."[2] The school was founded through a bequest to the American Episcopal Missionary Board by the son and daughter of Jane Bohlen of Philadelphia.[3]

The goal of the Jane Bohlen School was to produce a Chinese women's Christian vanguard that would, in the imperialistic and militaristic analogies of the day, help "conquer" China for Christ. Because these newly Christianized women could not be ordained into the ministry, their work would be ancillary to that of their minister-husbands. Hence, they would represent the idealized Western vision concerning the proper role of women in society—they would be good Christian wives, mothers, and helpers. In this way, it was felt by the missionaries that they would become positive role models for China's women to emulate. This was the dream, but the reality was very different.[4] Conversions to Christianity were few, the faculty was constantly in flux, and unless the American Episcopal Missionary Board took drastic measures, the school would fail. As a result, the Board decided to act; it recruited teachers specifically for the school and decided to expand its size. The result was that in 1899, the Jane Bohlen School became the Jane Bohlen Building of the newly christened "St. Hilda's School for Girls at Wuchang."[5]

While the goal of the school would be the same—the creation of a Christian women's vanguard—its focus would be different. St. Hilda's, like Jane Bohlen, would be a boarding school; however, it would be solely a middle school. Its students would be the children of missionaries and the fiancées of the boys at the adjoining Boone School, Central China's training school for Episcopalian ministers.[6]

In either of its two phases, the school was anathema to prevailing Chinese culture. It existed not only to educate girls, but also to mold *Christian* girls. Also, this education did not include the Confucian classics, the very basis of China's moral code. Thus, within the confines of traditional, Chinese orthodoxy, St. Hilda's represented a foothold for disseminating Christian heterodoxy.

Although the charge of advocating heterodox views could be leveled at all missionary schools, St. Hilda's could be accused of cultural subversion as well, because the continuation of traditional Chinese patriarchy depended upon the total subservience of women. Perpetuation of this system required that women remain ignorant, both in terms of academic knowledge and in terms of alternative social and cultural constructions. St. Hilda's thus represented a small crack in the foundation of Chinese patriarchy. Since the girls who attended St. Hilda's during this period were already the daughters of converts, the school had little chance of affecting Chinese conceptions of the world, as long as the existing social order that underpinned the Qing Dynasty remained unchanged.

With the founding of the Republic in 1912 came changes, however slight, in the cultural perception of women's roles in Chinese society that made it possible, if not desirable, for girls to be educated. As a result, wealthy, non-Christian families in the Wuhan area began to send their daughters to St. Hilda's, and with the sudden influx of new students, reports from St. Hilda's began to envision the imminent arrival of the long-awaited Christian vanguard. St. Hilda's was becoming "an oasis in a heathen city."[7] As enrollments swelled, a new St. Hilda's campus was established in 1914. This new campus, which included both a middle school and a high school, was located outside the city walls of Wuchang.[8] The enthusiasm for the socially transformative role to be played by the new St. Hilda's proved to be unfounded, however. In fact, it was not until the late 1920s that any tangible effects on the lives of St. Hilda's girls would actually be seen.

Nonetheless, this increased presence for St. Hilda's meant that more and more Chinese girls were now receiving educations that were designed to inculcate (1) a specific corpus of knowledge supporting a Western conception of the "way things are" (its worldview), and (2) a specific set of moral values supporting a Western, Christian conception of the "way things ought to be" (its ethos). The dual role of intergenerationally transmitting a culturally prescribed worldview and ethos represents the core aspect of any educational process. But at St. Hilda's, receiving an education meant that a foreign ethos and worldview were being learned and accepted by these girls. As a result, their education would have an extraordinary impact upon their lives. Thus, I have seen how my mother was resocialized through her education at St. Hilda's to embrace certain Western values concerning the role of women in society. It turned out that she was not alone.

As far as these women are concerned, however, this resocialization process was not without its costs, as it placed them in a unique (though not always necessarily beneficial) position within Chinese society.[9]

Auntie Chen: In the old society, who could afford to attend college? Am I not correct? The people who usually attended colleges were the sons and daughters of landlords and capitalists. They don't realize that in the old society, the churches provided the children of ministers and preachers free education so long as they attended schools and colleges that were affiliated with their denomination. That was the opportunity we had for obtaining an education. In our present-day society, they would say that such an education was enslaving us to the foreigners, what they call *"nuhua jiaoyu."* That is, they were using education to enslave you. *Nuhua jiaoyu.* Eventually, you would do their bidding. But at that time, I did not hold that opinion. I still don't hold that opinion.

Auntie Zhong: At that time, however, we were of the opinion that foreigners were invading our country, but all of our education came from the foreigners. (Laughs) At any rate, they trained many of our very talented people. Right? This is the truth.

Auntie Margaret Wang: From our very youth, we followed the religious life, Bible study, attending church services. From the point of view of today's society, of course, they feel as if we were anaesthetized *(mazui)*. But they did have a good influence upon us.

It is this "good influence" from St. Hilda's that had the greatest impact upon these women's lives. Neither "enslaved" nor "anaesthetized," these women were changed by their years at St. Hilda's, and this transformation paralleled the changes that occurred in China as well.

The first change came with the founding of the Republic in 1912 when a Western-style education was seen as a tool that could be used to help modernize China. As a result, wealthy, non-Christian families in the Wuhan area began to send their daughters to St. Hilda's. Traditionally in China, wealthy girls were sheltered from any contact with the world outside their family compounds, and if these girls were to receive more than just a cursory education, it could only happen at missionary boarding schools, where the existing cultural practice of female isolation was maintained. In fact, this isolation was almost total:

Auntie Zhou: [St. Hilda's was seen as] a convent. It was a boarding school and interaction with outsiders was not permitted. It was for this reason that, when I was still quite young, all of the girls [in my family] were sent to St. Hilda's to study. . . . At our school, you could not go home when you liked. We were not allowed to go home even on Sunday. We were only allowed to go home once every six months . . . once a school term. Every year there were two school terms, five months each.

The sense of separation from Chinese society was made even more complete as classes were taught in English, and Bible study was mandatory. Thus, the daughters of a portion of Wuhan's economic and social elite were being resocialized in an environment that fostered their acceptance of Western values.

It was not only their Western-centered education that distinguished St. Hilda's girls from the students in the public school system. As nationalistic fervor was increasingly sweeping over China, the school forbade the girls to engage in the political demonstrations that were common in the public school system; hence, their confinement to the school grounds effectively made them apolitical. Their social and political isolation continued until political events occurred in the country that altered the school's authority.

The second change that affected the lives of the girls at St. Hilda's came about because of the unique political situation in Wuhan. In the twentieth century, the Wuhan cities had been at the forefront of nationalistic movements in Central China, starting with the anti-Qing revolt that led to the 1911 revolution. Further, Hankou served briefly as China's capital following its liberation in 1926 from warlord control during the Northern Expedition—the Guomindang's nationalist revolution of 1926–1928.[10] Swept up in the apparent success of the Northern Expedition, mobs attacked the British concession in Hankou, and it was formally returned to the Chinese.[11] This capitulation by a foreign power could not have helped but swell nationalistic pride. However, factional conflict within the Guomindang was rife. This conflict led to a major split in the party in 1927 between the left-leaning political faction based in Hankou and the right-leaning military faction based in Nanchang.[12] In the end, the military faction won. Many Western powers began to reconsider their imperialist intentions in China and nominal stability began to return to the country. But in late 1926 and early 1927, mass demonstrations in Wuhan and other Yangzi Valley cities made the situation untenable for foreigners. Consequently, only five hundred out of eight thousand missionaries remained in the interior of China in 1927.[13] Thus, from the fall semester of 1926 through the fall semester of 1928, St. Hilda's held classes for only one semester.

The closing of St. Hilda's for this period had a direct impact on many of the girls. Released from their cloistered environment into a maelstrom of nationalistic fervor, the girls became more aware of political events occurring in Wuhan and became infused with a strong sense of nationalistic pride. When school reopened in the fall of 1928, the girls were no longer politically naïve. The closure of the school made it possible for them to become aware of and participate in the political demonstrations occurring in Wuhan. Thus, when the Japanese invaded China's Northeast *(Dongbei)* from their puppet state of Manchukuo in 1933, defeated the Chinese army, advanced on Peiping (Beijing), and forced the Chinese to agree to the terms of the Tangku Truce,[14] which "legitimated" the Japanese occupation of *Dongbei,* the girls were no longer politically indifferent. They consequently showed their heightened awareness by organizing a boycott of Japanese goods at the school:

Auntie Yi: I participated in [the anti-Japanese] campaign. Your mother was the president of the Student Body, and she initiated the campaign.

Mom Liu: During the Japanese occupation of *Dongbei,* there was a great deal of hatred of the Japanese because Chinese men and women were impressed into service and after the work was completed all of the workers were killed. While we were at St. Hilda's, we had several campaigns. One such campaign was a boycott of all Japanese products, an "Anti-Japanese Products Campaign." I would check the luggage of all incoming students and notate what Japanese-made products were in their possession. Each one of these items would be stamped with a chop stating "Japanese good" and the year, 1933. This campaign began in 1933 because the Japanese invaded *Dongbei* and the country was swept with anti-Japanese sentiment. Each Japanese-made product was stamped with the chop and the student was given a certificate. The following year, any products made in Japan that were brought back to school without the necessary chop and date were confiscated and sold. The money from the sale of such goods was donated to the wounded soldiers. There was a Chinese Red Cross that we would donate the money to. This campaign we did for three years beginning in '33. I was the Student Body President, and she helped me inspect the students' things.

Auntie Yi: Right, right. I remember that I participated in the anti-Japanese campaigns. And I remember accompanying your mother to make speeches about not purchasing Japanese goods. Then I participated in another campaign—I don't know who was the organizer for that campaign—but it was the campaign to assist the wounded soldiers.

Mom Liu: Correct. We would rip up old sheets to make into bandages to go into First Aid kits. I also would give haircuts to the students and save the hair to stuff into padded jackets for soldiers. Also, I embroidered the school's name on uniforms for twenty-five cents each. This money was all donated to the Chinese Red Cross.

With their increased awareness about political events occurring within China, the school's administration could no longer keep them quiescent within the school itself. When a student leader, my mother, was threatened with dismissal for disseminating information she had obtained from reading government bulletins that had been discarded—unread—by the school's headmistress, the students organized a strike to show their solidarity, and she was not expelled:

Auntie Liu: When I was in high school, there was an incident. I'm not exactly clear because I've gone through so many of the Communist movements that I have become confused. I remember there was the incident when I joined in a protest against Deaconess Clark. Right, right. . . . It had to do with your mother. Wasn't your mother once locked up? I don't quite remember.

Judy: Correct, correct. She was locked up by Deaconess Clark.

Auntie Liu: She was locked up and the remainder of the students refused to attend class. We would not listen to [the teachers]. Because we were on strike and refused to attend classes, it seems that they had no other choice but to let your mother go. It seems to me that was the case. That is how I remember the event.

The politicizing of the student body began at the time that secularization of the schools was at the forefront of Chinese nationalist policies. Once the Guomindang achieved nominal control over China, missionary schools became a target as the question of school registration arose. Registration meant the abandonment of two separate and distinct educational systems in China—the regular Chinese public school system and the foreign-supported missionary school system. With registration, missionary schools would become, in theory, secularized Chinese institutions. The significance of this transformation was not lost on the students:

Auntie Yu: We fought wars with foreigners. As a consequence, because China lost, we had to allow missionaries to enter China. [At St. Hilda's], it was an Episcopalian church and missionary group. Originally the school was organized by foreigners. All of the courses were originally taught in English. Do you understand? It was entirely taught by foreigners using English. With the exception of Chinese classes, everything was taught in English. . . . [After the Northern Expedition], all of the schools had to register with the government. They had to register that it was a foreigner-operated school; that it was a missionary school. Right? You had to register with the Board of Education; all missionary schools had to register. This registration demanded that the courses be taught in Chinese. From that time on, the courses, with the exception of English, had to be taught in Chinese.

Prior to registration, the goal of St. Hilda's had been to produce an evangelical vanguard of Chinese women. From this perspective, the school was less than successful. The girls who attended were primarily the daughters of converts already. With the exception of Chinese, all courses were conducted in English and the Chinese that was taught was *Putonghua* (Mandarin), not the indigenous Hubei dialect. How could the graduates of St. Hilda's be expected to proselytize in the countryside if they were unfamiliar with the local dialect?

With registration, the focus of the school necessarily changed. According to government regulations, classes had to be taught in Chinese, the principal of the school had to be Chinese, graduates of the school would receive Chinese diplomas, and chapel attendance and religious instruction had to be voluntary.[15] Further, the faculty became predominantly Chinese. Added to the curriculum were the Three Principles of Sun Yat-sen, which had to be taught by a Guomindang Party member, and a course in ethics that had to be offered as an alternative to religious studies.[16] While these rules were the law, the school was able to bypass some of them:

Auntie Hazel Wang: After St. Hilda's reopened . . . it was supposed to be supervised by the Chinese, [but] it was still Deaconess Clark who was the acting principal. They said she was the acting principal; however, all of the authority was still in her hands. She was supposed to be acting in Deaconess Chen-Jiang's place.

Mom Liu: I remember that I never saw [Chen-Jiang] while I was there. It was always Deaconess Clark. Everyone knew she had the power. We didn't even see Deaconess Chen-Jiang!

Auntie Hazel Wang: She was supposed to act in place of Deaconess Chen-Jiang. . . . [St. Hilda's] was supposed to be under the supervision of the Chinese. We had a Chinese Deaconess in charge only for appearance sake. It was one of the regulations. . . . But in reality, Deaconess Clark was the real principal.

Registration sparked great debate within the missionary community.[17] From the perspective of many missionaries, education was secondary to evangelism. To accept registration would mean placing evangelism in a subordinate role. Many schools chose to close their doors rather than to register. St. Hilda's, however, decided to remain open and registered in 1930.

Registration for St. Hilda's was not as traumatic as it was for many schools. The reason for this is the transformation that occurred in the religious orientation of the faculty members at St. Hilda's. The American women who taught at St. Hilda's were all college graduates, they were single, and they came to China to do good work. Because women missionaries could not preach, they assumed the role of educators. But these women were different from their predecessors; whereas many of their predecessors were the wives of ministers, which made teaching a mere adjunct to their lives as wives and mothers, most of these women came specifically to be teachers and to teach the social gospel.

Basic to the concept of the social gospel is the belief that social service is a legitimate means of evangelism and that evangelism can be an effective instrument for social change as well as for salvation. While previous attempts at evangelism dealt with the notion of personal salvation, the social gospel was directed toward an increased democratization of this world. The social gospel was predicated on the belief that a fellowship can exist between God and man and that this fellowship can be attained through the cultivation of correct attitudes and the development of the right skills.[18] Just exactly what these "correct attitudes" and "right skills" are is somewhat nebulous, but the proposed result—the creation of "purposeful activity . . . proceeding in a social environment"—is not.[19] It was hoped that service to the welfare of the whole community would result in a beneficial social reconstruction of the society along Western lines. While the spiritualism of pure evangelism went unheeded, the fusing of spiritual with secular in the social gospel had an explosive impact on these girls.

The secular aspect of the social gospel legitimated the nascent nationalistic views held by these girls and, in a sense, broke the element of cultural subversion that hindered the spiritual side of the missionary movement. By secularizing the religious message, the social gospel transcended the sectarianism inherent in pure evangelism. It was able to separate the moral basis of Christianity from its Episcopalian sectarianism. As a consequence, St. Hilda's produced a significant number of Christians; however, it produced very few Episcopalians. It was this inherent theological relativism in the social gospel that permitted the school to deemphasize its sectarianism in order to register with the government.

Religious indoctrination for personal salvation gave way to the principle of "Christian love and concern for the true welfare of the people."[20] A major emphasis on social service was stressed. Thus, the goal of St. Hilda's became the desire to create Christian educators, medical workers, and social workers who would work for the good of China. (Coincidentally or not, these were the only occupations available to educated women in China.) In order for these girls to successfully perform the "good works" dictated by the social gospel, another of its aspects had to be inculcated into them: the girls had to be self-sufficient and independent. Yet women still had a dependent and subservient role in Chinese society. Thus, instilling the values of self-sufficiency and independence would be no easy matter. Everything at the school was designed to promote these values, and the women themselves provide information as to how this inculcation occurred. Interestingly, it was their moral education—not the transference of knowledge per se—that had the greatest effect upon these women. As Auntie Zhou summarized it: "Many of my habits, my good traits were all developed while I was attending St. Hilda's." Or from Auntie Xiang: "What we learned in high school in terms of living influenced our later lives."

Students from St. Hilda's feel that they learned the value and desirability of working for their own well-being through their education. Thus, from the perspective of traditional China, St. Hilda's graduates epitomized the transformation in the role of elite women that was overtaking China:

Auntie Xiang: Women also have a position in the workplace. It was not like this in the old society. In that society, once you married, you were expected to stay at home and be the mistress. Then you were expected to hire someone to take care of you all. You understand. You were not allowed to work. Now being a nurse at that time was a relatively independent occupation. A nurse could find independent employment. It was also very easy to find work. . . . Moreover, the income nurses made was quite good. I could support myself. That was something I learned from school. I learned that I could and should support myself. Even though I was a girl, I could support myself.

Judy: Do you think this [desire to work] had anything to do with your education at St. Hilda's? Were you influenced by your education?
Auntie Zhou: In fact, definitely. At St. Hilda's they stressed that we should be independent. I wanted to work. I knew I could work. Even when I was pregnant with my first son, I wanted to work. I complained so much that my husband finally allowed me to go and teach at a middle school. I did not want to stay home and do nothing. It is a good thing that I did go to work or else I would be lost today. My education helped me.

Auntie Margaret Wang: Everyone should have self-motivation in learning. I think this also comes from [my education]. Also, everyone
should work; everyone should have their own work. Look at me, I
was only fifteen when I had my first job. This was taught to us. It
wasn't because my mother and father wanted the money. I wanted to
be a very good teacher. Therefore, this philosophy of being on your
own *(duli gongzuo)* came from my education.

Clearly, the school was successful in inculcating the values of self-
sufficiency and independence within these women, but these values were
tempered by a moral code that stressed that the women should be "conscientious and hardworking." Thus, Auntie Zhou could state that: "I feel
that I am an honest, hardworking, capable person because of my education at St. Hilda's." Whereas, Auntie Huang held that:

> St. Hilda's was very good. We received a very good education. Hon-
> esty—we learned that at St. Hilda's. When you work, you must have
> responsibility. These things were an integral part of our education at St.
> Hilda's. Honesty, keep your word—we all learned this at St. Hilda's.
> Have responsibility at work; have responsibility in all work and in
> dealing with people. These were all taught as part of our education
> there. I really thought St. Hilda's was very good. We were taught re-
> spect for order; this was very good.

Self-sufficiency and independence were promoted at St. Hilda's in a
number of ways. Abilities of any sort were recognized and nurtured by the
staff. Students with leadership abilities were encouraged to run for student association offices while others were made dormitory leaders, class
leaders, or the like. Those with athletic abilities served not only on teams
but also were made the exercise leaders who led the required daily calis-
thenics. Those with scholastic abilities were encouraged to be tutors for
their classmates or assumed teaching responsibilities in the community.
Each Sunday, a group of teachers and volunteering students regularly visited the homes of local families. They taught parents about sanitation, nu-
trition, and hygiene. They helped bathe the sick and elderly; administered
minor medical attention; groomed young boys and girls; and even cleaned
the homes of local residents. The school started a literacy program in the
neighborhood with both teachers and students serving as tutors for children, which evolved into a small neighborhood school in 1935. Although
many of the girls who initially volunteered were only doing it in order to

avoid boredom, many later chose professions that were subtly being promoted during these weekly excursions. Several women mentioned that their love for teaching or medicine was first stimulated by their community service activities. According to Auntie Hazel Wang, "It was during this time that I discovered I loved to work with children. That is one of the major reasons why I became a teacher." Moreover, students learned never to consider themselves better than anyone else. "We learned the principles of equality—not to denigrate the poor or elevate the rich."[21]

Social service was also fostered in the school by its emphasis on "health and hygiene."[22] With tuberculosis rampant in China, prevention of this illness at St. Hilda's was a paramount concern. Thus, the doctrine of the healing benefits of fresh air was rigorously employed. In fact, the rooms used for rehabilitation were surrounded by a porch, and girls were assigned two to a room. Given the temperature extremes in Wuhan, these rooms were definitely conducive to a speedy recovery. Dormitory rules dictated that bedding was to be aired daily as a means of sanitation. The following exchange indicates how this practice was enforced at St. Hilda's:

Auntie Huang: Also, the system of cleaning and fixing your beds was also a good system.

Mom Liu: Every morning, you had to air your blankets; you were not supposed to fold your blankets immediately. Each one of us had a white thermal-like blanket. Each one of us was required to purchase one before coming to St. Hilda's. Every morning we had to fold back our blankets and air them out. If you made your bed immediately, you were fined. I was often fined. (Laughs) Each room had a room leader. After she woke up and washed her face, she would examine each of the beds to see whether or not they were made properly. She would then report to the Boarding Matron. Once a month, you were issued a moral character *(pinxing)* grade. It was based on 100 percent. For sloppy beds, for instance, you were deducted 2 percent. I was always deducted. (Laughs) Also, every month the room that had the highest score was awarded a gold star, which was hung on the door. The room where I slept never could receive a gold star. (Laughs) For that reason, I was disliked by some of the students. Second place was a silver star. You had to receive high grades for moral character or you couldn't graduate. I almost didn't graduate because my moral character grades were low. (Laughs)

Auntie Huang: I remember that you had to air the blankets. After you had aired the blankets, then you could make the bed. That was a very good system.

The interesting fact is that even today, many of these women—my mother included—keep windows open year-round and still turn back their bedding first thing each morning. From this perspective, St. Hilda's had a lasting impact on the girls' lives.

Self-sufficiency and independence were also encouraged within St. Hilda's itself. Students who needed a haircut, laundry washed, shoes repaired, or clothing mended could seek the services of the student association's self-help organizations. Any girl, but especially one needing financial assistance, could earn income by working at these various services. Surprisingly, this did not serve as a wedge between the richer, tuition-paying students and the poorer, tuition-free students. Instead, it taught students to cooperate:

Mom Liu: Do you remember when you helped me wash my cotton padded blanket? I remember that I had already torn it apart and decided to wash it myself because it hadn't been washed in two weeks. I tore it all apart and put it in the water. And there it was. I didn't know how to wash it. And furthermore, I didn't know how to wring it out now that it was wet. I was in a panic about what to do when you showed up and said: "You big family girls don't know how to do anything. Let me in, and I'll take care of it for you." I never saw anyone who could handle a washboard as good as you. In no time, you had the blanket washed, wrung, and hung up to dry.

Auntie Chen: (Laughing) I remember that. You looked so helpless. Being from a large, rich family, you had never seen how it was done. You really would have been in terrible shape if I hadn't come along that day.

Besides encouraging the students to be independent and self-sufficient, the female teachers themselves proved to be exemplary role models. The foreign teachers were single, self-supporting women who made the trek from the United States to Central China. They were independent and self-sufficient themselves. If these foreign-born teachers could do it, the consensus of the girls at St. Hilda's was that they could do it as well. This spirit of independence was complemented by a spirit of caring. Thus, many of the students recalled the genuine care and affection that many teachers had for them:

Auntie Hazel Wang: [Some of the teachers at St. Hilda's] felt that I wasn't mature. "You're still not mature enough in your work. The best thing you should do is continue your education." They felt that I should continue my education. I answered, "I don't want to continue my education." Miss Sherman asked me, "Why don't you want to continue your studies?" "I don't want to continue my studies," I replied, "I want to be independent." She said, "You're still young now." I said, "I don't consider myself too young. I feel that I can work." Later, she said, "We all think it would be best if you continue your studies. Is it because you have some difficulties?" "Of course there are difficulties! Attending college requires a great deal of money." She later said to me, "If there was someone who was willing to help you, would you go? There is someone who is willing to help you." It was she, [in English] Miss Sherman. She told me to go home and ask my parents. I thought to myself, "This still isn't a good idea. After a person assists you, you are always under some obligation to listen to another person." I wasn't that type of person. I was never willing to listen to anyone else. I said, "I have to consider this. If I do accept your assistance, in what way will I be obligated to you in the future?" She said, "I'll tell you, we will just be very good friends." She said, [in English] "As a friend, I can help you; however, there is no obligation whatsoever." Under those circumstances, I could accept the money. I said, "I will take this into consideration."

For all its good points, however, students also recounted stories of aspects they did *not* like about St. Hilda's. Chief among the complaints was the poor treatment of Chinese male faculty members. Not only did students perceive them as not being treated with the respect that was their due but also their living quarters were far below the standards of the foreigners:

Mom Liu: We used to have Chinese teachers who worked there. They were taken advantage of. While the foreigners lived very comfortably in the foreigner house, the Chinese teachers lived in terrible quarters. In the winter, it was bitterly cold. The foreigners had steam and were quite nice and warm while the Chinese teachers didn't even have a stove. The students in my class banded together and protested that they were taking advantage of the Chinese. We created such a nuisance and such a fuss that eventually stoves were installed for the Chinese teachers as well.

Auntie Chen: Right, right. That was always the case. If we felt that an injustice was done, one of the students—usually your mother or another one of the leaders—would call a meeting and we would discuss. Then the entire group would go and see the headmistress and complain.

Some teachers as well as the headmistress were seen as currying favor with the parents of paying students and considering themselves "better than the Chinese."

Auntie Yu: There is one thing that I remember about the headmistress, Deaconess Clark. She was very conscious about money. She would always treat the daughters with money better than those who did not have money. . . . She was supposed to be a Christian, yet she treated the daughters of the Chinese missionaries and preachers far less courteously than those who paid. I never liked that. She would flatter, fawn on *(bajie)* the parents of tuition-paying daughters. Otherwise, she tended to look down upon us. I don't think that she really liked the Chinese very much. I never liked her very much.

From the recollections of the students, Deaconess Julia Clark seems to be the symbolic embodiment of all that was bad about Western imperialism and the Chinese sense of inferiority vis-à-vis the West. She catered to the wealthy, dispensed discipline, and undermined Chinese authority at the school. Yet it is clear that these stories are contradictory. For example, one cannot fawn on the wealthy and at the same time threaten to expel the daughter of one of Wuhan's wealthiest and most influential families. As a consequence, the character of Julia Clark represents one of the difficulties of doing ethnography through the use of oral history. By lacking the possibility of observing social interactions at the school, only the students' side of those interactions is told. If archival sources were not available, we would be left with the myth of the "negative" influence of Deaconess Clark, and this tale would not accurately depict the complexity of her life as a missionary.[23]

Good and bad role models alike, however, inspired the girls to do their best. The ethnocentrism of some of the teachers was matched by a nationalistically inspired ethnocentrism on the part of the students. Thus, some of the women interviewed stated that they became fierce in their determination "to prove that the Chinese were as good as [the missionaries]."[24] This paradox affected the students' lives at St. Hilda's. On the one hand, they had a strong dislike for the foreign teachers as embodiments of the results of China's military weakness and its inability to overcome foreign military cultural inroads. On the other hand, the moral education they received was clearly seen as impacting their lives beneficially. If nothing else, going to school at St. Hilda's taught these women how to deal with ambiguity and change.

The impact of self-sufficiency and independence on these girls was extraordinary. It is on this point that Chinese fears about the possibility of cultural subversion coming from a missionary education have some merit. The major message received by the girls at St. Hilda's was that they alone were responsible for their well-being. Their future success was, therefore, independent of the cultural traditions that defined a woman's social role as that of wife or mother. In fact, a small but significant number of these women chose not to marry or, if they did, they married in later life. While the reasons for this vary from fear of childbirth to having to support their family, the fact is that many of these women saw the tragedy of their mothers who, widowed early in life, could not remarry due to tradition. With no education and no sons to provide for them, it became incumbent upon their daughters to support them. If these women had married, their mothers would have been doomed.

Auntie Yu: Look at the old society; it really was quite cruel. [My paternal great aunt] never remarried, she couldn't remarry. My mother also grew up in that feudalistic society. My paternal grandmother, my mother, and my paternal great aunt were all widows. My mother was a widow and she never remarried. She never even mentioned it, never thought of it. They were all widows. . . . As a consequence, I had to be very independent. Because there were so many women, single women, in our family, I learned to be independent. Even though there were no men in my family, I believed that we could survive, that I could do something to help out the family. So long as I had a job, I didn't need to have a man around to help us survive. I didn't really mind not having a man around.

No matter what justification they had for not marrying, these women had been taught that they could succeed on their own, and they learned that lesson well:

Auntie Yu: When I was younger, I realized that if I could work, I could earn enough to support myself and be independent. That is something I learned while I was at St. Hilda's. They always stressed that we should be independent. I knew that I could take care of myself and my mother and paternal great aunt if I worked. We didn't need a man around because I was capable. That is one reason why I don't regret not marrying.

Auntie Xiang: Many [of us] did not marry. In that society, it was very unusual but if someone asked me I would answer, "If you liked to be independent and if you wanted to have your own profession, then you were much freer." Understand? You were much freer to do what you wanted. Then there was no one to place restrictions upon you. That is why many of us chose not to marry and chose to live alone. Furthermore, those of us who obtained our educations in missionary schools were different from other people in terms of our lives and our training. We had different circumstances than most and this perhaps had an influence. Speaking for myself, I really liked to travel. I would work one year at a place and then I would change jobs. Another year and I would change again. Understand? Therefore, I knew a lot of people, and I saw all types of people. In the course of my lifetime, I heard about a great deal of unhappiness about people who were trapped by their circumstances. I had some friends who used to tease me that I heard too many unhappy stories and that is why I chose not to marry. (Laughs) For that reason, I thought a single person had greater independence and that is the main reason why I chose not to marry. I wanted to be independent. I voluntarily chose to be independent.

That both Auntie Yu and Auntie Xiang felt that they could succeed on their own demonstrates the degree to which being educated at St. Hilda's influenced their lives, and they were not alone. Yet when these women refer to education, they mean moral education—education as an acculturating and socializing agent—and not education as a means for inculcating facts. When asked about the impact of their education at St. Hilda's, the women did not refer to course contents but referred to what Auntie Hazel Wang captured in her insightful statement that "[missionaries] gave me a model of behavior by which to follow. I am of the opinion that they gave me an excellent model by which to follow. This type of thing, this realization comes slowly. You don't realize it yourself, but you are constantly learning it." Thus, the girls learned to be honest, hardworking, and responsible women; to value work as an important and integral part of their lives; and to be self-sufficient, independent, and orderly in leading their lives. In other words, the moral education received by the girls at St. Hilda's resocialized them into believing that it was possible for women to take a more active role in society than existing Chinese patriarchal norms permitted, and they acted according to that belief.

Ultimately, what do these reminiscences of St. Hilda's School for Girls tell us? At their broadest level, they tell us that education is more than the transfer of knowledge from one generation to the next. These women rarely mentioned the actual course content of what they were taught. The inculcation of this knowledge is clearly incidental to them when compared to the moral aspects of knowledge that they were taught. This is not too surprising given the cultural history of China. Entrance into the bureaucracy—the basic structure of dynastic China—was based upon the ability to understand and recapitulate the Confucian classics. Thus, morality was irrevocably associated with education in Chinese culture by the time these women entered St. Hilda's. If anything, the moral focus of the school was more in line with historical Confucian educational concerns than were the government's attempts to impose Western-style educational content and practices on the developing public school system.[25]

That these women were socialized and acculturated into a new environment is clearly evident. While Chinese culture is strongly influenced by a collectivist ethos that places individuals rigidly within set social roles (for example, within the family or within the workplace), St. Hilda's varied this pattern ever so slightly. As a boarding school, the focus was inherently collective—these women were "St. Hilda's girls." Further, they were divided into "big sister" (girls in Grades Ten through Twelve) and "little sister" (girls in Grades Seven through Nine) cohorts, where a big sister in Grade Twelve was assigned to look after a girl in Grade Nine and so on. In the end, St. Hilda's produced, as most boarding schools do, a strong sense of belonging to a group that exists even until today.

The biggest impact upon these women, however, occurred in their reacculturation toward accepting more Western beliefs. The lives of many of these women are a fitting tribute to St. Hilda's ability to subvert Chinese patriarchy. The school provided women role models who showed their students that women could succeed on their own. This reacculturation is ironic, however, since the teachers themselves functioned within a strongly patriarchal system that held that married women could no longer teach because the roles of wife and mother were seen as far more important socially. Thus, a letter from the National Council of the Protestant Episcopal Church in the United States of America written in 1933 to Miss Dorothea K. Wakeman, who would become a teacher at St. Hilda's, stated, in contractual terms that:

> Because a surprisingly large number of our appointees have been
> married soon after arriving in the field, the Department of Missions
> feels that in justice to the work, it must ask that in the future young
> women appointees shall agree if the case should arise, not to be mar-
> ried within a period of three years after arrival in the field. This may
> seem like anticipating a question that is, to say the least, not uppermost
> in your mind; but we would like to have your statement that in the
> event of appointment, you are willing to agree to this request.[26]

Further, the strong class basis of traditional Chinese society was undermined by the egalitarian practices taught to these girls. Thus, it was not
difficult for many of these women to accept the Maoist variant of Chinese
communism. From the social gospel–inspired emphasis of the school,
these girls learned the value of social service—of working for the collective good. If any association with a deity is removed, then the goals and
practices of the social gospel are embodied in the Maoist dictum to "Serve
the People." Thus, the egalitarianism of Maoist ideology was similar to
the ethos that these women had become reacculturated to at St. Hilda's.

If we can conclude anything from this study of the women who attended St. Hilda's, it is that education is more than the mere memoriza-
tion and regurgitation of dates and facts. We are also taught, though less
directly, how to fit within our society and to learn what our society holds
dear. These are not educational outcomes that can be quantified for
analysis the way that graduation rates and test scores can be. In many
ways it is the moral components of education that have the most meaningful impact upon our lives, and these components are the least
amenable for statistical analysis. Studies that overlook these subtle aspects of education, whether qualitative or quantitative, may construct a
beautiful body of evidence, but that body has no heart.

At the level of the heart, reconstructing the past with these women
has given me a new appreciation for how inherently interesting people's
lives are. By teasing out the threads of a collective history from these
women's memories, I have been able to weave a tapestry of St. Hilda's
life as they remembered it. Yet that tapestry is replete with flaws, because
it is woven with the fragile threads of events that occurred over half a
century ago. Working with reminiscences has made me aware of the ten-
uousness of memory and the relativity of "truth." Truth is neither absolute nor fixed; rather, it is always subject to reinterpretation. Thus,
while the facts of the events that affected these women's lives remain
consistent, their meanings are fluid. Within the contingent, perspectival

world of St. Hilda's, I have come to find that whether one was a Chinese student or an American teacher affected how experiences were perceived both inside and outside the walls of St. Hilda's.

Given the perspectival differences that affect our constructions of the world, it is not surprising that reminiscences are clouded by the passage of time. Rarely does one consciously reflect upon the meaning of life events—particularly when they are occurring. That is, we tend to see our lives as continuous, not as something episodic. The act of reminiscing produces a reconstruction of the past that is often more appreciated in hindsight because it becomes placed within the context of the present. That specific details become embellished, forgotten, or inaccurate is inevitable.

If memories are inherently faulty, then doing an ethnography by means of oral histories requires that a researcher become acutely aware of the context of events surrounding informants' lives. Thus, it becomes necessary to know more than merely the people involved. A knowledge of both a general history of the country being studied and a specific history of the place being studied is imperative. To have studied St. Hilda's without an awareness of the historical contexts of Wuhan, of China, or of missiology would have produced a tapestry of all warp and no woof. However, if I have done my work well, then this written account will be a "faithful" representation of life at St. Hilda's at the height of Republican China.

NOTES

1. Unless otherwise noted, all the quotations used in this paper come from personal interviews audio-recorded by Judith Liu in the People's Republic of China in 1982.

2. Wuchang, along with Hankou and Hanyang, composes the urban industrial center commonly known as Wuhan. Wuhan is located about five hundred miles inland from Shanghai at the confluence of the Yangzi and Han Rivers.

3. Henrietta F. Boone, "The Jane Bohlen Memorial School," *The Spirit of Missions: An Illustrated Monthly Review of Christian Missions* 44 (1879): 174–175.

4. For a more in-depth look at the history of St. Hilda's, see Judith Liu and Donald P. Kelly, "'An Oasis in a Heathen Land': St. Hilda's School for Girls, Wuchang, 1928–1936," in *Christianity in China: From the Eighteenth Century to the Present,* ed. Daniel H. Bays (Stanford: Stanford University Press, 1996), 228–242.

5. "St. Hilda's School, Wuchang, China," *The Spirit of Missions: An Illustrated Monthly Review of Christian Missions* 65 (1900): 374–376.

6. For a discussion of the Boone School, see John L. Coe, *Huachung University* (New York: United Board for Christian Higher Education in Asia, 1962).

7. "Impressions of St. Hilda's," *The Spirit of Missions: An Illustrated Monthly Review of Christian Missions* 76 (1911): 318.

8. Dorothy Mills, "St. Hilda's, Wuchang," *The Spirit of Missions: An Illustrated Monthly Review of Christian Missions* 81 (1916): 227.

9. Because of their foreign educations, the patriotism of these women was frequently questioned during the many mass campaigns that were launched between the founding of the People's Republic of China in 1949 and the end of the Cultural Revolution in 1976.

10. The exact dates of the nationalist revolution are open to debate. For differing analyses, see Harold Isaacs, *The Tragedy of the Chinese Revolution,* 2nd rev. ed. (Stanford: Stanford University Press, 1961), and Donald A. Jordan, *The Northern Expedition: China's National Revolution of 1926–1928* (Honolulu: University of Hawaii Press, 1976).

11. See James T. Sheridan, *China in Disintegration: The Republican Era in Chinese History, 1912–1949* (New York: The Free Press, 1975), 180.

12. Ibid., 171. Nanjing became the Nationalist's capital in 1927.

13. Jessie Gregory Lutz, *China and the Christian Colleges: 1850–1950* (Ithaca: Cornell University Press, 1971), 260.

14. See Lloyd E. Eastman, *The Abortive Revolution: China under Nationalist Rule, 1927–1937* (Cambridge, Mass.: Harvard University Press, 1990 [1974]), 246–7.

15. Prior to registration, St. Hilda's graduates received diplomas issued in the United States.

16. The Three Principles of Sun Yat-sen were: (1) Nationality (the recognition of China as a nation); (2) Democracy (suffrage and the establishment of women's rights); and (3) Livelihood (equalization of land ownership, control of capitalism, and nationalization of public utilities). From H. Owen Chapman, *The Chinese Revolution: A Record of the Period Under Communist Control as Seen from the Nationalist Capitol Hankow* (London: Constable & Co Ltd., 1928; Hyperion Reprint Edition, 1977), 64. (From Chapman's title it is not difficult to see how the West viewed the political philosophy of the left Guomindang and why the protofascistic right Guomindang was viewed as a more favorable alternative.)

17. For a discussion of registration, see John W. Wood, D.C.L., "The Pro and Con of Registration of Christian Schools in China," *The Spirit of Missions: An Illustrated Monthly Review of Christian Missions* 93 (1928): 653–655.

18. Deaconess Julia A. Clark, "Voluntary Religious Education in China," *The Spirit of Missions: An Illustrated Monthly Review of Christian Missions* 95 (1930): 380.

19. Ibid.

20. *Handbooks on the Missions of the Episcopal Church,* rev. ed., no. 1, China (New York: The National Council of the Protestant Episcopal Church, 1932).

21. Liu interview, 1989.

22. "Health and hygiene" were the terms used by those who attended St. Hilda's to describe the emphasis on sanitation stressed by the school. From Liu interviews, 1982.

23. Deaconess Julia Clark was assigned to St. Hilda's following the death in 1923 of Deaconess Katherine Scott, her longtime friend who was in charge of St. Hilda's. Since Deaconess Clark did not enjoy working in a major city, each year she would request a transfer back to Yichang, Hubei, to work with training Chinese Bible women and was sent to Yunmeng, Hubei, in 1933. In her annual report during her furlough of 1932, she informed Bishop Logan Roots in Hankou that she had joined the Socialist Party in the United States because she believed that its views coincided more with her own Christian convictions of working with and for the people.

24. Liu interview, 1989.

25. For a thorough history of education in China, see Suzanne Pepper, *Radicalism and Education Reform in 20th-Century China: The Search for an Ideal Development Model* (New York: Cambridge University Press, 1996).

26. A. B. Parson, New York, to Dorothea K. Wakeman, California, 17 May 1933, from the private collection of Dorothea W. Howe, Solana Beach, California.

CHAPTER 8
Conclusion
VANDRA LEA MASEMANN

Now it is time to return to the original purposes of this book, to look at all the accounts we have read, to see how these purposes have been achieved. Donald Kelly, in his Introduction, states that the volume is somewhat Janus-faced, in that the book deals with the task of doing ethnographic research, as well as dealing with the task of writing about education in China. Thus method and content are the two sides of this face. It is important to reflect on these two aspects of the studies presented here, not only in each separate chapter, but in their entirety. In other words, what have we learned about ethnographic method, and what have we learned about China? Moreover, the melding of these two tasks yields a third possible question: What have we learned about doing ethnographic studies of education in China? This concluding chapter will examine the answers to each of these questions.

DONALD P. KELLY:
INTRODUCTION: A DISCUSSION ON ETHNOGRAPHY

Donald Kelly identifies five possible varieties of ethnography in his introductory chapter: classical, interpretive, feminist, postmodern, and critical. He also presents a historical overview of the changes that have taken place in the research stance adopted in each. The chapters in this book say a great deal about taking a stand on the particular uses of ethnography that are important to the writers, so there is no unitary view or reified notion of there being only one "real" ethnography.

Kelly notes the drawbacks of classical ethnography in its association with an essentially colonial relationship between anthropologists and the people they studied, with a belief in scientific rationality, and with the ideology of the inevitability of human progress, as in the idea of social evolution which was the foundation of the idea of "development." Kelly points out that in these conditions, "the author tends to disappear from a scientifically based, normative relativistic ethnographic text" (Kelly, 6).

This book represents various attempts to study education in China from the stance primarily of the second approach, interpretive ethnography. Kelly states that "ethnography's value lies in providing detailed interpretations" (Kelly, 2). He notes that the underlying epistemological assumptions in the interpretive approach are almost the opposite of the classical approach: a more personal, equal relationship between the researchers and those they research, a willingness to study the seemingly irrational and to allow for other forms of knowledge production than the formally scientific, and a less linear view of human progress than was fashionable during the heyday of the social evolutionists. He also discusses the influence these values have on the creation of the ethnographic text itself, in that the text itself can be seen as the product of the negotiation of meanings between ethnographer and informant, and in that the relationship between them has influenced the creation of the text itself. In Kelly's words, "ethnographies are not seen as realistic representations of cultural facts, but, rather, they are seen as creative fictions" (Kelly, 9). Several of the authors in this book grapple with the theme of their relationship with those they are researching and the creation of the account that results from their research endeavor.

The third approach to ethnography is the postmodern approach, or perhaps one should say postmodern approaches. Kelly discusses the impact of philosophical debates about the power relationship between ethnographers and the sociocultural context in which they work. He sees reflexivity not as a new invention but as having its roots in the *Verstehensoziologie* of Max Weber and in more recent sociologists such as Pierre Bourdieu, with his epistemological insistence on the need for researchers to be able to grasp the taken-for-granted cultural arbitrariness of their own society (Kelly, 11). Kelly argues in favor of an "authorized" discourse that "is a compelling representation that engages and informs the reader" (Kelly, 14), as long as it avoids the "potential descent into bathos" (Kelly, ibid.).

The fourth approach, loosely labeled "feminist," is an attempt to deal with the "issues of gender, color, voice, and power" (Kelly, 15). Kelly situates his discussion of feminism within the interpretive framework, and notes that it raises the same questions about the position of the researcher and the production of the text. Several of the authors, particularly Heidi Ross and Judith Liu, address these issues directly in their analysis of the relationship between themselves and those they interviewed. What is not addressed in this book is the positioning of forms of feminist analysis within the other ethnographic approaches, particularly the critical approach.

Kelly gives short shrift to critical approaches to ethnography, especially those that are linked with activist approaches to educational and pedagogical reform. He sees potential pitfalls in advocating for the groups one is studying in that the power differential is rendered overt and the resulting situation of the participants is sometimes fraught with danger. His analysis is, once again, embedded in the interpretive framework, and it omits any reference to structural analyses, for example, of the role of social class, race, or colonial factors in the reproduction of inequality in schooling. There are hints in the experiences of the researchers, particularly Heidi Ross, and Lynn Paine and Bryan DeLany, as well as Gerry Postiglione and Kai-Ming Cheng, that these authors ran into structures that prevented them from addressing some of the research questions in which they were interested.

If one looks at this entire collection of papers from the perspectives outlined in these approaches, it is clear that the interpretive approach is the main focus of the book. However, it is important to see them as a segment of the possibilities for ethnographic research. For example, the existence of power relationships between these researchers and those who had the authority to grant or deny them permission to do their research makes it clear that they were part of a much larger set of structures in China in which they were relatively powerless. Moreover, from a postmodern perspective, these mininarratives are quite overshadowed by the metanarratives of the long sweep of Chinese history and the debates over research methodology. However, we now turn to the individual chapters to see what the answers are to our original questions.

KAI-MING CHENG: UNDERSTANDING BASIC EDUCATION POLICIES IN CHINA: AN ETHNOGRAPHIC APPROACH

Doing Ethnography

This chapter presents the general overview of Chinese education, and its main contribution to the book is that it makes the case for using ethnographic methods to understand the actual process of education. It shows how difficult it is to do large-scale surveys of education in a country without first understanding the right questions to ask. It presents the case for doing small-scale pilot research in order to find out how people react to the wording of research questions, as well as to the content of the questions. It also shows that ethnographic methodology can be important in formulating an evaluation of policy, either before or after its implementation. Another use of ethnography in this study was in the researcher's ability to tap into the needs of the local people, rather than impose a top-down model of implementation. It was possible to speak with groups in the local communities and to hear firsthand what their perceptions of their needs were. This kind of research, which is somewhat similar to market research as it is known in North America, made it possible for policymakers to gain insights into the contextual factors and processes that affected basic education.

Studying Chinese Education

This chapter makes it clear how large a country China is, and how difficult it is to get an accurate picture of the way education operates in various parts of the country. The larger the research site, the more difficult it is to do small-scale case studies. However, the use of ethnographic methods to identify the characteristics of the sample one is studying is very useful, and makes overgeneralizations less likely.

It also gives the reader some idea of the complexity of the policy-making process in regard to education in China. In this particular case, the issue of the spread of basic education was an important policy question that could be researched in several countries, since the attention of the world was going to be focused on it at the Education for All conference in Jomtien, Thailand, in 1990. Chinese colleagues raised the issue of intellectual attainments not being the most important goals of education but, instead, moral norms, life skills, and other important factors essential for participating in the social life of China.

Another fact specific to China that was of interest to the researchers was the high attendance rates at school. When researchers probed the possible reasons for this, they found that the parents they questioned held a holistic view concerning the overall value of education, but did not express their aspirations for educational outcomes in relation to occupational status or economic utility.

The researchers concluded that it would be unwise for policymakers to recommend a fee for basic education, because it would probably lower the enrollment rate, and also that the addition of other elements beyond literacy and numeracy would be desirable. They also found that the conditions conducive to high educational attainment were not physical or social conditions, but the existing school culture of emphasizing the value of hard work and the mastery of basic skills, as well as the homogeneity of values supporting education of the various sectors of the educational system.

Doing Ethnography in China

This chapter shows some of the interesting differences in interpretation that researchers can have about the very meaning of the term *research*. Even though he realized that these differences in interpretation existed, the author decided to work with his colleagues because they would have better insights into the local culture. "It would have been contradictory to the aims of the study if the Chinese researchers had been excluded simply because they worked within a different methodological framework" (Cheng, 33).

After a period of intensive training with the local researchers, the author realized that the differences were more in relation to the purposes of the research. His local colleagues had been used to doing research that was "*prescriptive* in nature, aiming at definitive conclusions that would lead to immediate recommendations about educational policy." (ibid.). They were "not accustomed to *descriptive* studies aiming at general understanding and developing insights regarding educational processes" (ibid.). The actual research process went very well, and the project seems to have been an excellent example of team-building and cooperation. It was also a good example of how ethnography is not always done by one "lone ranger" ethnographer but can be done by teams of researchers who have a large area to cover.

This chapter also shows the value of including questions on surveys that express the cultural values of the society being studied, in this case, asking questions about the inculcation of moral and life skill values rather than just focusing on academic attainment.

GERARD A. POSTIGLIONE: NATIONAL MINORITY REGIONS: STUDYING SCHOOL DISCONTINUATION

Doing Ethnography

This chapter raises several issues about doing ethnography in a minority context that are relevant not only in China, but in any country. The choice of a sample is one key issue. In a situation of many possible field sites within a very large and polyglot area, the choice of the sample can be dictated by two criteria: ease of access and knowledge of the language. Within the research schools themselves, sampling was also a problem in that the school principals used their own method of constructing a random sample of students.

The issue of research in minority education is another one. When most of the previous research has been done by researchers who were themselves not members of minorities, there can be a decided bias in the research in favor of delineating the extent to which those in the regions are not keeping up with those in the more urban areas or at the center of power. One of the advantages of ethnographic methods is that the researcher may be gathering original data on cultural beliefs and practices of minority groups that have been ignored by previous researchers.

Closely related to this point is that of language. Postiglione emphasizes in this chapter the importance of learning and speaking a minority language (Postiglione, 54). He discusses the role of the foreign and Chinese researcher, and notes that both of them are handicapped if they do not speak any minority languages (Postiglione, 67). In his findings, he notes that the linguistic diversity of the students made it necessary sometimes for teachers to present concepts in four different languages (Postiglione, 66).

Other methodological problems presented themselves, for example, the development of concepts used in the research instruments, such as the contrast between the concepts of "nonattendance" at school (perceived as a temporary condition) and "dropping out" (perceived as a permanent condition). Even the terms used to label the progress of basic education in China were designed to "put the best possible face on the situation" (Postiglione, 60). Moreover, the answers to questions about distances to school had to be interpreted in the light of prevailing conditions of geography, such as flat or mountainous terrain. Thus, even data that are assumed to be objective can be liable to distortion or misinterpretation.

Finally, the issue of construction of meaning is very important under these circumstances. When the researcher is perceived as foreign or an outsider, the answers given in interviews or surveys may be stretched to accommodate the perceived wishes of the outsider, or the more distant dictates of policymakers in the central government. Ethnographic methods can be very useful in providing a context for the interpretation of research results and presenting a picture that is more accurate of the meaning assigned to these results by the actors themselves.

Studying Chinese Education

The most important contribution of this chapter is its focus on minority education in China. Ethnographic methods are often used to try to uncover ways in which minorities differ from the main ethnic or linguistic groups in a country, because ethnographers tend to try to discover that which is not obvious or taken for granted. In his introduction, Postiglione outlines the dimensions of the minority issue in Chinese education, and its importance to national policymaking. He notes that although minorities constitute only 9 percent of China's population, they inhabit over one-half of the total land area of China, an area that forms 90 percent of China's interior border region. Moreover, the area they inhabit is rich in natural resources.

One major problem involved in studying these minorities is that they are impossible to study as a single entity, because there are 55 identified minority groups. National policies for minorities are meant to be interpreted flexibly to meet the needs of each group. The focus of Postiglione's research was the identification of how regional, school, and family factors influenced school attendance and dropout within these regions. The research focused on the Inner Mongolian Autonomous Region (with Mongols forming 80% of the population), the Guangxi Autonomous Region (with the Zhuang forming about 40% of the population), and Yunnan Province (with many minority groups but no single dominant minority).

While the proportion of minority children initially enrolled in elementary school roughly approximates their proportion in the population as a whole, they are underrepresented in completion rates for all levels of schooling. This is true especially for females, and especially at the secondary and tertiary levels. While minority regions are deemed to be "autonomous," in reality they have to abide by policies set by the central government. The exploration of the gap between the goals of national policies and the realities of the minority regions was the central purpose of this study. The findings, which were to be understood as preliminary, focused on lack of qualified teachers, low teachers' salaries, factors specific to female students, parents' lack of financial resources, the perceived lack of relevance of academic education to everyday life, and parents' resistance to state schooling.

Doing Ethnography in China

The principal issue in this chapter concerning doing ethnography in China is the vastness of the country and the presence of 55 identified minority linguistic and cultural groups. While statistics generally indicated that academic achievement was lower and school dropout rates were higher in minority areas than the national average, the task of identifying regions in which to study these discrepancies was a very difficult one. Issues of sampling, representativeness, and generalizability were probably insurmountable. Even if a thorough small-scale study were done of one region, there is no guarantee that the pattern of school attendance and dropping out would occur elsewhere, or for the same reasons. This chapter makes a strong case for well-grounded, large-scale surveys that are adaptable to the cultural variations in the various regions.

IRVING EPSTEIN:
JUVENILE DELINQUENCY AND REFORMATORY
EDUCATION IN CHINA: A RETROSPECTIVE

Doing Ethnography

This is a chapter about "fact-finding," which the author considers not to be strictly ethnographic, but it does represent a branch of qualitative research. Even relatively short visits to field sites can have an advantage to the researcher over no visits at all. Access to information was a key problem in this study, as the author notes that no repeat visits were allowed, officials were always present when questions were asked, and difficult questions were disregarded.

In spite of these difficulties, Epstein was able to gather information about juvenile delinquency and reformatory education in China. However, he reflects from the vantage point of several years' distance how his own observer biases affected the interpretation he made of his own data.

Studying Education in China

The major part of this chapter focuses on the "facts" that were gathered during the author's visit to China. He found official efforts to find a monolithic cause for juvenile delinquency quite striking: the Cultural Revolution, poor parenting, peer group influences, the mass media, and so on. (Epstein, 74). Heavily influenced by the Chicago School of sociology, he was interested in investigating "whether the normative value claims that rationalized coercive treatment of offenders could continue to be effective during the post-Maoist era" (Epstein, 77) in the context of a society that is much more collective than Westerners are accustomed to.

He outlined the framework and operation of juvenile institutions, specifically reformatories and work-study schools, several of which he visited. As in Paine and DeLany's chapter in this book, he is able to give the reader a fairly detailed account of the daily life of the institution he is studying. Epstein comments that he found the work-study factory class he visited a less coercive institution than the reformatory, and was even quoted in the local press as having a favorable reaction. He concluded that the stigma of having been in one of these institutions presented former inmates with more of a problem after their incarceration than during it, and that it was an extension of the authoritarian collectivism that was found within the institutional settings. Since his visit in 1983, he noted that juvenile crime had increased, particularly in the urban and coastal regions, and in relation to gang and drug-based activity. The mechanisms of social control have become increasingly technologized and professionalized, although mass campaigns to identify and punish criminals are still much in evidence. He identifies certain social trends, such as increasing urban unemployment, urban and coastal migration, changing residential mobility patterns, and structural changes within the educational system (such as deterring students from attending university) as playing a role in the increase of juvenile crime. He notes the existence still of a traditional institutional culture's reliance on notions of the redemptive value of manual labor, the importance of character reformation in a general sense, and the need to respect collective authority, and contrasts this traditional institutional culture with the increasing professionalization of the legal system.

Doing Ethnography in China

Toward the end of the chapter, Epstein discusses Western research on Chinese delinquency. He cites recent research on China by Western researchers and notes that it is primarily statistical. However, the results of the surveys that have been carried out have convinced some researchers that Western theories of delinquency are applicable to the Chinese situation (Epstein, 91). Epstein notes that the results of survey research should be used with caution. He raises several issues about methods of gathering data and possible sources of bias, as well as issues of informed consent and freedom of delinquents to refuse to participate in such studies. It is evident that ethnographic studies of delinquency would provide some clearer definition of the context of large-scale studies, and would also make the interpretation of results clearer.

Epstein ends the paper by reflecting critically on his own assumptions while he was doing the research, assumptions that are linked with critical ethnography. He now considers arrogant his assumption that the observers can "unobtrusively use their authority as outsider to give voice to a group they view as marginalized and impotent" (Epstein, 88). Moreover, he sees these assumptions as having a negative impact on the researcher's "ability to grasp the fundamental nature of the research being pursued" (ibid.). On reflection, he feels that his earlier analysis failed to foresee the trends toward individuation of all aspects of life in China that have happened with the growth of the market economy. Epstein raises the point that it is important to counter the tendency "to totalize the foreign in the name of cultural distinctiveness or use the foreign to superficially reaffirm the primacy of Western paradigms" (Epstein, 91).

LYNN PAINE AND BRIAN DELANY:
RURAL CHINESE EDUCATION: OBSERVING FROM
THE MARGIN

Doing Ethnography

One of the most interesting aspects of this paper is its emphasis on long-standing cultural and social patterns in a rural village. This chapter attempts to investigate how these patterns are exemplified in the daily activities of one rural school. This is a somewhat classic task of ethnographic research. The authors also point to the associated issues of urban/rural differences and marginality in the life of the larger country as a whole. However, the life of Burntwood Central Junior High School is not conceived of as static, but as a dynamic reflection of changes occurring within the county and the country as a whole. The researchers were interested in the meaning attached to education by students, teachers, and parents. Interviews were also conducted with numerous administrative staff, as well as principals and teachers. On a later visit, intensive field work was also carried out with two groups of students and their teachers. The authors show how the students' families are highly committed to their educational success, although they may lack the skills with which to help their children. They document how the students are participating in processes that are steering them toward a life outside the village. However, they also show how the pedagogy and the social construction of the curriculum as well as the relationships among the students themselves are still rooted in traditional behavior patterns. They concluded that "Burntwood's rhythms, despite its apparent breaks with tradition, seem steeped in powerful, longstanding social and cultural patterns"(Paine and DeLany, 103).

Studying Chinese Education

The main focus of this chapter is on studying education in its rural context. The authors point out that rural education is placed at the margins in educational and policy discourse, and its characteristics are seen as problematic and in need of reform. The authors present an analysis of the ways in which rural education is viewed, a description of their experiences at a rural school, and an exploration of their role as researchers.

They note that while over 90 percent of all primary schools and even over 60 percent of all junior high schools are in rural areas of China, very little research has been done in rural education (Paine and DeLany, 98). Paine and DeLany cite the Chinese- and English-language literature review by Kai-ming Cheng and Lynn Paine that found certain recurrent themes dominated research on education in China. These themes were: education and the economy; school wastage rates; vocational education; coordinated reforms related to the educational, scientific, and agricultural sectors; economic concerns within the various regions; teacher-training issues; and educational planning issues (Paine and DeLany, 98–99). Because researchers were setting their sights on such macro-level questions, they were not able to focus on the minutiae of everyday school life, particularly in the rural areas. Paine and DeLany's study was an attempt to remedy this situation.

Doing Ethnography in China

The problem that presents itself in this chapter is the disjunction between urban-based policymaking in regard to education and the realities of the rural school experience. Paine and DeLany express the contradiction thus: "Both the formal curriculum and the hidden curriculum, as well as the pedagogical techniques used by teachers, tell students that the important work of school is learning knowledge that comes from a cosmopolitan, political center, one that is far removed from their villages and their daily experiences" (Paine and DeLany, 111). The value of this study is that it is able to show the disjunction between the observed realities of daily school life and the large-scale pronouncements about educational reform on a national scale. This is a particularly daunting task in a country as populous as China. The value of ethnographic research in portraying descriptive accounts of real-life situations in education is, of course, countered by the impossibility of drawing generalizations on the basis of one case. Nevertheless, the pattern documentation of a worldwide trend of education providing the means for rural students to leave their village lives and migrate to the cities is enriched by this case study.

Another aspect of doing ethnography in China, raised explicitly in this chapter, is the role of the foreign researcher who observes "at the margins." By examining a population that is already perceived of as marginalized, the researchers become doubly marginalized by taking a research stance that sees value in studying that population. They discuss both how they affected those they researched and how they in turn were affected by those they researched. Their differing facility in the Chinese language was also a factor in their success at interviewing. Moreover, they shared a complementary gender identity and were able to perform various aspects of gender roles in a manner acceptable to their hosts. Previous knowledge of classroom experience was a helpful factor in establishing rapport with Chinese educators, while their lack of agricultural knowledge was a distinct hindrance. Moreover, they discovered an urban bias in their initial research inquiries, which had been shaped by their interaction with their urban Chinese colleagues. Thus, they are quite open about admitting the layers of their "otherness" in their research context in China: being Americans, being of urban origin, and studying a population that was an "other" to their Chinese colleagues. This theme of "layers of otherness" is one that will be taken up in the discussion of the subsequent chapters of this book.

HEIDI A. ROSS:
IN THE MOMENT—DISCOURSES OF POWER,
NARRATIVES OF RELATIONSHIP: FRAMING
ETHNOGRAPHY OF CHINESE SCHOOLING, 1981–1997

Doing Ethnography

Whereas the previous chapters in this book have rested on some notion of empiricism, this chapter moves away from the assumption that there is a separate apprehendable reality outside of the observer, and raises some of the questions about ethnography that pertain to the relationship between the observer and the observed. The chapter also raises important questions about the nature of discourse(s).

The organization of this chapter differs from the others, in that it focuses on four different "ethnographic moments" in the author's life between 1981 and 1997, in which she occupied various roles as teacher-researcher, narrator, collaborator, and consultant. She perceives these roles as having raised different questions about the nature of field research and the nature of ethnographic research and writing, but also sees this period of time as having taken place in the sweep of historical events in China during which the metanarrative of Communist ideology gave way to "multiple, locally inspired narratives of schooling for private interest and representation" (Ross, 123).

The author takes as her theme in this chapter the tension "between top-down, moralized, and rationalized discourses on Chinese education and fragmented, local, ambiguous narratives of individuals finding meaning in the processes of schooling" (Ross, 124–125), even while she claims that this characterization may create a false dichotomy. Nevertheless, for heuristic purposes, she presents her four "moments" in this frame.

An important point the author makes concerns the notion of "field" in fieldwork. She notes that the field is more than just a geographical area. It is the entire context in which fieldwork is done: the relationships between the researcher and the researched, the set of obligations "in which the researcher's identity and understanding develop as a process of negotiation" (Ross, 125). She also emphasizes the importance of "thick description," a term used by Clifford Geertz to describe ethnographic writing in which the ethnographer has astutely observed and portrayed cultural actors in the process of going about their daily lives.

The first "moment" concerns the author's experiences in a Shanghai secondary school, in which the principal, in the process of approving an open-ended interview schedule for twelve questions for all the school faculty, scheduled the names and times of faculty along with the one or two questions the individual staff were, in the principal's opinion, best qualified to answer. She notes that this "top-down" view of schooling was at odds with her own training in critical ethnography, and she was not prepared to be the object of her colleagues' attempts to transform her teaching practice. A key point she admits in this "moment" was her inability to see "how firmly [her] colleagues' views of research were anchored in the evaluative nature of Chinese society" (Ross, 127). The principal had assumed that she would want to interview those who were best able to answer each question.

The second "moment" was in 1991, when Heidi Ross recounted to a colleague from her university how she had been conducting very intense and moving interviews in New York of alumnae of a Shanghai school, after which her colleague questioned whether such methods could properly be called "research." She herself had seen these interviews as part of the laborious project of doing a historical ethnography of the school, by interviewing alumnae. She recounts how the school's " 'official' history was being rewritten by its graduates through their efforts at coming to terms with their own histories"(Ross, 134). She continues by saying that she began to conceptualize research as storytelling and to look more closely at phenomenological methodologies. She was convinced to replace the notion of "discourse" with that of "narrative" as her concept for "identifying how meaning is created through the relationships that sustain the research process" (ibid.) and as a model for cross-disciplinary communication. She describes how she became the narrator of the stories her informants told her and how she felt a great responsibility for her informants and her audience.

The third "moment" occurred when she was collaborating with a Chinese-speaking colleague on the final details for a workshop on qualitative methodology. Her colleague, who was born and raised in China but who is now a Canadian citizen, was accustomed to moving around in Chinese schools without having her foreignness "marked," whereas the presence of her blond-haired American collaborator caused other Chinese people to treat her as a "handler" or "guide" of the author's. She reflects on the meaning that is signalled by her physical body moving around "in the field" and relates it to "traveling theory," a concept of Edward Said, who locates it in the "postmodern moment of destabilized nation-states, cultural and economic diasporas, and increasing disparities of wealth and power" (Said, quoted in Ross, 138). She concludes this section by emphasizing how important it is to collaborate with Chinese teachers, parents, administrators, and students.

The fourth "moment" occurred during a day of filming at a Shanghai school, when the vice-principal expressed his rage at their lateness. The author feels that the usual niceties of ethnographic access and the building of relationships had been completely overlooked, but she was powerless to remedy the situation. She realizes the difference between the slow process of crafting an ethnographic account and the speed of the electronic media, which gathered a very partial vew of a fragment of a day in the life of a school.

These four "moments" are relevant to the life of any ethnographic researcher. They compel the reader to think about the process by which one insinuates oneself into the life of the scene that one is studying, and how in turn one is perceived. These perceptions go well beyond simplistic accounts of "access to the data."

Studying Chinese Education

There is not a great deal in this chapter that is strictly applicable only to the Chinese situation. Ross does note that the rapid expansion of private and all-girls' schools reflects the increasing plurality of Chinese schooling (Ross, 136). She discusses the varying experiences of girls in these schools, from those who learn gender-stereotyped skills such as making beds or pouring drinks, to others who are taught driver training and martial arts. What they have in common, however, is outrage at being silenced by parents and teachers. Ross also notes that private schools vary greatly in curriculum, quality, and intent, from altruistic and liberal motivations on the part of their founders to market- and profit-driven ones.

Ross discusses briefly the impact of market socialism on popular culture at various points in the chapter. She notes the infiltration of many aspects of teenage popular culture in music, dancing, and consumer products, and the impact these have on the taste and lifestyle of the private school students.

In her conclusion, Ross states that the fact that "communities and individuals are usurping social functions of education previously monopolized by the state is . . . the most intriguing, and most significant outcome of the conjuncture between market and educational reforms" (Ross, 146). Her chapter itself demonstrates the tension between top-down discourses of state control and the lived, contested experiences of both educators and researchers. The chapter in its entirety gives us four moments or "windows" into seeing the results of this tension.

Doing Ethnography in China

Ross describes her difficulties in writing up her "moments." Overarching each detail was the realization that even when her account was able to frame the research on her own terms, she knew that "the objects of [her] analysis [were] also analyzing subjects" (Rosaldo, quoted in Ross, 128). She recounts several examples of how her former students reflexively commented on their perceptions of her effect on them. This is a part of classical fieldwork that an ethnographer does not usually recount, because in colonial days, either those who were researched never saw the published account of themselves, or else the ethnographer never was reunited with them. In a country like China with a long history of literacy, and with the increased use of communications technology, this one-sided version of ethnography is far less likely to occur.

Heidi Ross discusses the "crisis" in ethnographic representation as a response across the disciplines to what constitutes a depiction of social reality, but she also situates it in the Chinese context of power relations in the world, and writing about another culture is also a part of these power relations. Moreover, she notes that the present interest of Western scholars in postmodernity clashes with the interests of "mainland Chinese scholars, whose disciplinary and methodological claims remain guided by a faith in modernity, with its core belief that human beings can progressively shape themselves and their worlds" (Ross, 131). Moreover, she notes that the critical posture adopted by some scholars who see their work as embedded in a series of power relationships is in contradiction with the beliefs of Chinese scholars who are interested in finding and celebrating what constitutes "good" educational practice.

JUDITH LIU:
RECONSTRUCTING THE PAST:
REMINISCENCES OF MISSIONARY SCHOOL DAYS

Doing Ethnography

The central problem in this chapter is the doing of "dialogic ethnography" in which the researcher's analysis and the subject's story become interwoven into a mutually agreed-upon account of a particular historical moment, in this case the reconstruction of the life at a missionary girls' school in China circa 1930. Judith Liu did an ethnographic study of a cohort of women who attended an American Episcopalian missionary school in Wuchang, Hubei province, in the 1920s and 1930s. The serendipitous origin of these research subjects was that they were all friends and classmates of her mother, who turned out to have a role as interlocutor in her interviews with all of these women.

Specifically, it eventuated that her methodology had a three-tiered format in which her mother asked questions of the interviewees on her behalf, questions that she as researcher could not have asked because she would not have been able to maintain the decorum of respect for the elders so important in the culture. This method proved particularly fruitful in eliciting more information from informants and re-creating a experience that her mother had shared with her classmates during a historical period that occurred before Liu was born. Moreover, since the study was historical, the use of archival records in the Episcopal Archives in Austin,

Texas, gave an additional view (the administrative version) of the school's history.

This historical aspect of the project also made it possible for the researcher to assess the long-term impact of the school experience, in a way not possible when only a short time frame is taken. The women's accounts of how far-reaching the moral lessons were and how profoundly they had altered their lives for years to come are evidence of this.

Studying Chinese Education

Although the main focus of this chapter was not the effect of missionary educational practices in China, it raises some very interesting points about the context and effects of such educational endeavors. For example, Liu points out that the school's curriculum did not initially include the Confucian classics and thus represented a foothold for disseminating Christian heterodoxy. Since the school's founders had also envisaged the goal of producing Christian wives and mothers who would be in the vanguard of Christianizing China, their view of women's roles was also in contradiction to the conception of the classic subservient role for women. Moreover, as St. Hilda's expanded, an increasing number of girls were receiving an education that contained a foreign ethos and world view, which were to have a profound effect on their values, particularly those concerning the role of women (Liu, 158).

Liu outlines the various stages and conceptions of Western-style education at St. Hilda's. First was the stage in which people achieved education for their children by sending them to St. Hilda's as a missionary school, but in return their children had to espouse Christian religious beliefs. Second was the stage in which education was seen as part of modernization, and wealthy non-Christian parents began sending their children to St. Hilda's for pragmatic reasons, such as being resocialized into Western values. They also remained effectively apolitical, as they were sheltered from outside political activities. However, political unrest from 1926 to 1928 resulted in the departure of many missionaries and the closing of St. Hilda's for an extended period. These events and the rise of Wuhan nationalism effectively spurred the political awareness of girls from St. Hilda's and their subsequent political activity, such as the boycott of Japanese goods in 1933 and sending first-aid kits to soldiers.

With the rise of nominal Guomindang control of China, missionary schools had to register with the state and in effect became secular Chinese schools. This change meant that henceforth all classes were to be taught in

Chinese instead of English, and the principal and curriculum had to be Chinese. Some of these rules were circumvented in practice, particularly with the appointment of a titular Chinese Deaconess, while the original Deaconess continued to run the school. The religious values of the school became transmuted in some way to a philosophy of social reconstruction along religious lines, with an emphasis on the roles of educators, social workers, and medical workers (Liu, 164). The difficult part, however, was the emphasis on women's roles of self-sufficiency and independence in a society that promoted dependence and subservience. Liu notes that it was the transmuted secular ethic that had the most profound effect on the women she interviewed. The informants reminisced at length about the ways self-sufficiency and independence were inculcated both within the school itself and in community service projects. They also recalled the influence their teachers had had on them as role models. But they noted the poor treatment of the Chinese faculty and their attempts to have conditions improved. Moreover, their own version of Wuhan nationalism spurred them to efforts to prove they were "as good as" the missionaries (Liu, 170).

Liu concludes that the intended subversion of traditional Chinese values did in fact take place, and theses students did absorb the lesson that they had important roles other than wife and mother. Some of these women chose not to marry, so as to support their own mothers who had been widowed and who had no other means of support. One informant sums it up well: "[T]hose of us who obtained our educations in missionary schools were different from other people in terms of our lives and our training. We had different circumstances than most and this perhaps had an influence" (Liu, 172). Liu echoes her thoughts in this conclusion: The moral education received by the girls at St. Hilda's resocialized them into believing that it was possible for women to take a more active role in society than existing Chinese patriarchal norms permitted, and they acted according to that belief. Thus, the moral lessons learned at St. Hilda's were stronger than the curricular lessons, an ironic commentary on the value placed in Chinese culture on the importance of schools as moral training grounds.

Doing Ethnography in China

The methodology of this chapter is inextricably caught up in the cultural context of Chinese culture. The participation of the author's mother as her interlocutor when she was interviewing all of her Chinese "aunties" is of particular note. She emphasizes that it would have been impossible for her to address these women and ask them questions about their lives in a way that would have been considered polite enough in the cultural context. Moreover, the fact that they and her mother had experienced St. Hilda's together meant that they wove together the tapestry of their common experiences. Liu also notes that it is impossible to know how much of this shared account is "true." She points out how important it is to have another account of the historic events that the informants are remembering, such as the institutional histories of schools and the regional histories of the countries in which they are located.

CONCLUSION

In the discussion of the various chapters of this book, and in the opportunity that the authors have had to discuss their contributions with one another, this book has begun to take on a coherence in its structure that was not so evident when the chapters were first collected together. There is a spectrum in this book of uses to which ethnography can be put. In the chapters by Cheng and Postiglione, the task is to define how ethnography can assist researchers who are doing very large-scale projects and who need assistance in generating relevant questions for surveys or in understanding the local cultural context, or who need to communicate more effectively, both with local minority groups and with fellow researchers who may be culturally different. In the middle section of the book, the paper by Epstein and that of Paine and DeLany are focused at a more middle level of generalizability, and the task is more to understand a local cultural scene that may differ in some profound respects from its equivalent in other countries, or not as the case may be. The role of the researcher and his or her assumptions become more evident, and the research is affected greatly by the assumptions the individual researcher has before, during, and even after the project. The retelling of the story of the conduct of their studies allows the researcher to explore how these assumptions have changed over time. The last two papers are at the other end of the spectrum, the more phenomenological end. Ross and Liu are able to reflect on the extent to which they were able to interact with their research subjects and the extent to which the "tale" they produced was "true," or in what sense truth was the point of the exercise.

In all of these cases, the reader has gained valuable lessons in the complexity of the ethnographic endeavor, and has been privileged to peer at some fragmentary and incomplete pictures of some aspects of the great undertaking that is education in China. It is hoped that this book will inspire the next generation of researchers to carry on with this task.

Contributors

Kai-ming Cheng is Chair and Professor of Education and Pro-Vice Chancellor at the University of Hong Kong. He is also currently Visiting Professor of Education at the Harvard School of Education. He was named an Honorary Fellow at the University of London's Institute of Education, where he completed his doctorate in educational planning and policy analysis. His research projects are largely in the People's Republic of China, where he is comparing the effects of culture on education.

Brian DeLany is an Associate Professor of Teacher Education at Michigan State University. He is interested in organizational decision making and in schooling's contribution to social stratification. His work examines how schools cope with turbulent policy and resource environments, how students and teachers become resources to be used in the process of institutional coping, and how recent efforts to decentralize decision making by government have affected schools. His current work addresses these issues in comparative perspective through the study of educational ordinance and governance in the United States, the People's Republic of China, and the United Kingdom.

Irving Epstein is an Associate Professor in the Department of Educational Studies at Illinois Wesleyan University. In addition to his interests in Chinese education, his recent publications have focused on issues of methodology and theory in the study of comparative education, educational provision for street children, and representations of street children in commercial film. For the past ten years, he was an associate editor of the *Comparative Education Review.*

Donald P. Kelly is a doctoral candidate in the Department of Sociology at the University of California, San Diego. His fields of specialization include education, culture, and social movements. His dissertation is on the knowledge bases that structure antismoking discourses. He has coauthored articles published in the *Comparative Education Review,* the *Review of Education,* and the *Journal of Contemporary Ethnography.*

Judith Liu is a Professor of Sociology at the University of San Diego, where she teaches theory and gender courses. Her research interests include missionary education in China, multicultural education in the United States, and pedagogy. She is the recipient of several teaching excellence awards, including the Council for the Advancement and Support of Education's California Professor of the Year for 1991. She has coauthored articles on women and HIV/AIDS, comparative education in the People's Republic of China, and critical pedagogy.

Vandra Lea Masemann is an anthropologist of education whose first ethnographic study was of a girls' boarding school in Ghana, West Africa. She has taught Anthropology of Education at the Ontario Institute for Studies in Education, the University of Wisconsin-Madison, the State University of New York at Buffalo, and Florida State University in Tallahassee. She has been president of the Comparative and International Education Society and the World Council of Comparative Education Societies. She has published several theoretical papers on ethnographic research, in the *Comparative Education Review* and in the forthcoming textbook on comparative education edited by Robert Arnove and Carlos Torres.

Lynn Paine is Associate Professor of Teacher Education and Affiliated Faculty in the Sociology Department of Michigan State University, where she specializes in the sociology of education and international comparative education. Her research interests include the relationship between educational policy and practice, the links between teacher education and teaching, and the connections between educational reform and social change. She has conducted extensive field research in China, England, and the United States.

Gerard A. Postiglione is an Associate Professor of Sociology and Education and Director of Advanced Studies in Education and National Development at the University of Hong Kong. His books include: *China's National Minority Education* (Falmer, 1999), *Hong Kong's Reunion with China* (M. E. Sharpe, 1997), *Higher Education in Asia* (Greenwood, 1997), *Social Change and Educational Development: Mainland China, Taiwan, and Hong Kong* (Center of Asian Studies, 1996), and *The Hong Kong Reader: Passage to Chinese Sovereignty* (M. E. Sharpe, 1996). He is associate editor of the journal *Chinese Education and Society*. He has been a consultant on minority education to the United Nations Development Program and the Asian Development Bank.

Heidi A. Ross is Associate Professor of Education and Director of Asian Studies at Colgate University. She teaches courses in comparative education and contemporary Chinese society and has served on the board of directors of the Comparative and International Education Society. She conducts research on Chinese secondary schooling, and gender and education.

Index

REFERENCE BOOKS IN INTERNATIONAL EDUCATION
EDWARD R. BEAUCHAMP, *Series Editor*

EDUCATION IN THE PEOPLE'S
REPUBLIC OF CHINA
PAST AND PRESENT
An Annotated Bibliography
by Franklin Parker
and Betty June Parker

EDUCATION IN SOUTH ASIA
A Select Annotated Bibliography
by Philip G. Altbach, Denzil
Saldanha, and Jeanne Weiler

TEXTBOOKS IN THE THIRD WORLD
Policy, Content and Context
by Philip G. Altbach
and Gail P. Kelly

TEACHERS AND TEACHING
IN THE DEVELOPING WORLD
by Val D. Rust and Per Dalin

RUSSIAN AND SOVIET EDUCATION,
1731–1989
*A Multilingual Annotated
Bibliography*
by William W. Brickman
and John T. Zepper

EDUCATION IN THE ARAB GULF
STATES AND THE ARAB WORLD
An Annotated Bibliographic Guide
by Nagat El-Sanabary

EDUCATION IN ENGLAND
AND WALES
An Annotated Bibliography
by Franklin Parker
and Betty June Parker

UNDERSTANDING EDUCATIONAL
REFORM IN GLOBAL CONTEXT
Economy, Ideology, and the State
edited by Mark B. Ginsburg

EDUCATION AND SOCIAL CHANGE
IN KOREA
by Don Adams
and Esther E. Gottlieb

THREE DECADES OF PEACE
EDUCATION AROUND THE WORLD
An Anthology
edited by Robin J. Burns
and Robert Aspeslagh

EDUCATION AND DISABILITY
IN CROSS-CULTURAL PERSPECTIVE
edited by Susan J. Peters

RUSSIAN EDUCATION
Tradition and Transition
by Brian Holmes, Gerald H. Read,
and Natalya Voskresenskaya

LEARNING TO TEACH
IN TWO CULTURES
Japan and the United States
by Nobuo K. Shimahara
and Akira Sakai

EDUCATING IMMIGRANT CHILDREN
*Schools and Language Minorities
in Twelve Nations*
by Charles L. Glenn
with Ester J. de Jong

TEACHER EDUCATION IN
INDUSTRIALIZED NATIONS
Issues in Changing Social Contexts
edited by Nobuo K. Shimahara
and Ivan Z. Holowinsky

EDUCATION AND DEVELOPMENT
IN EAST ASIA
edited by Paul Morris
and Anthony Sweeting

THE UNIFICATION OF
GERMAN EDUCATION
by Val D. Rust and Diane Rust

WOMEN, EDUCATION, AND
DEVELOPMENT IN ASIA
Cross-National Perspectives
edited by Grace C.L. Mak